EVERYDAY LIFE IN
GLOBAL MOROCCO

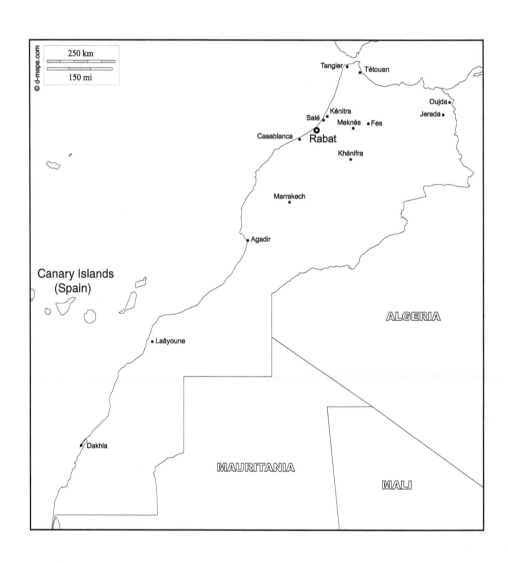

© d-maps.com

250 km

150 mi

Tangier

Tétouan

Oujda

Kénitra

Jerada

Salé

Meknès

Fes

Casablanca

Rabat

Khénifra

Marrakech

Agadir

Canary Islands
(Spain)

ALGERIA

Laâyoune

Dakhla

MAURITANIA

MALI

PUBLIC CULTURES OF THE MIDDLE EAST AND NORTH AFRICA
Paul A. Silverstein, Susan Slyomovics, and Ted Swedenburg, editors

RACHEL NEWCOMB

EVERYDAY LIFE
IN GLOBAL
MOROCCO

INDIANA UNIVERSITY PRESS

This book is a publication of

Indiana University Press
Office of Scholarly Publishing
Herman B Wells Library 350
1320 East 10th Street
Bloomington, Indiana 47405 USA

iupress.indiana.edu

The paper used in this publication meets the minimum requirements of the American National Standard for Information Sciences—Permanence of Paper for Printed Library Materials, ANSI Z39.48-1992.

Manufactured in the United States of America

Cataloging information is available from the Library of Congress.

ISBN 978-0-253-02952-2 (cloth)
ISBN 978-0-253-03123-5 (paperback)
ISBN 978-0-253-03130-3 (ebook)

1 2 3 4 5 22 21 20 19 18 17

Chapter 4 appeared in an altered version as "Modern Citizens, Modern Food: Taste and the Rise of the Moroccan Citizen-Consumer" in *Senses and Citizenships: Embodying Political Life*, editors Susanna Trnka, Christine Dureau, and Julie Park, published by Routledge in 2013. It has been reprinted here with permission of the publisher.

*This book is dedicated to Lorraine Gorrell,
the most wonderful editor, role model,
supporter, and mother I could ask for.*

CONTENTS

Note on Transliteration

Moroccan dialectical Arabic (*darija*) varies from region to region and does not have a standardized written form, unlike Modern Standard Arabic. For words from Modern Standard Arabic, I have relied on the *International Journal for Middle East Studies*. For darija, I refer to Heath 1987 and Harrell 1962 for transliteration. Where there are standard spellings for words that occur in English texts, such as *tagine* or *Alaoui*, I use the Anglicized versions. I have followed those guidelines. Diacritics that do not occur in English have been simplified to make them accessible to readers.

EVERYDAY LIFE IN
GLOBAL MOROCCO

INTRODUCTION

What is past is gone, what is hoped for is absent, for you is the hour in which you are.
        —Moroccan proverb

Ordinary lives do not confront the global as such. They face more immediate issues.
        —Friedman and Ekholm Friedman 2013, 249

If a man told you that a dog had run off with your ear, would you go after the dog or search first for your ear? The year is 2011. All around Morocco, the so-called Arab Spring is making its presence felt, with frequent Sunday demonstrations in major cities organized by the February 20th Movement. So far, the movement's demands have been modest: more accountability in government, an independent judiciary, jobs, and other reforms. When a few demonstrations turned violent, some of the attacks were directed at businesses, including a French company in Tangier that had begun privatizing water and charging higher prices than the municipality.

The city of Fes has also seen its share of demonstrations, but Khaled has little interest in joining them. Although he is unemployed, the movement's concerns do not seem to resonate with him, and he generally dismisses its rhetoric. What truly inflames him, and the project to which he devotes his summer, is getting his neighborhood together to protest the addition of a bakery on their street. He has organized petitions, visited city government officials, and canvassed among friends, acquaintances, and nearby businesses. He does not know the businessman, an outsider, who wants to open the bakery, and

1

that, to Khaled, is a major part of the problem. What was once, during his childhood, a small city of old French buildings with neighbors who all knew one another has become a place overrun by gleaming, unaffordable new high-rises owned by strangers. What he knows is that the city in which he grew up is changing, and soon, he worries, rising costs will force everyone he knows to relocate.

He who eats when he is full digs his grave with his teeth. 2013. In the morning, Ilham rises first, straightening the kitchen from the previous night's meal and putting a pot of coffee and milk on the stove. She unwraps yesterday's baguettes and places them on a plastic tray with jam, small silver packets of La Vache Qui Rit cheese, and glasses, then rouses her family from sleep: her husband, Brahim, and her two children, Sara and Samir, ages ten and fifteen. They snatch bites of breakfast between taking turns in the family's small bathroom, then everyone is off to work and school. At lunch, Brahim returns home for the *tagine* Ilham has prepared, which they eat together. An hour later Samir arrives; he eats a pressed panini sandwich and fries Ilham bought from the frozen food section of the Marjane supermarket, then returns to school. Sara, who eats lunch at school, does not come home until three in the afternoon, when a bus brings her back to the house. She nibbles on cookies and Danone yogurt while doing her homework. When Samir arrives a little later, he downs a soda and a bag of chips before going back out again to meet his friends. For tea at around seven that evening, Sara helps Ilham fry up some fresh *malawi*, a multilayered pancake with large quantities of oil and butter between each layer. Samir returns to do his homework, and his mother makes him a sandwich with *cacher* (processed meat) and cheese, along with a Fanta orange soda. After returning from having coffee with his friends, Brahim also has a piece of malawi before drinking a glass of hot chamomile tea to help him sleep.

For the sake of a single rose, the gardener becomes servant to a thousand thorns. 2009. Hanane wants a baby. She has been married twice. She has no children and has had one miscarriage. She has visited doctors, healers, and herbalists, taking careful note of their prescriptions, even if there are some she will not be able to follow. She does not place the medical doctors' expertise higher than that of anyone else. "If I could afford it, I'd do the expensive treatments," she says, referring to in vitro fertilization (IVF). But one cycle of IVF costs more than she makes all year as a teacher in a primary school. And she is skeptical about the success rates of any one treatment over others: all the doctors and herbalists she has visited claim similar success rates and exude expertise. In fact, the health practitioners, both traditional and modern, all offer advice and counseling to their patients, and from them all she hears a common message: *Our treatments offer your best chances for success, but if they don't work, stay together. A marriage doesn't need children to be happy.* In her mother's day, she says, her condition would have been devastating: her husband would have left her or taken another wife. "If I can't have children, of course I will be sad, but he says it's not important to him, and if it doesn't work out, he won't leave me," she says with certainty.

Three Moroccan proverbs open these vignettes into everyday life in a globalized Morocco: about pursuing the wrong targets, the excesses of our modern diets, and the multiple options that globalization seems to provide (although not to everyone). The stories themselves have been chosen to represent slices of everyday life in which average Moroccans confront larger issues related to globalization. What connects the broader contexts of the upheavals in the Arab world in 2011, a national protest movement, and a man who is concerned about the opening of a bakery in his small corner of the city of Fes? What can a typical day in the life of a middle-class Moroccan family tell us about culture, cuisine, health, and the changing dynamics of food and family? What is global about the life of a woman who still chooses from among traditional therapies to try to have children?

Khaled, Ilham, and Hanane Benjelloun are adult siblings from a middle-class family, born during the forty-year reign (1960–1999) of King Hassan II.[1] They have two other brothers: Rachid, a migrant who has struggled since the 2008 recession to make ends meet in Europe, and Mourad, a small-scale entrepreneur who sells used clothing out of a tiny shop in a suburb of Fes. They came of age around the time of the fall of the Berlin Wall, a moment that marked the end of the Cold War and the beginnings of the era of globalization. Their lives reflect many of the challenges and opportunities of living in a globalized world. They are children of the era of structural adjustment programs in Morocco, when Morocco borrowed heavily by agreeing to the terms of the International Monetary Fund (IMF) and the World Bank: cutting the government jobs an earlier generation relied on and encouraging private investment. They have lived through a time when the main language of instruction for Morocco's educational system switched dramatically and suddenly from French to Arabic, through the birth of the internet, and through a dramatic population shift when average family size fell from around seven children per woman in the early 1970s to slightly over two in 2014. Although middle class, the Benjellouns are subject to the same forces of globalization that have scattered families in search of better opportunities to support themselves and their loved ones. Their diet is affected by worldwide trends toward processed foods, and the resulting health problems are those increasingly shared by countries in both the Global South and the Global North. When they are sick, the medical care they seek also represents the middle tier of income: they do not need to use public hospitals, where the quality of the treatment is often abysmal. Instead they rely on a medium tier of private clinics that provide acceptable care yet do not offer the latest technologies, which are within the means of the upper class but not the rest of the population.

The Benjelloun patriarch, Si Mohammed, worked for years in a steady government job with benefits, a position that was eliminated when he retired. His wife, Latifa, raised their five children and was known around their middle-class neighborhood for her excellent cooking and fine embroidery, which she occasionally sold to make extra income. Since Si Mohammed passed away from a heart attack several years ago, Latifa divides her time among her children's houses, and until recently she and Khaled shared the small apartment in the city center where all her children grew up.

This ethnography explores how everyday lives in urban Morocco are affected by globalization.[2] We will see how global factors come into play as individuals navigate activities that are both timeless and human: marrying, having children, working, eating, and finding shelter. With globalization, these activities have all grown much more complex. Cultures, however, give their own meanings to biological activities, and exploring those meanings can teach us about a culture's distinctiveness while revealing the underlying facets that unite "us" with "them." As globalization connects us through technology, trade, and travel, it possesses potentially homogenizing effects as well. Work schedules around the world come closer to resembling a Euro-American model, corporations spread their reach nearly everywhere, and technology offers simultaneous access to news and media.

The Benjellouns are part of Morocco's middle class, living modestly but in adequate comfort, in jobs and circumstances that are quite different from those of their parents' generation. They bear an illustrious Moroccan family name and are members of an extended family that, in other cities, has enjoyed power, influence, and wealth beyond their reach. A billionaire, a soccer star, and a writer all share the same name but are relations so distant that the Benjellouns cannot trace the exact family connections they might have shared in the distant past. For this branch of the family, the Benjelloun name implies a higher social class than their economic status actually conveys. They often tell the story of their grandfather and his three brothers. The brothers left Fes to seek their fortunes in Casablanca and Rabat, while their grandfather stayed behind, marrying a local woman and starting a large family of ten children that included their father, Si Mohammed. When the grandfather died, his property was divided among his many heirs, some of whom managed to build their wealth with astute (or lucky) business decisions, while others sold their assets and spent their inheritance. Si Mohammed himself held onto the family's apartment in the center of town, where Latifa and Khaled lived until the building was sold. Latifa used some of the proceeds she received from the sale to rent a small apartment on the outskirts of the city, where she lives with Khaled whenever she is not visiting her daughters. Rachid, who is frequently in Morocco as a result of the economic downturn in Spain, often stays with them as well. But even without the residential connection to the city center, Khaled still returns daily to spend time in his favorite café, networking with people from the old neighborhood.

The three vignettes that begin this book—Khaled Benjelloun's protest against the opening of a bakery, Ilham Benjelloun's efforts to feed her family despite disjointed schedules and multiple dietary preferences, and Hanane Benjelloun's quest to have a baby—relate to larger globalization issues in Morocco. They reflect gentrification and rising inequality; the disappearance of the Mediterranean diet, leading to an increase in health issues such as obesity and diabetes, and new ways of dealing with infertility and its effects on marriage and family. Later chapters focus on the lives of the other siblings: of Rachid Benjelloun's forays into migration and transnational marriage, and of Mourad Benjelloun's experiences with the Moroccan labor market. Along the way, I explore situations Moroccans face as they navigate globalization-related dilemmas, including an increased emphasis on consumer culture, the presence of conflicting discourses on female virginity and premarital sex, and the perils of the informal labor market. These are issues people confront everywhere around the world, yet they do so in locally and culturally specific ways.

Globalization is an abstract concept, often described in terms of processes such as flows of capital and technology. But what is often lost in theoretical discussions of globalization is its lived reality, portrayed in a way that humanizes the struggles of individuals navigating an increasingly globalized world. Everyday life has changed as a result of discourses interacting on multiple levels: local, national, and global. The global permeates both the local and the national in ways that are not always obvious. People do not usually perceive themselves as encountering globalization head-on. Yet globalization makes its presence felt in numerous ways, in a chain reaction of sorts. Barriers to trade and investment are removed as governments withdraw from being the main provider of jobs and services to their people. Multinational supermarkets and shopping malls open, while neighborhood markets disappear. People change their shopping and eating patterns, and new health concerns emerge. Using the internet and satellite media, people form connections with each other in cyberspace and learn about other ways of living and other goods to covet, or about the possibilities for political action or "correct" religious observance. Through all of these processes, cultures are both resilient and malleable, maintaining aspects of their uniqueness while also finding themselves dramatically altered by global encounters.

These processes are common to countries such as Morocco that occupy the territory known as the Global South, the term applied to most nations within Africa, Latin America, and much of Asia.[3] Many governments embarked on structural adjustment programs in the name of "development" so that the Global South could become part of the high-speed international world of trade and commerce that characterizes life for the Global North, which comprises the wealthier countries of the Northern Hemisphere, plus Australia and New Zealand. What effect do these processes have on people in these countries? How are their everyday lives affected by globalization, and what are the core facets of Moroccan identity that remain stable amid flux and change? What is globalization, and what can an anthropological view of one family tell us about its larger meanings?

A Brief History of Morocco

Located in northwest Africa, 7.7 nautical miles across the Strait of Gibralter from Spain, Morocco is a stunningly beautiful country with a varied geography, three major mountain ranges, extensive beaches on its Atlantic and Mediterranean coasts, rich, flat agricultural land, and arid deserts in the south. Bordered by Algeria on the east and Mauritania on the south, Morocco has long been a crossroads of cultures. Inhabited since Paleolithic times (190,000– 90,000 BCE), its original indigenous population were Berbers, with the Phoenicians settling in the area as early as the sixth century BCE. The word "Berber" comes from the Greek *barbaroi*, and designated those who spoke no Latin or Greek (Ilahiane 2006, xxx). Subsequently, Morocco was occupied by Carthage, and then the Roman Empire from the first to the fifth century CE, and was briefly part of the Byzantine Empire, although Berber tribes in the hinterlands generally continued to live unaffected by these waves of occupation. Some Berbers converted to Christianity during the Roman Empire. There were also preexisting Jewish populations, whereas other Berbers followed animist religious practices. That was to change in the seventh century with the arrival of the Arabs, who brought with them the new religion of Islam.

Today, 99 percent of the country is Muslim, and all but a few thousand Jewish Moroccans, most of them now living in Casablanca, have emigrated. There are no significant Christian populations except for foreign residents. Moroccan Islam has historically been moderate in nature. Like all Muslims, Moroccans follow the Qur'an, hadiths, and sunna, or sayings and customs of the Prophet. They follow the juridical school of Maliki Islam for

Islamic law. But the country is also home to a variety of popular religious practices often loosely associated with Islam, such as Sufism or mysticism, the seeking of blessings at the tombs of holy men, the writing of amulets as a protection against black magic, and trance and spirit possession.[4] Both the internet and migration have caused many Moroccans to attempt to eradicate or "correct" such religious practices, often in keeping with a more hard-line, conservative Islam learned in the mosques of Europe, which are frequently funded by Saudis.

The first attempted conquest of Morocco was by the Umayyad Caliphate in 670 CE, and over the next century Morocco was claimed by various caliphates originating in the Middle East until the establishment of the Idrisid dynasty in 788. From the eleventh century onward, ruled by both Berber and Arab dynasties, Morocco was a substantial power in the region, commanding not only its own territory but parts of Spain and Algeria as well. In 1492 Spain reclaimed its land, expelling both Muslims and Jews from the country. Many settled in Morocco's "imperial" cities—Fes, Meknes, Rabat, and Marrakech— so named because they have all served as national capitals. Throughout history, there has been tension among the rural and urban areas, with the urban areas being under control of the *makhzen* (the central state apparatus), while the rural areas were often under tribal control and only nominally subject to the ruling dynasty.[5] In 1666 the current ruling dynasty, the Alaouites, took power. They first came to Morocco in the thirteenth century and trace their lineage back to the Prophet Muhammed.

Long coveted for its strategic position at the mouth of the Mediterranean, Morocco was eyed as a colonial possession by several European powers, but in 1912 France gained control of most of the country as a "protectorate," while Spain colonized the north and far south of Morocco. As a protectorate, Morocco was not considered a full colonial possession by the French, who built new cities (*villes nouvelles*) alongside the existing Moroccan ones rather than razing the Moroccan cities. The French did, however, take advantage of Morocco's rich agricultural and mining resources, and they created a substantial infrastructure in the country, including railways, government offices, and an educational system. In 1956, after an active independence movement, Morocco gained its freedom from the French, and the Spanish ended their Protectorate in northern Morocco later that year (although they continued to occupy parts of the country and did not leave the Sahara until the 1970s). Sultan Mohammed V, who had become popular when exiled to Madagascar by the French, became king. After his death in 1960, his son, Hassan II, ruled until 1999. Hassan's son, Mohammed VI, has ruled ever since.[6]

The king of Morocco is believed by Moroccans to rule by divine right because of his status as a descendant of the Prophet. Mohammed VI is moderate and generally well liked by the Moroccan population, although some human rights violations have characterized his regime, such as the arbitrary detention of journalists and crackdowns on freedom of speech in the name of protecting Moroccans in the war on terror. Relative to other Middle Eastern and North African regimes, however, the monarchy is tolerant of some social criticism, as long as that criticism does not specifically attack Islam or the royal family, or involve the conflict in the Sahara.[7] While political scientists consider Morocco to be an authoritarian regime, there is a bicameral parliament and a nominally independent judiciary. Revisions to the constitution after the "Arab Spring" of 2011, following greater demands for accountability and democracy, granted more power to the prime minister, who is appointed by the king from the party with the most votes. Morocco's response to the revolutions of 2011 is discussed in more detail in chapter 5.

Ethnically, most Moroccans consider themselves to be either Berber or Arab, with Imazighen, or free people, being the preferred term for Berbers. Multiple languages are spoken, including three dialects of Tamazight (Berber), spoken by 35–40 percent of the population; formal Modern Standard Arabic; colloquial Moroccan Arabic (*darija*, spoken in the home); and French. Many Moroccans also speak English and Spanish. Modern Standard Arabic and French are considered the prestige languages, with French still the preferred language of commerce among the elite. Language use is not a neutral issue, however. Although French is no longer an official language of instruction in public schools, Moroccan elites still send their children to French schools, giving them a considerable career advantage, particularly in business. Additionally, although Tamazight was recognized as an official language in the 2011 revisions to the constitution, its usage has historically been considered controversial and a "threat" to the Arab identity and social cohesion of the country. Since 2003 the language has been taught in schools to about 12 percent of Moroccan children, but many Moroccans feel that it hampers those children from full participation in a society that still privileges Arabic (Lindsey 2015). To ameliorate this, some believe the language should be taught to all schoolchildren in Moroccan society, although this is unlikely to happen.[8]

This study is situated in the city of Fes, whose *medina* or old city was first constructed in 808 by Sultan Idris II. An ancient, predominantly Arab city that served as a capital under various dynasties, Fes has a reputation in Morocco for social conservatism and religiosity. The medina is designated as a World Heritage site, yet Fes also has a large Ville Nouvelle, where the Benjellouns and their extended family now live. Longtime residents of Fes like the Benjellouns are known as Fassis, and they trace their lineage back to the expulsion of Muslims from Spain, or even further. Today, many influential government officials and businesspeople in Rabat and Casablanca have origins in Fes, yet the city itself has been in decline since ending its final stint as capital after the French moved the capital to Rabat. The second-largest city in the country, Fes has a population of 1.4 million, with a large number of rural-urban migrants, an unindustrialized economy largely consisting of artisanal, commerce, and civil service positions, and levels of unemployment that are generally higher than the national average (Newcomb 2009, 17).

Globalization, Modernization, and the Moroccan Middle Class

At the most basic level, definitions of globalization generally stress the increased integration of markets, ideas, and cultures, made possible by technological innovations and economic agreements among countries. New technologies facilitating globalization include air travel, ships that can hold up to 18,000 containers (the type that are hauled by eighteen-wheeler trucks), the internet, and satellite media. Economic aspects of globalization involve the integration of world markets, the free movement of capital across borders, and the (less free) movement of people through migration. This integration of world markets accelerated after the fall of the Soviet Union in 1989, which is a date that many consider to be a starting point for contemporary globalization. While trade, immigration, and exchanges among cultures have been happening for centuries, the speed of these processes is one of the hallmarks of contemporary globalization. Another unique feature of globalization is how highly integrated world economies are today. Past processes of trade and exchange (such as the famous "triangle of trade" that linked the slave trade in Africa to the colonies in the United States and back to industrial England) created links between specific parts of the world, but now the global economy itself is so interconnected that domestic events in one country can send shock waves throughout the entire world economic system.

Free trade agreements allow money to be transferred instantly across national borders, speeding up the rate at which people are able to do business. Loans granted to developing economies from international monetary organizations such as the IMF and the World Bank often require that Global South countries agree to remove their trade barriers, reduce obstacles to foreign investment, privatize their economies, and eliminate government jobs, subsidies, and social support. These loan packages and free trade agreements, and the idea that an integrated market unrestricted by governments is the best prospect for world prosperity, underlie the principle of neoliberalism, also known as the Washington Consensus.[9] Privatization and the elimination of government jobs and services, as we shall see, have resulted in many Moroccans losing their jobs, facing an uncertain economic future, and turning toward the informal economy to seek their livelihoods.[10]

Free trade benefits consumers, who now have access to a variety of goods that they were unable to buy in the past. Not so long ago, markets were local or regional. In the 1990s, for example, people in countries such as Morocco had to go to Europe to find specific products; but now international retailers such as Zara and fast-food restaurants such as McDonald's are found in Global South countries as well. The same free trade agreements that may benefit consumers also allow multinational companies to locate their factories in countries that offer the cheapest sources of labor. While in the past an entire product might have been made in one factory, various components of a single product are now often produced all over the world, to be assembled at a final destination. Outsourcing, in which manufacturers look for the cheapest place to produce their goods, often results in factories opening and then closing when a cheaper source of labor is found in another country. This has happened not only in countries like Morocco but also in places like Mexico and China, the countries most of us think of when we picture the outsourcing of labor. Moroccan textile factories produce goods for international retailers, but, as we shall see in chapter 3, most of the formally registered factories have closed, leaving only informal factories, which are often hidden from authorities and therefore beyond the reach of government safety regulations that would protect their workers.

In compliance with the conditions of loans received from the IMF and the World Bank, countries like Morocco drastically reduced the number of jobs available in the public sector. Private investment was supposed to create jobs to replace those lost under structural adjustment. Yet the much-vaunted private sector jobs did not magically appear to replace those lost, and despite economic growth, unemployment also rose dramatically. Meanwhile, as a result of free trade agreements, countries in the Global North were able to export their own products to the Global South, often for lower prices than it would cost to produce them in the Global South. Those whose employment once depended on industrial and agricultural products that can now be imported for less subsequently find themselves among the unemployed. As a result, legal and illegal international migration has increased.

Many governments in Global South countries, Morocco included, encourage emigration, both because it serves as a pressure valve for high unemployment and because migrants send back remittances that stimulate their

home economies. In Morocco during the summers, television specials celebrate the return of migrants from Europe for their vacations, with returning
families being interviewed as they reenter the country. For 2015, the World
Bank estimated that there were over 250 million migrants in the world, with
those migrants sending $601 billion back to their families ("International Mi-
gration" 2015). Morocco is ranked fourth in the entire Middle Eastern and
North African region for the number of its migrants, after the West Bank and
Gaza, Syria, and Egypt. Many of the jobs available for immigrants are low
skilled, in construction and farming for men and in care work for women.
However, the vagaries of the world economy affect overseas opportunities as
well, and in the case of Moroccans like Rachid Benjelloun, who has lived in
Spain off and on for over a decade, work became sporadic after the worldwide
economic crisis of 2008.

Prior to globalization, scholars used modernization theory as a way to
understand the contemporary world. This theory posited that formerly colonized Global South countries could "modernize" and become economically
successful if given money, technology, and education. Modernization theory
has its roots in postwar and postcolonial economic practices, which kept
colonial and postcolonial economies tied to the parent colony but lacked larger
integration with the world economy. Although modernization also involved
loans from international agencies, the goal was not integration with the
world economy but rather for local economies of what was then called the
Third World to catch up with already developed First World economies.
The goal of foreign investment was not so much to integrate developing
countries with the world market, as is the case with globalization, but to help
strong states to develop and become more "modern," like their former colonial
occupiers. Apart from implying a hierarchical notion of progress, in which
"traditional" people progress and become "modern," another issue with modernization theory is that many of these "developed" economies were able to
become wealthy because of their colonial investments. Labor and raw materials from the colonies enriched the economies of the colonizing power, while
the colonies themselves were often steered toward producing only one thing
for direct export to the colonizing power, a condition that did not help to
diversify their economies post-Independence.

Another major difference between the period of modernization and the
current era of globalization is that during modernization, governments were
expected to invest directly in employment and infrastructure, rather than cutting their workforce and services and turning toward privatization, as international lenders require today (Cohen 2003, 169). After gaining independence
from the French, Morocco invested in its own citizens, resulting in an

upwardly mobile, newly educated middle class, with the government serving as the primary employer of this group. These middle-class citizens formed strong attachments with the nation-state, and the idea that one could rise above one's origins and lack of resources created "a mystique around university and secondary education" (174). The Moroccan state was the largest employer, offering benefits and a generous pension for government employees that are still highly coveted, even as those jobs have dwindled to a small fraction of what they once were. Today, by contrast, most university graduates must enter the private sector, which is characterized by job insecurity, a lack of benefits, and unpaid internships that never turn into employment.

Shana Cohen writes of the newly modernized middle class of Moroccans who were the first in their families, post-Independence, to get an education and employment in the public sector (2003, 171). The creation of a "modern middle class," in fact, was one goal of modernization, as it was believed that this new middle class would consist of hard-working, loyal citizens eager to participate in national development (Adam 1968, 730). Prior to Independence, Morocco was highly stratified, with an elite class who worked closely with the French or with the royal family, and a working class who were either farmers or, in the cities, craft producers (artisans) and repair people (Boufous and Khariss 2015, 2). After Independence, the emerging middle class was educated bilingually in an adopted French educational system and consisted of "middle functionaries, employees, modern merchants and technicians, teachers, and some skilled laborers" (2). Education led to public sector employment with the state, but while this first generation benefited from heavy government support, with the coming of globalization that investment in human capital dried up. The children of this first generation of middle-class Moroccans are the ones who now find themselves struggling to achieve the same economic level as their parents, and in an era of privatization the government no longer provides anything beyond an education.

Who are the middle-class Moroccans of today? According to a Moroccan government study from 2008, "the middle class is constituted of individuals whose consumption, expenditure, or income levels are in the middle range of the social distribution of those indicators" (quoted in Boufous and Khariss 2015, 3). The study measured the middle class in two ways: by self-identification and by income surveys of 7,200 urban and 4,320 rural households. Self-identification was found to be somewhat inaccurate, as income levels showed that many people defined as poor placed themselves in the middle class, as did others whose income would qualify them as wealthy. The income surveys, however, indicated that 53 percent of the population was middle class (4). Within this class, there was a wide range of income levels, further divided into thirds, such that middle-class incomes ranged from 5,308 dirhams (approximately $545) per month on the higher end to 3,500 dirhams ($360) on the lower end (4). It is important to bear in mind, however, that even if the cost of living in Morocco seems much lower than in Western countries, the prices of many goods and services are similar. In large cities, rent for a centrally located apartment can be well above a monthly middle-class income. According to the survey, two-thirds of middle-class income was spent on food and housing (5). Middle-class households now have access to credit, something that was uncommon thirty years ago, with 31 percent of them indebted and borrowing at a faster rate than they are reproducing their incomes (6). Finally, around 25 percent of the middle class is unemployed, with the levels even higher for those with advanced degrees (4).

The Benjellouns, a prominent family in Morocco, originally came from the elite social class in Fes who, prior to Independence, owned property, had access to education, and worked as traders. Today, however, this particular branch of the family now finds itself in almost the same circumstances as those middle-class Moroccans without connections. This situation is echoed by the 2008 Moroccan government study, which concludes that the middle class now consists of both former elites and those who became middle class after Independence (Boufous and Khariss 2015, 6). While the Benjellouns still own a few modest properties and maintain some connections to friends in locally high places, for the most part they are just as challenged by the new economy as are members of the "new" middle class. Rachid Benjelloun, for example, has worked off and on in Spain for years, doing the same types of labor as many other undocumented Moroccan migrant laborers, on farms, in construction, and in security. Yet instead of arriving in Spain with a smuggler on an inflatable raft, he was able to get to Europe on a tourist visa due to some familial assistance, with property ownership and finances rearranged to seem as if they belonged to him. Hanane Benjelloun received a coveted government teaching position in part because of a family connection in Rabat, whereas the vast majority of teachers have to search for work in the poorly compensated private sector. Aside from Rachid and Hanane, the other siblings have struggled on their own to make ends meet, Mourad in setting up his own business after years of failures, Khaled warming the café seats for years despite his university degree, and Ilham taking the path of marriage and children rather than attempting to enter the workforce.

The fate of the middle class in Global South countries is a crucial barometer in determining the success of globalization. The Benjellouns are a solid example of what the middle class has become: a group clinging to its status through participation in the global economy, ranging from labor-related migration to consumption of material goods. While colonialism may have created a middle class, and although Moroccans still talk about their country as a "modern Muslim nation," the modernization discourse has been increasingly replaced by a globalization-focused rhetoric of "consumer, investor, and social entrepreneur (as well as *chômeur-diplomé*, or unemployed university graduate)" (Cohen 2003, 171). We see this in the status of Mourad Benjelloun, a small-scale trader and entrepreneur, and his unemployed brother Khaled. Modernization has created a sense of insecurity among many Moroccans, aware of the ways that their country does not measure up in terms of positive indicators such as development and negative ones such as corruption. Because globalization involves different processes than modernization, many have also internalized globalization's neoliberal encouragement that individuals take control of their own economic future in the private sector. Although arguments that the government should provide for its people still remain strong, Moroccans simultaneously blame those who are unable to find work for being lazy or "too good for anything," as one person told me in criticizing a friend who had turned down restaurant work because he considered it beneath him. It remains to be seen, however, if the lack of decent private sector jobs in Morocco will cause middle-class families to slip further down the social class ladder.

GLOBALIZATION: SOME ANTHROPOLOGICAL OBSERVATIONS

How have theorists explained and analyzed globalization's social effects, particularly in anthropology? While much writing about globalization outside anthropology has been focused on the macro processes of globalization, anthropologists have been interested in local effects: in other words, how individuals navigate globalization on a local level (Povinelli and Chauncey 2009) and in culturally specific ways (Inda and Rosaldo 2008, 7). In the introduction to an influential collection of essays about globalization, the anthropologists Jonathan Xavier Inda and Renato Rosaldo (2008) highlight several of the most prominent theories about globalization, which can be broadly summarized as those dealing with conceptualizations of time, culture and community, mobility, and exclusion.[11]

The geographer David Harvey (1989) proposed the idea that globalization has changed the experience of time and space, resulting in "time-space compression," in which the pace of life under globalization seems to move faster and space and distances become compressed.[12] New forms of communication and travel have lessened the amount of time it takes to get something accomplished, which has economic effects as well. Harvey asserts that this effect is due to mass production and overaccumulation in capitalism. He traces over-accumulation specifically to crises in the 1970s when factories around the world produced too much, flooding the market with goods, which then led to a decline in prices, corporate profits, and government revenues (Inda and Rosaldo 2008, 8). The result was a transformation in worldwide economies to a process of "flexible accumulation," in which corporations are more nimble and can attend to consumer demand by making just enough of a product, outsourcing, and hiring and firing the exact number of workers necessary to meet consumer demand but also dictating that demand by constantly producing new goods for the market. An example of this is the "fast fashion" practiced by clothing stores like Zara, in which Spanish designers pay close attention to runways and street trends, creating clothes that can rapidly be made in Morocco and placed in stores within days. This process, however, creates financial insecurity in the lives of factory workers. Moroccan factory workers must be flexible, responding to requests to speed up or slow down production depending on demand for orders, and working with no guarantee of a steady income, since factories are likely to drop workers when there is a slowdown. For other Moroccans, exposure to the latest consumer goods and technologies through media increases the desire to consume new products despite the fact that many such products may be out of reach financially.

The experience of time as compressed and sped up better describes life in urban areas than in rural places. To a tourist, village life in Morocco may seem picturesque and out of another era, with colorful red mud houses rising up from dramatic, rocky landscapes and shepherds tending flocks of sheep and goats in verdant oases. Yet despite surface appearances, rural Moroccans also experience globalization and are connected to the same processes as urban Moroccans. Labor migration is common in rural areas, with villagers leaving to seek economic opportunities both in the cities of Morocco and in Europe. Cell phones and satellite dishes are present in even the tiniest villages of Morocco. But rural populations lack the same level of access to health care, education, and economic opportunities available to people in the cities. Indicators of human development, measured by the Human Development Index (HDI), are quite poor for people in the Moroccan countryside, who have higher rates of maternal and infant mortality, greater levels of malnutrition, and a lower life expectancy than those in urban areas (United Nations Development Program 2014). Thus, while time in the villages may seem to outsiders to have slowed down compared to the bustle of Moroccan cities, generational time has actually sped up, since life cycles are much shorter. As the anthropologist David Crawford writes, "The compression of time associated with globalization is limited to certain types of interactions, certain types of time. The general

argument that time itself is being compressed is an artifact of urban experience, and the mistaken assumption that a high density of proximate interactions is the same thing as speed" (2007, 30). In rural Morocco, childhood is a
time of hard work and limited schooling, and reproduction and death happen
at much younger ages than in the cities. While not excluded from globalization
or the global economy, rural Moroccans often find other aspects of globalization, such as health care advances and education, to be physically inaccessible
or unaffordable.[13]

Under globalization, what happens to local cultures? Most anthropologists agree that cultural imperialism, in which local cultures are obliterated by
the colonizing effect of powerful Western imports, is a myth. Cultures change
one another in contact, and there are also exchanges between non-Western
cultures that do not involve the West. But the idea that cultures have to be geo-
graphically bound by particular places has been shattered. Culture, Inda and
Rosaldo point out, has the potential to be deterritorialized. Anthropologists
have proposed numerous definitions for culture, but the definition that, despite its age, is most likely to be cited in introductory anthropology classes is
that of Edward B. Tylor (1920 [1871]), who wrote that culture is "that complex
whole which includes knowledge, belief, art, morals, law, custom, and any
other capabilities and habits acquired by man as a member of society" (1). In
other words, the particular practices, behaviors, and ideologies that individuals learn throughout life come to constitute a person's culture. Throughout
anthropology's history, cultures were also associated directly with places, such
that one traveled to Morocco to learn about Moroccan culture but did not
think of it as belonging to other spatial locales beyond the country's national
borders. However, with globalization and mass migration, cultures are no
longer linked so closely to single territories, a concept that has fascinated
anthropologists as they think about how culture "travels" and often becomes
reterritorialized in new places.[14]

Cultures are not simply wiped out by global processes but respond in
creative ways to global discourses and constraints. Some of the "local-level
responses to global processes" have included "migration, gender-role transformations, nationalism, the emergence of new or revitalized ethnicity, revolution,
riots, the assumption of transnational and even global identities, and religious
revivalism" (Lewellen 2002, 26). Anthropologists have focused on global
"flows" of people and capital, on transnational social movements, and on globalization's effects on the environment. Many anthropologists have demonstrated that cultural identity and distinctiveness are alive and well, and that
cultures have unique ways of receiving, rejecting, or transforming cultural
imports from elsewhere. While this is certainly true, there are ways that the

Global North and its financial products have sent dramatic shock waves throughout Global South societies.

Another debate in globalization theory has been the extent to which the nation-state has withdrawn from the lives of its people. At first, it appeared that multinational financial agreements tied the hands of governments, allowing investment and private enterprise to operate freely without government interference. While the nation-state may have been constrained by the demands of its financial overseers under structural adjustment, it has not withdrawn from public life entirely but rather attempts to manage its citizens in new ways. For example, in the case of Morocco, the most intimate domain of marital life, family planning, has been subject to extensive government programs that encourage women to adopt birth control in the interests of promoting national development by encouraging them to go to work instead (Rinker 2013, 102). This started in the 1970s but continued well into the neoliberal era of structural adjustment. Another example concerns the ways government promotes investment and development. As we shall see in chapter 5, it is the nation-state that allows the bulldozing of shantytowns and facilitates investment in desirable neighborhoods by encouraging or even forcing residents to leave their homes. It is also the nation-state that fosters a shift in consumption practices, again by facilitating the opening of fast-food chains and supermarkets and the closing of local traditional markets, even if the supermarkets are also peddling convenience foods that have not been a part of Moroccan diets in the past.

This book looks at the creative ways that one family and its associates have dealt with the transformation of their country and its economy, and at their expectations for their relationship to the nation-state. Anthropologists have often used the term "resistance" to describe local responses to globalization, but there are moments when people also embrace it, generally when they are able to participate in aspects of globalization that they find beneficial. There are also moments when that embrace can cause a collapse of some former way of life that was arguably better for people than its globalization-informed replacement. But rather than adopting a simplistic "resistance" to globalization, people often vacillate between acceptance and rejection, between assimilation and integration. Moroccans attempt to make the most of globalization-related changes by choosing from among the best possible options for their survival. Local responses to globalization we will see throughout this book include nostalgia for the colonial past and a rejection of the present, an eager embracing of consumerist behaviors, and an ambivalent acceptance of new health technologies that, for pragmatic reasons, exist alongside traditional therapies. The Benjellouns struggle to make a living among the limited options available to them, without a clear sense of the best path toward a stable career. And in forming a family, both women and men face a marriage process complicated by a mix of traditional expectations and new legal reforms, by increased freedom of choice combined with the existence of patriarchal expectations. Discourses that did not originate in Morocco—such as the emphasis on increased religiosity and correct Islamic practice disseminated through media and migration, ideas of universal human rights and women's rights, and consumer culture—all come into play as Moroccans grapple with questions of both cultural and personal identity.

Against the background of these constraints, the Benjellouns have maintained strong local family ties but a decreased connection to the nation-state. The nation-state is still present as the arbitrating body that legislates and allows global processes and investment, but it has withdrawn from its role of providing assistance to its citizens. "Local" for the Benjellouns means maintaining kinship networks and trying to protect face-to-face relations, as well as a sense of identity and tradition in the face of challenges from imported customs and ideas. Ideas such as "identity" and "tradition" are invoked in nostalgia for the past, and for an ideal country in which everything was predictable, work and family life were stable, and one's life trajectory was clear and easy to follow. "Identity" and "tradition" are invoked when the Benjellouns make "local" choices because the global is too expensive or out of reach. At other moments, when the global is accessible, within means, and nonthreatening, one hardly hears talk of "identity" and "tradition," and instead people welcome innovations, touting the superiority of new over old, and of the global over the local.

GLOBALIZATION IN MOROCCO: A PANORAMIC VIEW

Morocco's own economic history, as well as its interactions with institutions such as the World Bank and the IMF, set the stage for globalization. In 1974 phosphate prices quadrupled on the world market. This resulted in a temporary windfall for Morocco, as phosphates are one of its most significant natural resources. The government used these profits to fund dams and to develop "a chemical industry based on phosphate derivatives and capital-intensive import substitutions such as sugar," in addition to funding military engagement with the Polisario Front in the Western Sahara (Claassen and Salin 1991, 193). This led to tremendous budget deficits in 1976 and 1977. A drought in 1981 devastated the country's other major export, agricultural products. Beginning in the 1980s, the Moroccan government introduced austerity measures and began structural adjustment programs to reduce its indebtedness and boost its economic productivity. As in so many other countries, these structural adjustment programs involved receiving loans from the IMF and the World Bank on condition that Morocco reduce its public services, privatize state-owned industries, remove its trade barriers, and devalue its currency.[15]

Although Morocco was considered a model by the IMF for its successful implementation of the conditions of structural adjustment, there was a subsequent increase in unemployment and poverty (Pfeifer 1999, 26). The resulting economic instability and hardship led to increased migration to the cities of Morocco, and to the massive growth of cities ill prepared for such challenges. At the time Morocco received independence from the French in 1956, 70 percent of Moroccans lived in rural areas, but by 2015 this had declined to 40 percent ("Rural Population" 2015). The Benjellouns, who lived through this era, remembered the bread riots of 1981, when falling phosphate prices and drought, combined with an agreement with the IMF to raise food prices, led the government to raise the price of wheat, a dietary staple for Moroccans (Alam 2011). In all the major cities there were demonstrations, which ended in violence and people being gunned down. After further experiments with reducing food subsidies also ended in violence, the government ceased pursuing this austerity measure and continued to subsidize wheat.

The latest phase of neoliberal economic development in Morocco has contributed to an increase in investment in the economic development of the cities. People may have bread for their dinner tables, and nobody is starving, but life in the cities becomes more and more expensive as outside investors snatch up desirable real estate in city centers, thus driving up prices. Everything is available, but at a price. The latest technologies, whether a new iPhone or the most recent medical advances, are available, but at prices comparable to those in Europe, how can a middle-class Moroccan with an income of around $600 per month afford them?

Whether globalization is considered a new phenomenon or just the latest phase in a cyclical wave, the current moment in Morocco is nonetheless one characterized by conflict, nostalgia, and a struggle to maintain local identity. These themes unite the chapters of this book, as do some of the new experiences people have that would never have been possible even fifty years ago. Globalization is the political and economic backdrop to the quotidian struggles that take priority here. The Benjelloun family members fight earnestly to hold onto local culture, while at the same time embracing other aspects of global culture. People are eager to consume new products, to soak up the latest popular media (whether from Europe, America, or the Middle East), or to correct Islamic practice based on information imported from elsewhere. As Shana Cohen has written, participation in global market capitalism "is founded in economic insecurity and consumption, with market actors strategizing to overcome insecurity through consumer choice, whether of a school, an appealing 'look,' an insurance plan, or a type of job" (2004, 11). Moroccan culture is at times fragmented, at others unified, with individuals frequently shifting their alliances among practices common to specific neighborhoods, cities, and social classes. While local culture remains resilient, there is also considerable evidence that smaller moments of resistance are not enough to keep change from sweeping through people's lives.

MOROCCO: ETHNOGRAPHIC CONTEXTS

Over forty years ago, the political scientist John Waterbury wrote *North for the Trade: The Life and Times of a Berber Merchant.* This ethnography followed the life of a Berber grocer from southern Morocco who lived through many of the important changes of the twentieth century: migration, nationalism, the independence movement, and economic change. The Benjellouns, similarly, have not only lived through significant moments in Moroccan history but also were born in an era when women had more children, when the government was a major employer of its citizens, and when migration, both to cities and to other countries, had not yet become the force it is today. As adults, they find that the opposite is true: families are much smaller, the state has slashed jobs, and nearly every family has at least one member residing abroad. The subsequent closing off of opportunities to most middle-class Moroccans is a process that affects them profoundly, and the networks and resources that give the Benjellouns a minor advantage in some situations have not been sufficient to change their class status or increase their wealth and prosperity. Focusing on one family's experiences with marriage, reproduction, work, food, and housing offers a perspective on a global Morocco that is connected to the rest of the world in unprecedented ways.

Morocco has a long tradition of being open to anthropological research. Consequently, anthropologists have produced a rich trove of ethnographies over the past one hundred years, almost out of proportion to Morocco's size as a country. It has also been an important site of theory production for the entire discipline of anthropology. Some of the major theoretical trends in anthropology have been based on fieldwork in Morocco, including structuralism and structural functionalism, interpretive or symbolic anthropology, Foucauldian and post-Foucauldian approaches, and the anthropology of gender.[16] In addition to theoretical contributions, however, these ethnographies have also offered a look over time at how Moroccan culture has changed. Many topics that were of interest to early anthropologists—tribal kinship, for example—were later replaced by other concerns, such as gender relations, the strength of patriarchy, and human rights.[17]

Several useful ethnographies on Morocco target in greater detail topics that I touch on in this book. In *Searching for a Different Future: The Rise of a Global Middle Class in Morocco* (2004), Shana Cohen focuses on the rise of an alienated middle class in Casablanca whose primary allegiances lie outside the nation-state.[18] Cohen finds that the nation-state competes for attention with transnational options for social relations, ranging from Islamist movements to development organizations (11). Similarly, Emilio Spadola's 2013 book, *The Calls of Islam: Sufis, Islamists, and Mass Mediation in Urban Morocco*, also set in Fes, explores in a religious context how the Moroccan state competes to present a state-sanctioned version of Islam, based on Sufi traditionalism, with alternative types of Islam from outside the country, including Islamism and Qur'anic exorcisms. In both books, globalization draws people's attention and loyalties away from the nation-state, whether in terms of participation in the global economy or through different forms of Islam.

In *In and Out of Morocco: Smuggling and Migration in a Frontier Boomtown* (2001), set in northern Morocco's Rif mountain region in the 1990s, David McMurray shows how wealth brought home by migrants from the city of Nador alters gender dynamics, social status, and consumption habits at the expense of a disappearing sense of local history. The onslaught of Western consumer goods, entertainment, news, and other media events, representing Western power and authority, obliterates local memory, and McMurray argues that "hyperimportation" or "the consumption of so much Westernalia . . . has the effect of devaluing all things local" (141). Ironically, much of the new construction in Fes is financed by Moroccans from the Rif Mountains, whom Fassis often disparagingly refer to as "drug dealers," a reference to that region's agricultural status as a source of hashish. As McMurray's Nadoris forget their pasts in the consumer-driven haze of the present, in Fes, globally accumulated wealth from elsewhere has caused a retrenchment into localism and a sense of nostalgia for Fes's past prominence.

Another globalization-related book, M. Laetitia Cairoli's *Girls of the Factory: A Year with the Garment Workers of Morocco* (2011), describes the lives of young women working in factories for multinational corporations. While factory work opens up new social and professional spaces for these women, it also challenges their dependence on patriarchal communities, who question the morality of women who leave home to go into the workplace (6). Their newfound employment also requires them to be subservient to the authority of the factory, where some of the same patriarchal patterns are re-created. In the

global economy, women are preferred in factory labor because of their perceived docility.

Two other notable works that place Moroccan culture in the global marketplace focus on music and fashion. Deborah Kapchan's *Traveling Spirit Masters: Moroccan Gnawa Trance and Music in the Global Marketplace* (2007), for
example, looks at Gnawa musicians and healers who induce trance through
music, and how they emerge on the global stage. Similarly, M. Angela Jansen's
Moroccan Fashion: Design, Culture, and Tradition (2015) examines the com-
moditization of the Moroccan fashion industry, its influences both within and
outside the country, and its reception and transformation according to local
and global influences.

What sets *Everyday Life in Global Morocco* apart from these other works
is the way it moves among multiple themes of globalization, rather than focusing on a single theme, as expressed in an urban setting by members of the
middle class. Based on several research trips to Morocco from 2007 to 2013
and on continued correspondence between visits, this book focuses on the issues that were preoccupying the Moroccans I know during this time.[19] Other,
larger world events were occurring at the same time, such as the revolutions
that wracked the Arab world in 2011. While people avidly discussed those
events and how they might influence their own lives, they also remained pre-
occupied with everyday life in its local contexts: seeking shelter and finding
work, or getting married and having children. People were not always aware of
when and how everyday life was affected by globalization, but as someone who
knew the families involved in this book and visited them at least every other
year, I often felt that the changes were dramatic: a local building demolished,
its history suddenly erased from the landscape; a beloved friend whose health
had suddenly begun to deteriorate from years of poor eating, or what we in the
United States might call "lifestyle choices"; or a person suddenly home all day
due to the loss of a job he had held for many years.

Chapter 1, "Transnational Suspicions: Marriage and Changing Gender
Roles," offers a look at the complexities of marriage and divorce in Morocco,
particularly in the case of transnational marriages. This chapter also examines
how globalization has led to uneven changes in laws and social practices regarding women and gender roles, attending to the rights of married women
while neglecting those of unmarried ones. Morocco's family laws (*mudawana*)
were revised in 2004, resulting in a code that is considered progressive internationally but is viewed with mixed feelings within Morocco. While the
revised laws give women more rights in marriage and divorce, they have
been applied unevenly, resulting in continued marriage inequities for women
in some places while privileging women in other settings. Further, marriages

can be complicated by migration. In particular, I tell the story of Rachid's un-
successful marriage to a Moroccan expatriate who took several thousand dollars from him and then left the country, promptly asking for a divorce and
claiming her "new rights" under the revised mudawana. The stories of men are
often ignored in studies concerned with gender inequities in society, yet their
experiences of marriage (and masculinity) are also important. Globalization
has created significant changes in gender dynamics in Moroccan society, specifically in the areas of education, marriage and divorce, and women's status,
yet increased options and roles for women coexist with patriarchal attitudes
that also significantly limit women's freedom and mobility.

Chapter 2, "Reproduce: Changing Conceptions of Reproduction and Infertility," asks what we can learn about contemporary relations in marriage
and kinship when people approach the obstacle of being unable to have
children. I follow Hanane Benjelloun's quest to conceive to show how traditional practices coexist with global medical technologies that are still out of
reach to all but the wealthiest members of the population. Aware of the possibilities presented by assisted reproductive technologies, women like Hanane
often adhere to local treatments, not out of a mistaken belief in their effectiveness but because the global technologies are unaffordable. Infertility often results from women marrying later, and changing ideas about the purposes of
marriage also affect how a diagnosis of infertility will be received. While the
actual technologies brought by globalization may be unaffordable, new regimes of biomedicine and law have placed the locus of authority and decision
making outside the extended family unit, privileging the expert opinions of
physicians in convincing childless couples to stay together. In the past, an infertile couple might have been pressured to divorce, or the husband compelled
to take another wife, but now kin groups have less power than before to determine whether a couple should stay together or not.

In a globalized world, how do people earn a living? What types of jobs
exist that were unheard of a generation ago? The uncertain paths Moroccans
take to find employment in an era of neoliberal restructuring are the topic of
chapter 3, "Labor: Migration and the Informal Market." Migration remains
one strategy, with remittances from family members working abroad representing approximately 7.8 percent of Morocco's GDP and serving as an important means for lifting families out of poverty (Bouoiyour and Miftah 2014). Yet
since the economic downturn in 2008, many Moroccans overseas have been
jobless, and remittances have remained flat over the past few years. This chapter contextualizes those statistics with the stories of Rachid, who migrated to
Spain in search of work, and his brother Mourad, who has become a small-
scale entrepreneur selling used clothes after losing his job with a multinational

automaker. The precariousness and instability of Rachid's and Mourad's working conditions in the informal economy, compared with the unemployed status of their brother Khaled, are indicative of dilemmas faced by many Moroccan families. To make ends meet, many Moroccans participate in what has been called "low-end globalization," described by Gordon Mathews as "the transnational flow of people and goods involving relatively small amounts of capital and informal, sometimes semilegal or illegal, transactions commonly associated with 'the developing world'" (2001, 20).

Chapter 4, "Consume: The End of the Mediterranean Diet," explores changes in shopping, cooking, and eating for middle-class Moroccans. Using a sensory perspective that attempts to capture the feel of changing Moroccan cuisine, from the supermarket to the dinner table, I follow Ilham Benjelloun, a middle-class mother of two in her thirties, to show how her family's patterns of eating and sociability differ from those of preceding generations. What effects do time-space compression, new work regimes, the availability of packaged and fast food, and the constant rush of modern life have on the ways people come together around food? And where women are associated with the work of feeding their families, how has the changing diet affected their relationship to food? Moroccan cuisine is both distinctive and internationally renowned, yet in everyday life the increased availability of processed foods is having dramatic effects on Moroccan diets. I explore the implications of those changes, both for health and Moroccan culture, and for how the Benjellouns themselves perceive cultural change through food.

The final chapter suggests that nostalgia can be a particularly strong emotional response to globalization. Chapter 5, "Dwell: Urban Nostalgia as Neoliberal Critique," draws us into local, national, and global contexts by showing gentrification firsthand, from the perspective of a group of individuals who are witnessing their local neighborhood and city changing before their eyes. The chapter explores the perspective of Khaled Benjelloun as he tries to keep a developer from opening a bakery in his neighborhood. Khaled's protest took place during the so-called Arab Spring of 2011 and is all the more interesting because the same people who fought so ardently to save the character of their neighborhood from changing felt that they had no stakes in the national protest known as the February 20th Movement. At the heart of both movements was a frustration with neoliberal governance, yet Khaled and his friends did not see any connection between what was happening in their neighborhood and the February 20th Movement. This chapter shows how globalization's abstract qualities make it hard for individuals to see themselves as sharing common concerns with others who are also protesting the same issues. Through Khaled's attempts to protect the character of his neighborhood, we can see how the ideal urban spaces of the past represent a critique of neoliberal governance in the present.

Morocco, while culturally distinctive, is inextricably bound to global processes that have conflicting results, both positive and negative. An ethnographic, localized study of everyday life is crucial to highlighting the ways the global and the local interact, in both overt and subtle ways. By using the Benjelloun family's stories to illustrate the themes of each chapter, this book attempts to enliven abstract debates about globalization, showing that globalization-related processes are woven into the fabric of everyday life, whether people are cognizant of them or not.

What some have called "globalization from below" or "grassroots globalization" entails considering globalization from the perspectives of people rather than multinational corporations. It is hard not to see globalization at work when speaking to the Benjellouns, whether in hearing the exhaustion in Rachid's voice as he talks about the end of his most recent short-term contract of farm labor in northern Spain or when Hanane tells me in hushed whispers about a cousin in France whose child is "not really hers," but the product of sperm donation, a process that is forbidden in Morocco due to Islamic prohibitions against adultery. Globalization is at work when Mourad talks about his venture in the early years of the twenty-first century to open a cybercafé with money from a "young entrepreneurs'" program, a microfinance loan that allowed him to buy ten computers and rent space in a rundown office building near the Place Florence, where he collected approximately a dollar per hour from each customer, a calculation that in the end was not enough to keep his business afloat. And it is at work when Ilham and her mother argue over whether her youngest child, who seems to subsist on heavily sweetened Danone yogurt and packets of Spanish cookies, should be eating more meat-and-vegetable-filled *tagines* to gain weight.

Market reform, Shana Cohen suggests, has led to the creation of a "detached" middle class in Morocco, in which middle-class citizens, having lost their association with the nation-state as a result of structural adjustment, not only lack "identification with any overarching collectivity" but also direct their actions toward "individual movement for opportunity and security within the imaginary and real possibilities of the globe" (2003, 169). While the Benjellouns are not fully detached from the nation-state and still profess their loyalty to the king, the family's allegiances nevertheless shift depending on the situation: at one moment they embrace globalization, while at another they decry it as a process that is disrupting the strength of local, traditional life. In conversation, they never personally connect it with the decisions of the monarchy but instead view globalization as the abstract changes wrought by outside influences, technology, investment, and modern life.

While the global economy encourages individualism and the pursuit of economic gain to enrich one's immediate family, Moroccans still have a strong sense of the need to support extended family. Migration to cities may mean diminished family ties for some rural-urban migrants, but as families reestablish themselves in a new region, extended family generally live together and pool their resources, a circumstance of economic necessity that also serves to maintain a strong familial aspect of Moroccan culture. The family is what remains, even when entrepreneurial Mourad is unable to create job opportunities for his other brothers, even when nobody can lend money to Hanane for expensive fertility treatments. As jobs with benefits disappear, and as citizens negotiate their changing relationship to the nation-state, the resources of kin should not be underestimated, even as the government pushes for smaller families, and even when resources are not available to those in precarious circumstances. The Benjellouns continue to struggle, helping out family members in the absence of assistance from elsewhere. They find that they have just enough income for shelter, food, and clothing, and for the modest consumption of material goods that are not necessities. Is this, then, what globalization promises?

Notes

1. "Benjelloun" is a pseudonym for the extended family whose experiences are central to this ethnography. I have changed many identifying details at the request of the family. Some of the events described in this book happened to other members of the extended family, including cousins, aunts, and uncles.

2. A total of 60.6 percent of Morocco's population lives in cities, according to the United Nations ("Urban/Rural Division of Countries" 2015).

3. "Global South" and "Global North" are preferred over previous terms (such as "First World" and "Third World," or "developed" and "developing) used to distinguish between those countries which were the targets of aid and development and the countries from which development loans originated. Previous terminology often contains an implicit judgment of progress, implying that one set of countries is attempting to measure up to the standards of the other.

4. See, for example, Spadola 2013; Cornell 1998; Kapchan 1996; Mernissi 1977; Crapanzano 1973.

5. The term *makhzen* has complex meanings. Its literal meaning is "storehouse," referring historically to the central authority who collected taxes and tribute from tribes, but today it refers not only to the king but also to those who surround him, including influential notables, business people, army figures, and other members of the royal family. Many episodes in Moroccan history reflect a tension between *bled al-makhzen*, or "land of the central government," and *bled as-siba*, the tribal "land of dissidence" that was not always under the control of the sultan.

6. Since Independence, the Moroccan kings have "adopted a policy of political fragmentation" in which various groups and interests compete for access to the monarchy (Abdel-Samad 2014, 796). This fragmentation is both overt in terms of "divide and conquer" approaches toward different political groups and more subtle in cultural terms. While Moroccans may unite in the face of perceived external threats such as terrorism or political tensions with Algeria (see Newcomb 2009), there remain long-standing cultural hostilities among Moroccans from different regions, social classes, and ethnicities as well as between those from urban and rural areas.

7. Morocco has been involved in a dispute over large parts of the Sahara since 1975, when Hassan II led a march of 350,000 Moroccans, called the Green March, into the Spanish territory to claim it for Morocco. The Spanish left, but the Algerian-backed Polisario Front, a group calling for independence and self-determination, waged a sixteen-year war with Morocco and Mauritania that ended in a cease-fire agreement in 1991. Morocco controls large parts of this territory, and its position is that the entire territory is Moroccan Sahara, but the United Nations has called for referendums and still does not recognize Moroccan sovereignty or that of the Sahrawi Arab Democratic Republic, the part of the territory governed by the Polisario.

8. See Silverstein 2012a and 2012b for more on the issue of Berber activism in Morocco.

9. The term "Washington Consensus" was coined in 1989 by the British economist John Williamson to refer to ten specific conditions required by Washington, DC–based lending agencies such as the IMF and the World Bank when they loaned money to developing Global South countries. These included suggestions that these countries should engage in privatization, tax reform, trade liberalization, and redirecting of public funds into initiatives such as health care and education. "Washington Consensus" is a contested term now more broadly used to refer to the principles of neoliberalism.

10. The informal economy consists of employment activities that fall outside the domain of state protection, taxation, and regulation.

11. Examples of key works exploring general anthropological understandings of globalization include see Appadurai 1996; Lewellen 2002; and Inda and Rosaldo 2008. For a survey of earlier anthropological literature on the topic, see Kearney 1995.

12. Equally influential has been Anthony Giddens's (1990) theory of time-space distanciation, which argues that distant localities are connected by global events, and oftentimes what is happening far away has more meaning than local events. He also argues that although new technologies have enhanced our abilities to connect globally with people who are far away, this has been at the expense of local, face-to-face relations.

13. David Crawford's excellent *Moroccan Households in the World Economy: Labor and Inequality in a Berber Village* (2008) highlights the many ways rural Moroccans interact with the world economy, shattering the stereotype that rural people have little contact with globalization.

14. See Deborah Kapchan's *Traveling Spirit Masters: Moroccan Gnawa Trance and Music in the Global Marketplace* (2007) for an excellent example of how Moroccan spiritual and musical practices take new forms in other geographical locales.

15. From an anthropological point of view, structural adjustment programs are problematic, as they place a "one size fits all" model of development on all countries, regardless of particular circumstances (Lewellen 2002, 26).

16. A partial list of significant contributors includes early functionalist and structuralist-functionalist anthropologists Robert Montagne, Jacques Berque, and Ernest Gellner, interpretive and symbolic anthropologists Clifford Geertz, Lawrence Rosen, and Vincent Crapanzano, and Foucauldian and post-Foucauldian anthropologists Paul Rabinow, Dale Eickelman,

and Abdellah Hammoudi. Scholars who have worked on gender issues include Fatima Mernissi, Deborah Kapchan, Susan Schaeffer Davis, Elizabeth Fernea, Elaine Combs-Schilling, and Fatima Sadiqi.

17. See, for instance, the work of Abdellah Hammoudi, Katia Žvan-Elliott, Susan Schaeffer-Davis, Deborah Kapchan, and Susan Slyomovics.

18. See also Shana Cohen and Larabi Jaidi's *Morocco: Globalization and Its Consequences* (2006) for an examination of globalization's effects on society, particularly in the areas of political reform and development. While it thoroughly covers larger trends and processes, especially those related to economics and politics, it does not offer ethnographic accounts of individual lives, nor does it examine how global processes affect more intimate domains such as those of family and marriage.

19. I first began conducting fieldwork in Morocco in 1994. My long-term engagement with Moroccan society has allowed me to keep up with multiple families over time and to watch them as they move through different stages of life. This longitudinal study has enabled me to see how global processes have affected the lives individuals once imagined for themselves, and how many of their lives have taken a different course from what they expected.

I

***

TRANSNATIONAL SUSPICIONS

Marriage and Changing Gender Roles

AFTER THE WORLDWIDE ECONOMIC DOWNTURN of 2008, Rachid Benjelloun, with more time on his hands, began to think it was time for a life change. Although he worked when he could, frequently returning to Spain to keep up his residency requirements and to search for short-term labor contracts, the steady six-month contracts he had depended on had become a thing of the past. He started going to the mosque regularly, and when he was in Fes he stopped spending as much time with his old friends who still drank alcohol and were going nowhere with their lives. He also began to think about marriage. In the past, he had dated women in Spain and even had a girlfriend or two whom he'd been serious about, but now he decided it was time to settle down with someone who shared his values: hard work, family, and a pious life.

In 2011, on an internet dating site for Muslims, he met Nejma, a Moroccan in her thirties who lived in Texas and worked in an insurance office. Nejma wore the hijab and told Rachid she had been engaged to a Moroccan but had never married. Her former fiancé, Nejma claimed, was not religious enough. After an internet courtship of a few months, during which they spoke frequently on Skype, Nejma and Rachid became engaged. Rachid was looking forward to starting over in America and had begun studying English in his spare time but wanted to meet her in person before getting married. Applying for a tourist visa to the United States was out of the question, since he knew that his recent patchy work history would definitely cause the consulate to refuse him. Nejma promised she would come to Morocco to spend time with him, but she continued to postpone her visit, citing the inappropriateness of dating before a proper Islamic marriage. A *shaykh* she had consulted said it was better to marry first than face the temptation to commit sins during an engagement. She insisted they do things properly, with him speaking to her family first and then setting a date for the wedding. Rachid had mixed feelings about marrying her without having seen her in person, but he agreed to visit her family in Casablanca to formalize their engagement. Together with his uncle and mother, he traveled to Casablanca, but when they arrived at Nejma's family home in a modest working-class neighborhood full of identical five-story buildings, the family did not invite him inside. Rachid's mother, Latifa, was particularly insulted, saying that even if the family insisted on separating men from women, at least she should have been invited inside to meet the women of Nejma's family.

Instead, they joined Nejma's brother and uncle in a café, where her family laid out the terms of the marriage, including a substantial bride price (*sadaq*) of several thousand dollars as well as jewelry.[1] If Rachid wanted to marry her, they insisted, he would gather the money to show that he respected her reputation and her good name, since she was, in their words, "still a girl [*ma zal bint*]." This was an assertion on Nejma's family's part that she had never been married, that she was still a virgin, and that therefore she could demand a higher bride price than someone who was divorced. They agreed tentatively to a wedding four months away.

Latifa had concerns about the fact that the relationship between their two families was almost nonexistent. Was Nejma's family just inhospitable? Why had they not invited Rachid's family into their home? And why had no one in Nejma's family come to Fes? Rachid brought up the issue with Nejma, who, in response, sent her mother, sister, and aunt to Fes to visit his family. The Benjellouns prepared a dinner in their honor, inviting several members of their immediate family, but only women, respecting Nejma's request to Rachid that no men be present. Nejma's mother and aunt arrived two hours late, citing problems with the train. They stayed only about an hour, refusing the several hours of socializing that the Benjellouns had expected, and departed shortly after drinking their after-dinner tea.

Latifa had a bad feeling about the marriage and was convinced that the two families were incompatible. By Fassi standards of hospitality, had Nejma's family really been interested in forging an alliance, they would have been friendlier, at the very least staying a few hours to make up for being two hours late. The Benjelloun family did not practice gender segregation, and aside from funerals, most ceremonies (such as weddings) and parties were mixed. Rachid and his sisters, however, convinced Latifa to put aside her reservations. Rachid was in his thirties, after all, and it was time to marry. There would be more work for him in the United States, where the unemployment crisis was not as severe as it was in Spain. Privately, although his sister Ilham had also found the family to be rude, she invoked regionalism and speculated that it might have something to do with their origins from a city near the Algerian border, saying, "People from there don't have the same manners as people from Fes. And they probably think we're snobs from Fes, so it might take them some time to warm up to us."

Among them, the Benjellouns raised the money agreed on in the marriage contract.

"If they're so religious," Mourad pointed out, "why are they demanding such a large sadaq for her?" Many Islamists decried the fact that materialism and the high costs of weddings were leading to fewer people getting married, so there had been a move in recent years to encourage Islamic marriages without all the associated forms of consumption, particularly the sadaq or expensive weddings. Some highly educated Moroccans also eschew the custom of the bride price, writing down only a symbolic token in their marriage contracts, such as a wedding ring. But most members of the Benjelloun family did not question this, accepting the basic cultural fact that Moroccan weddings came with the custom of money changing hands in preparation for setting up a new household.

To afford the sadaq, Rachid returned to Spain, working as much as he could in the months leading up to the wedding, while his mother gathered family heirlooms and sold a dilapidated apartment she had owned in the medina, which brought in a modest monthly income. His siblings contributed what they could as well. In June Nejma arrived. She had been talking on Skype with Rachid for a year now, and by his account their first in-person meeting went well. He found her just as attractive and modest as she seemed on the internet, wearing a fitted headscarf and a long but stylish skirt and blouse. The night she arrived, he met her in Casablanca, where he took her to a seafood restaurant a friend had recommended. He stayed overnight with a cousin in Rabat, and then he and Nejma spent the next day together, walking around the city and talking about the future.

"She said she'll go right back to America and apply for the green card for me to move over there, so we can be together," he reported. He was nervous about his lack of English, but she assured him that in Texas his Spanish would give him a good start, and the English would come with time. The wedding was to take place in two days, and her family members, who were arranging it, had been uncommunicative with him about the details. When he asked if they might go to her house and visit them, she refused, saying they were too busy working on preparations. He respected her wishes and returned to Fes to wait.

For a few months now, his only contact with her family had been when she sent over documents necessary for the marriage permit. When the wedding day approached, the Benjelloun siblings, their mother, and a few other relatives traveled to Casablanca, unsure of what to expect. The wedding was held on two floors of an apartment that belonged to someone Nejma's family knew, and, as expected, the men's party was on one floor, the women's on the other. However, aside from the gender segregation, there was still music and dancing. Rachid's family had paid for the catering at considerable expense, even though the bride's family traditionally covered wedding arrangements. The couple signed the wedding contract and left around eleven that night in a borrowed car, to spend their wedding night in the four-star hotel Rachid had reserved for them. The next morning, they traveled to southern Morocco for their honeymoon.

For the next few days, while the couple was on their honeymoon, no one in the family heard from Rachid, except for brief text messages and photos. The couple looked happy in the photos. But a few days into the marriage, Rachid called Mourad and asked him to send money, around the equivalent of $500. Mourad sent it to him, no questions asked, but after five days, two days earlier than expected, the couple returned to Fes, completely out of money. Rachid and Nejma would stay in the family apartment with Latifa, but Nejma was visibly unhappy with this arrangement, complaining about the tight quarters, the uncomfortable bed, the lack of pillows, and the fact that Rachid did not have any money left to put them up in a hotel. She was waiting for jewelry and an antique gold belt (typically worn with caftans) that his family had given her, which had been at the jeweler's to be fitted. Rachid, Latifa, and Nejma went to the jeweler the evening the couple returned but found the shop closed.

The next day, they returned to the jeweler. The jewelry would be ready later in the day, and Rachid asked Nejma if she wanted him to show her around the city or meet some other members of his family, but she said she just wanted to go to a café and wait. They sat together, not speaking, for an interminable amount of time, and then returned to Latifa's for lunch. After lunch the jewelry was finally ready, but then Nejma announced she was returning to Casablanca. She refused to stay another night in the family apartment, she told Rachid, which she found uncomfortable. He assumed she was just tired from the strain of the past week's travel, but when he called her later that day, her phone was turned off. He left several messages, sick with worry, but she did not return his call until the next day. Nejma was supposed to spend another week in Morocco but announced that her plans had changed and that she had to return to Texas in two days. He offered to come to Casablanca to try to make things up to her, but she told him, "Only if you can support me like a real man, which doesn't seem possible, so I don't want to see you."

He was stunned by her comment and, in truth, by the events of the week of the honeymoon. From the first moment they arrived in Agadir, everything had gone badly. Nejma found the three-star hotel he'd reserved to be not nice enough for her standards, and she insisted on moving to a four-star resort. Rachid was too ashamed to tell her it was beyond his ability to pay. At the resort, food was included in their bill, but after one meal there, Nejma told him the buffet was unappetizing and demanded they eat at restaurants she had researched in advance, all of which were expensive and filled with foreign tourists. Rachid was easygoing and had envisioned that they might go to cafés or modest restaurants, or even eat fresh grilled fish at the port, but Nejma was horrified by this suggestion and accused him of not valuing her. She had no interest in walks on the beach and spent most of her time shopping, bent on acquiring as many things to take back to Texas as possible, ranging from clothes to expensive purses to Moroccan souvenirs for her friends at home. The morning he called Mourad in desperation, Rachid had spent all of the $1,500 he had brought with him to cover the honeymoon expenses. The $500 Mourad sent lasted only another two nights, after which Nejma had to put part of the cost of the final night at the hotel on her credit card, which had infuriated her. She again accused Rachid of not valuing her sufficiently, going back to the day of their wedding, when, she said, his family had chosen an inferior catering company which had delivered food that was of low quality. She cited the first hotel in Agadir and most of his ideas about restaurants as evidence of his cheapness, claiming he had deceived her about his income and the amount of money he had.

"I wouldn't have married you if I'd known you were so cheap," she said. "You deceived me, with your Benjelloun name and your work in Spain. I thought you were someone else."

"And I thought you were religious and didn't care about money and gifts," he argued back. "You told me you liked me for who I was, and that the most important thing was to be a good Muslim, not to be so obsessed with money."

Rachid realized too late that Nejma and her family had assumed his family was wealthy based solely on their family name and Fassi origins. His side of the story was that he had never deceived her about his own wealth, and that he had explained to her that he worked in Spain when he could but had not had the same job opportunities that had been available only a few years before.

"I don't know what else she wanted. We had an agreement about the sadaq. I found a way to cover that. All our other conversations were about how we would start a life together and support each other. I told her I was a hard worker, and that we might start our new lives with nothing but we would grow with time. And as for her, I thought she was a religious girl. I didn't see anything religious about her when she got here. She only asked to go to the mosque once, for Friday prayers, but all I saw was someone who treated me like I was a bank."

For the rest of her time in Morocco, Nejma avoided Rachid. He went to the airport on the day she was scheduled to return to the United States but could not find her, and after driving around Casablanca visiting all the places he knew her family might be, he finally found her brother at his workplace; the brother admitted that Nejma had not left but told him to stay away from her. She had lied to Rachid about returning early and stayed another week in Morocco, her mobile phone turned off.

Soon after that he received an official notice that she was petitioning for divorce and spousal support. In the petition, she claimed she was unemployed, which he knew was not true, and she asked for the equivalent of several months' rent, alimony, and several thousand dirhams for damages to her reputation.[2] She also stated that he had only wanted to marry her to immigrate to the United States.

"I'm divorcing you because we're incompatible, and also because you didn't respect me," she told him one of the few times she agreed to communicate once she left Morocco. He asked her what she meant by a lack of respect.

"You were so cheap on our honeymoon," she explained. "And when you took me to the cheap fish restaurant in Casablanca the first day we met. You never bought me one present except when I had to ask. And the catering your family ordered for our wedding was horrible; the chicken was cold. And because of the new mudawana I'll get everything I'm asking for. All I'll have to do is come back and sign the papers. You're going to pay!"

Rachid consulted a close family friend who was a lawyer, who looked at the conditions of the marriage contract. Rachid pointed out that the contract said she was unemployed. It also, he said, claimed she was a virgin, though he had found out on their wedding night that this was not true. Nejma had been briefly married in the States, he learned, although she had divorced right away. Originally, she had told him only that she had been engaged to someone. The lawyer consulted a colleague who often handled transnational divorce cases, and the colleague explained that marriage and divorce records in the United States were public. At considerable expense, Rachid paid the second lawyer, who had connections in America, to obtain copies of both the marriage and divorce decrees. To his surprise, he discovered that Nejma's "brief" marriage had lasted more than two years. He filed a countersuit for marriage fraud, since virginity in Morocco still makes a woman more "marriageable" than someone who is divorced, so for Nejma to claim that she was a virgin significantly increased her value in the eyes of Moroccan law. Additionally, it was technically illegal for a Moroccan who married abroad to neglect to register a marriage in Morocco. In his petition, he asked for the return of the jewelry his family had given her.

What followed was a legal nightmare that took up much of Rachid's time and energy over the next year, as he pursued both cases through the courts of Casablanca (where she filed) and Fes (where he filed). Nejma came to Morocco once, and they met in court. The judge urged them to stay together, which Rachid was willing to do, but Nejma refused and said she would never stay married to him. Most of the time he was in court alone, with his lawyer facing her lawyer, and the cases were repeatedly deferred as the lawyers asked for more time or the judges asked for more paperwork. During this time, Rachid was unable to travel to Spain for work, even when his friends there had called to let him know about available work contracts. He worked in Fes when he could but was now receiving very little income. The Moroccan courts repeatedly refused to accept the marriage and divorce documents from the United States, often for puzzling reasons, such as too few stamps on the documents, or that the documents looked like photocopies (which they were, although with stamps certifying them). Nejma's lawyer repeatedly filed for delays, a strategy that Rachid realized only too late was meant to delay the clock on the divorce so that he would be responsible for support during the time they were legally married. He spent several hundred dollars obtaining translations and multiple copies of the marriage and divorce decrees from the United States. Rachid and his lawyer tried several times to have the police question Nejma about her first marriage in the United States and serve court papers to her house in Morocco, particularly when they were aware she would be in the country, but the police were never able to find her.

Ultimately, the Moroccan courts granted Nejma her divorce, but they ordered both Nejma and Rachid to pay nominal sums that ended up canceling each other out. Several months later, through her lawyer, Nejma served him with an additional lawsuit seeking support (*nafaqa*) for the time they had been married, in which she claimed again to be unemployed in Texas. Even though she was no longer in Morocco, the money would be transferred to her through her lawyer. Rachid and his family had spent over $10,000, he said, on the wedding, on jewelry, on the honeymoon, and then on legal costs, and he admitted to feeling completely blindsided by his ex-wife's actions.

"If she didn't like me in person, then why did she allow the wedding to take place?" Rachid asked. "What did she get out of it in the end? She probably spent more on plane tickets and on her own lawyer. She accused me of deceiving her and of not being what she thought I was. But I don't know what that means, except that she must have believed I had money because of the family name. I never led her on. And she's the one who deceived me. When we talked on Skype, she always presented herself as religious. If you're truly religious, you shouldn't care so much about money."

Rachid believed that Nejma's reasons for marrying him were solely materialistic, which he did not realize until after they were together in person. Over the internet, she seemed to him like a deeply spiritual woman interested in meeting a pious husband and starting a new life together. In person, she was happy only when he bought things for her. He had envisioned a romantic honeymoon full of walks on the beach and discussions about their future together, but "even when she had just put her bags in the hotel room, she asked if we could leave to go shopping," he said. "I bought her a Prada bag. It cost one night in the hotel, which I also couldn't afford, but when I questioned that, she said I shouldn't have gotten married if I couldn't afford to be married. The next day she wanted diamond earrings. She said when her best friend was on her honeymoon, each day the husband bought her a special gift to show how much he loved her. She suggested the value of those special gifts should each be several hundred dollars and said I should have planned for this as part of our honeymoon. She accused me of being cheap and not loving her. Is this what an Islamic marriage is supposed to be?"

Family Law and Divorce Strategies

What globalization-related changes to Moroccan marriage can be illustrated by Rachid's short-lived marriage to Nejma? Additionally, what do their divorce proceedings demonstrate about the workings of the 2004 mudawana reforms, designed to give women more rights and a more equal footing with men, yet within the contexts of an "Islamic" marriage?

Previously, for a woman to petition for her own divorce was difficult, requiring proof of the husband's abuse or neglect, although a man's right to divorce was unilateral. Women in lower socioeconomic classes were and still are highly vulnerable in the event of a divorce, since many lack viable professional skills or education. Under the revised laws, women not only have the right to a judicial divorce but also are granted financial support, whereas before only their children would receive support, and women were entitled to support only for the time they had been married. This initially affected the divorce rate in Morocco, and in 2005, one year after the new laws went into effect, the number of divorce applications plummeted 72 percent from the previous year ("Divorce Applications in Morocco Plummeted 72%" 2005), as men had become wary of the increased financial obligations that divorce incurs.

Numerous anthropological accounts have detailed the gender imbalances and inequalities in Moroccan marriages, usually from the point of view of the women. Indeed, one of the reasons for the reform of Morocco's family code, the mudawana, in 2004, was that women were often taken advantage of by their husbands, who could divorce them with little explanation, expel them from the marital home, and easily shirk any financial responsibility for their wives, who did not have the same ease of divorce as men did. Women were required to document that men physically abused them in order to ask for a divorce themselves, something that the 2004 revisions changed by allowing women to petition for *chiqaq* divorces, or divorces for reasons of "discord" or "irreconcilable differences" (Foblets 2008, 151). In research I conducted in the early 2000s, I heard many stories from women consulting with a Fes national governmental organization (NGO) who were trying to figure out how to get a divorce or whether they had any rights to support after being abandoned by their husbands, some after marriages that had lasted decades (Newcomb 2009).

The mudawana reforms of 2004 were designed to prevent these situations, providing women greater protection. Approved by King Mohammed VI and spearheaded by years of political agitation on the part of women's rights activists, the revised mudawana raised the minimum age of marriage from fifteen to eighteen, allowed women to marry without the permission of a male guardian (*wali*), and made judicial divorces on the grounds of discord (shiqaq) easier for women to obtain. Within two years of the implementation of the mudawana reforms, in fact, judicial divorces (which women could now petition for) had increased 113 percent, from 9,983 in 2005 to 21,328 in 2007 (Deiana 2009, 77).

The movement to change the mudawana was local and distinctively Moroccan, but activists drew on global networks and a global knowledge base for support. The revised mudawana adheres to some international standards for equality, acknowledging the fact that Morocco has signed the United Nations Convention on the Elimination of Discrimination against Women (CEDAW). Although women's uneven access to inheritance violates CEDAW principles, the higher age for marriage and the ability to obtain a divorce both stem directly from CEDAW.[3] However, since the new mudawana was implemented, responses to the reforms have been mixed, and the reforms have not been evenly enforced across the country.

Examining Moroccan marriages from the perspective of men, however, there have been numerous examples of women successfully petitioning to their advantage from their more limited legal positions, even prior to mudawana reform. Although widespread statistical studies of courtroom outcomes do not exist, studies by the anthropologists Ziba Mir-Hosseini (1993/2002) and Lawrence Rosen (2016) both examined court cases from different historical periods and regions of Morocco and demonstrated that women won their legal cases a majority of the time. Women did not lack for strategies in navigating divorce cases from their inferior position under the previous mudawana, but the revised laws have given them additional tools with which to pursue an advantage. Some of the strategies used by Nejma, however, have little to do with any new advantages granted by mudawana reform. For example, delaying the divorce by having her lawyer question the validity of Rachid's documents is not a new tactic but later proved to be an excuse for the couple to stay married long enough to force Rachid to pay her the maximum support.

In a discussion of transnational Moroccan divorce cases taking place in the 1990s, Lawrence Rosen writes:

> The usual image of Muslim countries is that all of the legal power is in the hands of the men. This is far too simplistic. Though the range of variation across the Muslim world is considerable in this regard, the situation in Morocco is not altogether unusual. Delaying tactics may run up support charges, corruption can be used to tactical advantage, willful disappearance can be used to a woman's benefit, and a wife may even be willing to go to jail rather than obey an order to return to her husband[,] thus drawing other relatives into the fray and restarting the support clock. These are tactics born to a considerable degree out of statutory inequality. But the question as to who has the greater power is not susceptible to a stereotypical Western answer. (2000, 8)

Rachid and Nejma's divorce reflected many of these strategies, and Nejma's distance from Morocco worked to her advantage, as the Moroccan courts had no record of her previous marriage or the fact that she had lied about being unemployed.

Told from the perspective of the husband, Rachid's marriage story reflects a number of themes that characterize many Moroccan marriages, particularly transnational ones. With Moroccan women migrating with greater frequency, women like Nejma can pursue a legal case from the safety of a country that does not recognize Moroccan law or communicate in any way with the Moroccan legal system.[4] Divorce proceedings have often involved both men and women negotiating for influence within a legal system prone to corruption and insufficient communication among courts and law enforcement agencies, yet these processes become even more complicated when marriages are transnational. Rosen writes that in giving notice about divorce proceedings in transnational marriages, movement both within and outside Morocco "becomes a very significant problem, one that is compounded by the quest for advantage" (2000, 8). This clearly happened with Nejma, who could not be questioned in Rachid's lawsuit against her for breach of contract. In fact, the address he had for her family became invalid several months into their divorce proceedings when her remaining family members moved and could not be located.

Using Rachid's story as an illustration, this chapter examines the complexities of Moroccan marriage practices as a result of women's changing roles in an era of globalization. In addition to being a transnational relationship contracted over the internet, Rachid and Nejma's marriage demonstrates the global influences of both the Islamization movement and consumer culture. As a migrant to Spain, Rachid had been influenced by his peer group to become more religious, citing the messages he heard in Spanish mosques and among friends that Moroccans were insufficiently religious and needed to return to their Islamic roots. In Nejma he attempted to find a pious spouse, but although she maintained the outward symbols of religiosity (such as the headscarf), he found her to be heavily influenced by consumer culture. While increased religiosity and materialism take local forms, both are also reflective of larger global processes. Nejma's independence and the fact she lived abroad, far from her family, are illustrative of Moroccan migratory practices that affect both men and women. The marriage's rapid failure, followed by the lengthy struggle to get a divorce, highlights the issues Moroccans face in navigating the actualities of the legal system, in which courts in different parts of the country are not even in communication with each other, let alone with the legal systems in other countries.

The mudawana reforms led Nejma to believe that claiming her rights meant suing Rachid for large sums of money, whereas to Rachid the laws illustrated that the new mudawana offered greater potential for women to exploit men by marrying and then divorcing them to gain a financial advantage. While the new mudawana has ostensibly given women greater freedom to divorce, it has also created an increased climate of fear and suspicion on the part of men. Although there is no evidence that women in Moroccan society suddenly have greater rights than men, in gossip and urban legend, stories like Rachid's are cited as evidence of women's venality. The girls of yesterday, they conclude, were more obedient and supportive of their husbands, whereas today they are materialistic and clamoring for men's resources. Many men now claim to be hesitant to marry for fear that, in the event of a divorce, their former spouses will take all their money.

Globalization-related changes in women's lives have influenced the changes in family law, which, activists maintain, demonstrate the fact that women deserve more independence and autonomy within a patriarchal system that tends to favor men. However, there has been a backlash against the new mudawana among Moroccans, who often decry the current state of marriage and criticize the laws as leading to women's supposed immorality and unbridled freedom. Moroccan society is still patriarchal, and Rachid's experiences feed into a narrative I heard from many Moroccans in which Western-influenced women have adopted a secular stance of equality in order to take advantage of men. Rather than accepting ideas of gender equality asserted by women's rights activists, men continue to assert traditional forms of masculinity, even if their own social positions have become insecure. Among Rachid's friends and family, for example, Nejma was described as having "forgotten her culture," in the words of Mourad, or as "not a real Muslim," according to one of Rachid's friends.

"She made him think she was a religious person, and a real 'girl of the people' [bint an-nas]," Rachid's friend Mustapha said. The expression "bint an-nas" describes a girl who is faithful, dutiful, and the ideal Moroccan for marrying. It was a phrase people used often to describe a young woman of excellent character, and there was even a famous song dedicated to "Ya Bent Nass" by a singer from Fes, Abdelhadi Bilkhayat. Nejma "sent him pictures from the mosque on Friday prayer day, or during Ramadan, to show him how much she was into her religion. But it was just for show. She's forgotten her culture, her religion, everything. She's a fraud," Mustapha continued.

Outside of marriage, women are blamed for social immorality, including an overwhelming rise in the number of single mothers, who are unable to petition the fathers of their children for any form of child support. In an imagined past, some Moroccans describe a harmonious, local form of marriage in which the values of Islam are universally agreed-upon premises for marriage, gender roles are clearly defined, and conflict is absent or, if present, resolved by families. However, globalization has complicated this idealized picture, leading to confusion on the part of both men and women about what marriage should entail.

GLOBALIZATION, WOMEN'S RIGHTS, AND MALE EXPECTATIONS

Transnational marriage is one of the more obvious ways that globalization has affected men's and women's lives in Morocco. Traditional urban family arrangements prior to Moroccan independence kept women largely at home, out of the workforce, and subservient to the authority of men. Even shopping for food was a male activity, and women were seldom in the public space. In rural areas, women worked hard in agricultural pursuits, but labor was generally segregated by sex, while in cities, prior to independence from the French in 1956, seclusion was the norm among middle- and upper-class families. Legal arrangements reflected male authority. While Morocco largely adheres to a legal system inspired by European civil and criminal law, for issues related to family, marriage, and inheritance, the mudawana is taken directly from the Islamic law, specifically the Maliki school of jurisprudence. The mudawana was not formally codified nationwide until independence. Formalized, it protected the authority of senior males over the family and over women in an attempt to appease the tribal notables needed to support a fragile monarchy building its support base after independence (Charrad 2001).

The recent legal reforms to the mudawana, the product of years of organizing on the part of women's rights advocates, reflect the fact that women's roles have changed considerably in Morocco since Independence. Since the 1970s, women have entered the public sphere to an unprecedented degree for both education and employment. Women can now be found in the universities in numbers equal to their male counterparts, and many work out of both choice and economic necessity, although their representation in the official workforce is much lower than that of men. In urban areas, women's official employment rose from 5.6 percent in 1960 to 17.3 percent in 1994, a figure that does not include women working in the informal economy (Ennaji and Sadiqi 2004, 67). Other statistics also demonstrate that women's roles in Moroccan society have changed. The average age of marriage for Moroccan women rose from 17.5 in 1960 to 26.2 in 2004, whereas the average age for Moroccan men was 24.4 in 1960 and 32.1 in 2004 (Haut Commissariat au Plan du Maroc 2012; Ouadah-Bedidi, Vallin, and Bouchcoucha 2012). Since the 1970s, the birthrate in Morocco has also decreased dramatically, from an average of seven children per woman in 1970 to slightly above two in 2014 (Adjamagbo, Guillaume, and Bakass 2014, 5).

Transnational migration patterns also increasingly affect women. The first phase of out-migration to Europe in the 1960s was largely male, but family reunification processes brought women to Europe throughout the 1980s. Since then, many women have migrated independently to Europe or North America, generally for economic reasons. Nejma had gone to the United States as a student, and her subsequent marriage to an American gave her permanent resident status. While initially it was uncommon for Moroccan women to migrate on their own, since the 1980s migration has become a strategy women have used to enhance their economic position or in search of greater freedom from the strictures of a conservative society (Salih 2001, 660).

Yet, while there have been many positive changes that have allowed women the chance to travel, work internationally, and participate in public life, globalization-related poverty, as in other countries, has also tended to hit women the hardest. Structural adjustment measures, implemented throughout the 1990s, have contributed to increased rural-urban migration, a reduction in social and health services, and sizable cuts in government-sponsored employment. Decreases in social spending have meant that women have had to increase both the time spent on care work and in low-paid industries or informal sector jobs to make household ends meet (Cairoli 2011). Migration, both internal and out of the country, has resulted in a rise in female-headed households. In 2004, the most recent year for which statistics are available, the World Bank estimated female headed households to be at 17%, and this amount has likely risen to around one in five households since then. ("Female Headed Households" 2017). Many poor women from rural areas have migrated with their families to cities, where they often lack the support of extended family or kin in the event of abandonment by their husbands. While women of urban origin have benefited from the increased emphasis on education and literacy, poor rural-urban migrants have not. As Ennaji and Sadiqi write, "Whereas upper and middle class women generally worked outside the home as a result of years of education and have felt proud of their work, poor women worked outside the home out of necessity and were not generally proud of this work" (2004, 67).

The number of Moroccan NGOs assisting women has increased dramatically since structural adjustment measures were implemented beginning in the 1980s. One worldwide by-product of globalization has been that as governments decrease social services, NGOs spring up to address unmet needs, generally with far fewer financial resources than the government has. In Morocco, many of these NGOs have been staffed by activists who view their mission as not only to help women who have lost the traditional safety net of family resources through migration but also to agitate to change laws that discriminate against women. Morocco's women-focused NGOs typically offer resources such as literacy and job training, legal advice about divorce and custody issues, domestic violence support, and psychiatric counseling. These NGOs can be roughly divided into two groups: those staffed by secular activists seeking rights for women closer to those that align with international human rights dictates (such as CEDAW, of which Morocco is a partial signatory); and Islamist groups that also aim to assist women but believe that legal reform not only goes against Islam but is also an import from the West.[5] It should be noted, however, that these Islamist groups do not operate in a vacuum and are themselves inspired by transnational Islamist movements (Moghadam 2012). Both camps draw on groups in other countries for solidarity, knowledge, and support.

One of the most significant accomplishments of these NGOs has been the revision of the mudawana, yet across social classes, the reforms have met with responses ranging from negative opinions to outright rejection, frequently with the approval of local authorities.[6] In addition to the objections of men that the reforms give women too much leeway in petitioning for divorce, reforms are unevenly applied depending on the court, region, and preferences of the judge. The eighteen-year-old age requirement for marriage, for example, can be over-ruled by a judge, and in recent years the number of underage marriages has actually increased. From 2007–2012, the number of underage marriage petitions rose from 38,710 per year to 42,783 (Haut-Commissariat au Plan, 2012).

Another change—that women no longer need the permission of a male guardian or wali to get married—has also been largely ignored. Most mar-riages are still taking place with a guardian, and many Moroccans feel that weddings without a wali demonstrate the lack of blessings from the parents, thus giving women less support in the event of conflict.

While reforms to the mudawana have granted married women more room to maneuver in divorce negotiations, single women are virtually ignored in terms of legal rights, health, and sex education. Females are still considered legal minors and dependents until marriage. As Katja Žvan Elliott points out, reforms in marriage laws affect only married women; they do not grant rights or autonomy to unmarried women (2015, 6). The Moroccan government, inspired by international development agendas that emphasize women's empowerment, encourages young women to seek higher education and em-ployment, even if it means traveling from their villages to the city. Yet Elliott notes that unmarried Moroccan women continue to be socially marginalized as "girls" well into adulthood in their villages of origin, where their education (and time spent living away from families) renders them unmarriageable (12). Continuing to live with their families, who often view them as a burden and strictly control their movements, these young women are forever legal minors, and any income they receive from employment goes to support their families. Elliott writes that "delaying marriage for girls may in fact translate into spinsterhood for life. A girl's (young) age and inexperience, rather than her education and employment, continue to define her as a suitable bride" (15).

The lack of rights and attention single women receive extends to health care. Morocco's national health ministry does not take the health of single women into account at all, either in terms of statistics or in national programs that would target them (Adjamagbo, Guillaume, and Bakass 2014, 28). The result, when it comes to sexual health, is that single women are uninformed and lack access to birth control, although it is widely available to married women. Family planning, promoted by the government since the 1970s, has been highly successful in Morocco, such that by 1992, 35.5 percent of married women used contraception, and 54.5 percent did so by 2005 (5). As mentioned earlier, there has been an accompanying decrease in births, from seven children per woman in 1960 to 2.3 in 2003 (5). Yet family planning programs are accessible only to married women, despite the dramatic rise in the number of single mothers and unplanned pregnancies.

Urban lifestyles and demographic shifts, whereby marriage for both men and women is delayed, and women are more likely to be in the public space, have made premarital sexual activity increasingly likely. There is little data available on contraceptive use among single Moroccans, in part because of assumptions that premarital sexual activity should not be taking place in an Islamic country. For reasons of both familial and personal honor, women are still expected to be virgins before marriage.[7] However, a survey of 776 young people in 2006 found that among youth aged sixteen to twenty-nine, 86 percent of men and 34 percent of women had had sex prior to marriage (Bakass and Ferrand 2013). Respondents also stated their awareness that hymen reconstruction surgery could be a viable option for young women who needed "evidence" of their virginity reinstated prior to marriage. Yet the denial of sexual activity outside marriage makes contraceptive access and use difficult. Among unmarried couples, the most common forms of birth control used were the most ineffective: the rhythm method or withdrawal, and condoms only on rare occasions. Estimates from 2009 indicate that abortions in Morocco take place at a rate of between 400 and 1,000 each day, although legally abortions are restricted to married women whose health is deemed to be in danger (Adjamagbo, Guillaume, and Bakass 2014, 7).

Modernization, education, and economic migration have led to larger numbers of women in the domestic labor force, in both high- and low-skilled professions. Many of these women live far from their families in a culture that still discourages female independence and questions the reputations of those who are not living under the protection of parents or husbands. Several problems have resulted from this, including the increased burden on women with children born out of wedlock and the lack of legal and social rights single young women have when not under the guardianship of a father or husband. Living on their own or working as maids, young women are vulnerable to sexual exploitation and often have no understanding of or access to birth control. In 2009 an estimated 27,000 babies were born to women without husbands, a situation that carries extreme social stigma (Jay 2012). Until a recent change in laws, those children were unable to get identity cards or claim a last name. Single mothers are still unable to petition a father for a paternity test or child support unless they have documentation to prove that they were married to or engaged to the father. Requiring the father to take a paternity test is considered an accusation of adultery, and adultery is still a crime for which both mother and father could be imprisoned. Single mothers are socially marginal-ized, yet aside from the efforts of the few NGOs that have been created to support them, such as Aicha Ech Chenna's Solidarité Féminine (McTighe 2011), they receive no assistance or support. Thus single women, many of whom are poor, uneducated, and unqualified for most forms of employment, bear total re-sponsibility for the care of their children.

Although Moroccan women now live very different lives from those of women thirty years ago, alterations to their legal rights and social status have been uneven. While women's NGOs have made major strides in pursuing legal reform, social attitudes have not necessarily followed suit. Globalization may have resulted in new lifestyles, de facto independence, and increased economic responsibilities for many women, but the patriarchal social structures that pro-mote traditional familial expectations are still strongly present. This results in a social identity that some Moroccan intellectuals have described as "schizo-phrenic."[8] The outside world views Morocco as a modern and progressive Mus-lim society, but inside the country public opinion often shows little support for the legal reforms widely celebrated in the international community. Further, there is considerable denial that social problems, such as alcoholism or children born outside of marriage, exist (Allali and Hamdani 2006, 45). This "schizo-phrenic" identity conflict can also be found in the contradictory messages of equality and education for the sexes as well as in the necessity for upholding tra-ditional roles in marriage. Although premarital sexual activity takes place, Moroccan society disapproves of it, insists that women should be virgins prior to marriage, and denies access to birth control to unmarried people even as birthrates out of wedlock skyrocket. Women are held to be solely responsible for premarital sexual activity, with no legal recourse to petition the father for paternity.

Returning to the marriage story of Rachid and Nejma, Rachid's friends cited what happened to him as evidence that Moroccan women were turning the tables on men where marriage was concerned, and, in a sense, getting away with behavior that had once been possible only for male migrants. One story several Moroccans told me was about a woman living abroad who had been in the national news; she had been arrested for marriage fraud after contracting serial marriages with men in different regions, getting them to pay her a high bride price, and then successfully petitioning for divorce and alimony from all of them. Domestically, rumors also flew about women tak-ing men for every dirham they owned.

Nejma, whose side of the story we do not have here, represented a contra-dictory mix of traits that men claimed exemplified what was wrong with the "modern" Moroccan woman: she lived away from her family, and thus her honor could not be vouched for; she had lied about her previous marriage and her virginity; and she planned to use the new mudawana only to extract as much money from Rachid as possible. The hard-working bint an-nass of the past who stood by her man and demanded little was the ideal, mythical wife these men hoped to find. While Rachid said he was surprised by Nejma's behavior on their honeymoon and reported being stunned at her materialism, his friends insisted that this was typical behavior for Moroccan women.

"It's hard to find a Moroccan woman who isn't constantly trying to get something from you," Rachid's friend Ali, himself unmarried, said. Like Rachid, Ali also moved between the European Union countries and Morocco. He had worked in agriculture in Spain until jobs for Moroccan men dried up, at first because employers were hiring women from eastern Europe, and then, ironically, because they were employing Moroccan women in short-term contracts.[9] Ali had briefly been engaged to a woman in Morocco but had broken the engagement because the she was "too demanding" and because her family had asked for too much compensation, including a car. In his thirties, he was now sporadically employed and said he was not interested in getting married. Other friends of Rachid's who were married, particularly to women who did not work, described the challenges of having to constantly give money and gifts to their wives so that they could keep up with their social aspirations. The money these men gave their wives, they claimed, either went immediately to clothes or to their wives' families.

"I constantly find [my wife] giving her family money that she had just told me she needed for the children," one man said. "She'll say the kids need new shoes, or they've grown out of their clothes, but then I don't see anything new on the kids. I'll ask what she did with the money and she's vague about it, but then I'll overhear her mother asking her to get more from me. When I confront her I find out she's given it to her mother."

Another man, Hassan, reported that his wife had bothered him for months to get her a car because her best friend's husband had given her one. "So finally I was able to buy one, but it doesn't end there. She just finds something new she wants, and she makes my life hell until she gets it."

In urban middle-class contexts, I suggest that this perceived materialism is the result of a culture that continues to insist on the traditional patriarchal roles of men as breadwinners (still enshrined in the mudawana, which requires only that men support their wives and not that working women contribute to the family income) combined with strong messages from satellite television, the internet, and other media that happiness can be obtained only through the acquisition of material goods. While Nejma lived in the United States, she acted, according to Rachid, "exactly like a Moroccan woman here. She was only interested in buying things, and in taking pictures to send to her friends back home of us at the nicest restaurants." Rachid's friends' opinions of Nejma were somewhat contradictory, although all emphasized her materialism: she was too Americanized, she was a fraud, she was too much like a materialistic Moroccan woman, she was not enough like a traditional bint an-nass Moroccan woman, and she was not a good Muslim.

This materialism may no doubt be exaggerated by men, who acutely feel the social pressure of needing to demonstrate their financial status beyond simply providing a roof over their families' heads and food and clothing for their children. Conversely, women still expect to be provided for, while additionally receiving social messages that a husband's love is demonstrated not in terms of time and affection but in terms of what he can buy. While in the past, and in the absence of their own incomes, amassing jewelry and other valuables was a strategy women could use as "insurance" in case they were divorced, today this practice is enhanced by the greater availability of material goods. This is also true outside urban areas, and Elliott notes that among rural women in southern Morocco, "materialism in terms of both owning and showing off one's assets was an important aspect of self-definition for particularly the younger and middle-aged married women" (2015, 182). She adds that among the married women she knew, "being poor . . . was thus expressed in the lack of possessing consumerist goods rather than in social deprivation" (183). Nejma repeatedly berated Rachid for being unable to truly "care" for her by showering her with luxury gifts during their honeymoon. Loubna Skalli writes: "Women have grown to inhabit a cultural context increasingly riddled by what Zakia Daoud calls 'a schizophrenic cohabitation of a desire for change and a no less strong desire to obey traditional values.' . . . In the case of women, schizophrenia is further sustained by a politico-economic order that embraces global capitalism and its technologies and a socio-cultural logic that reaffirms 'authenticity' and its traditional (gender) values" (2006, 62).

Moroccan men also experience a conflicting mix of societal messages concerning women, which is reflected in their own ideas of marriage. In their comments to me about Rachid's story, as well as in other contexts, they expressed interest in a companionate marriage with a modern woman who nonetheless deferred to her husband and could keep up a home the way women of their parents' generation did. Don Conway-Long, in his analysis of a survey of forty-eight men from three Moroccan cities in the 1990s, notes that many were insecure about women's changing position in Moroccan society and the effect it would have on men's social positions. Most of them believed that men's power is granted by politics and religion, while women exercise power through their sexuality. Additionally, many felt that the media's emphasis on women's rights, already beginning in the 1990s, combined with women's slightly enhanced abilities to get a divorce, was emasculating for them. Conway-Long writes: "The irony of the position is that it is women who are far more likely to be physically endangered by men's behaviour, not the other way around. Men who see women as such a threat as to necessitate fantasy or real actions of vengeance are, in some sense, the vanguard of patriarchal privilege. Their interpretation of male-female interaction is derived from perception, not fact; from ideology, not statistical reality. But the experience of the power inversion is a reality for those who feel it" (2006, 148).

Men also believed that changing educational and economic practices in Morocco were leading to demands for equality that they were uncomfortable with. Women, they felt, were taking all the good jobs (Conway-Long 2006, 155). Globalization had led to women acting and dressing less modestly, which, in the words of one man, "made men weak with sexual desire, and thus their masculinity is shaken" (156). They further argued that women had become more materialistic and demanding of luxuries due to exposure to Western ideas. Interestingly, the majority of the men in Conway-Long's study who expressed "anger at Western pressures, Western styles, [and] Western consumption patterns" were under thirty years of age at the time (157). Economic insecurity was also an important factor, as those making more money were also less concerned about the perceived effects of globalization on women's roles.

For Better or for Worse: Marriage in Twenty-First-Century Morocco

Although the average age of marriage has increased and it is often difficult for men to marry until they are financially stable, and despite popular portrayals of the institution of marriage as declining in the region, researchers have not found this statistically to be the case (Assaad and Krafft 2014, 2). Yet in Morocco, compared with other North African countries such as Egypt and Tunisia where marriage is nearly universal, one-quarter of the population never marries (5). On average, Moroccan women are eight years younger than their spouses, which can give women less power to negotiate within a marriage (6).

The Benjelloun siblings are somewhat representative of Moroccan marriage patterns. Only 75% of Moroccans marry, and there is a one in six divorce rate. Of the five siblings, one (Khaled) has never married, two (Rachid and Hanane) have experienced divorces, and two (Ilham and Mourad) have been in only one marriage. Khaled, although an adult, has never married due to unemployment. Ilham, a housewife, and Mourad, a trader, have been married for many years to the same person, and both have children.

Ironically, Hanane had been through a situation similar to her brother's several years before. Her brief marriage, to a Moroccan immigrant living in France, had been arranged through extended family who knew the husband from their neighborhood in the outskirts of Paris. Anas had lived in France for almost twenty years and was fifteen years Hanane's senior. He had been married to a Moroccan in France, had two children, and later divorced. Most of Anas and Hanane's courtship, like Rachid's, took place over the phone and the internet. In her early twenties at the time, Hanane had just completed university and hoped to move to France to join her new husband and then obtain a teaching certification there. Anas came to Morocco for a large traditional wedding, took Hanane on a honeymoon to Asilah, in the north, and then returned to France, supposedly to finalize the paperwork to bring his new wife home with him. However, less than two months later he sent word through his family that he wanted a divorce. Hanane was devastated by this turn of events, not only because she had assumed everything was going well with their relationship, but also because now she was no longer a virgin. Because this happened prior to the 2004 revisions of the mudawana, when Anas divorced her, he also claimed that unemployment in France prevented him from paying her even the few months of support she was entitled to during their marriage. Under the revised laws, men now have to pay all the necessary support and court fines before being able to finalize a divorce they have initiated. The Benjellouns knew from their extended family in France that Anas had a job, but they had no way of proving this in court. Thus, Hanane received nothing, and she was devastated that she had "wasted" her virginity on a man who was so *khafeef* (flaky).

These transnational Benjelloun marriages, separated by a period of nearly ten years, shared a number of commonalities but reflected gender-based differences as well. Both Hanane and Rachid felt that their spouses' status as residents abroad allowed them to be more easily abandoned, although Rachid pointed out that before the mudawana changes, it would not have been so easy for Nejma to divorce him. The two marriages also shared not only the spouses' migrant status but also the fact that Rachid and Hanane were marrying Moroccans whom the family did not know well. This was a contrast to "traditional" marriages, according to all of the siblings, which were believed to be more harmonious because spouses were members of the same community. Marrying someone not only from outside the community but also outside the country involved a tremendous leap of faith, one that was not always justified by the outcome.

"Fes used to be small," Mourad said. His wife came from a large Fassi family, and they had been acquainted for years, seeing one another at weddings and other events where extended family got together. The marriage was set up by the two families, although the couple had time to get to know each other beforehand. "You married someone whose family you knew, and that was it. You married someone who had been known to the family since they were young. Or marriages were between cousins. If something went wrong, the whole family got involved." This was not to say that Mourad's marriage was entirely without conflict, but for the most part, he felt that it was harmonious and that he and his wife shared similar values because they were from the same social group.

Latifa blamed Nejma's family, whom she felt were only interested in money. She was of the opinion that Nejma's family wanted to scam the Benjellouns and assumed they had more money than they did.

"They had no interest in us. You could see even when they came here that they were just looking around, trying to figure out how much money we had. And when we went to Casablanca to set up the engagement, they didn't even receive us!" She shook her head. "The next time Rachid gets married we'll make sure we know the family. Two of my children have had bad luck with *muhajereen* [immigrants]. I won't let him make that mistake the next time."

Transnational marriages are extremely common between Moroccans and first- and second-generation Moroccans residing abroad. While statistics are not available for marriages between Moroccans and United States–based migrants, research shows that in Europe, a large number of marriages take place between first- and second-generation immigrants and Moroccans. A study of Moroccan and Turkish migrants in France, Germany, Belgium, and the Netherlands showed that one-third to one-half of the marriages of first- and second-generation migrants were to spouses from the country of origin (Carol, Ersanilli, and Wagner 2014, 388). Reasons include a desire to help other Moroccans emigrate as well as a sense that second-generation Moroccans in Europe have been overly Westernized. Researchers also found that a strong identification with religion meant that Moroccan first- and second-generation migrants were more likely to choose a transnational spouse (Carol, Ersanilli, and Wagner 2014, 401).

Conclusion

The practice of transnational marriage can disadvantage Moroccans in the event of marital conflict, as it becomes difficult to pursue a spouse across borders. Despite certified legal documentation from the United States of Nejma's previous marriage, Rachid had a difficult time convincing the authorities of the reliability of his documents. Marie-Claire Foblets has argued that the new mudawana should require Moroccans who marry abroad to bring proof of the marriage and its permissibility from the country in which they reside: in other words, birth certificates, proof that neither party is married, and, in the case of a Moroccan woman, proof that her spouse is a Muslim (Foblets 2007, 1405). Foblets writes: "The aim seems clear: it should be difficult for a Moroccan national to commit fraud with regard to marital status. The purpose of registering marriage certificates (and the dissolution of marriage) is namely to allow the competent administrative and legal bodies of Morocco to know with certainty the civil status of a person. At least, this is the ambition. This ambition will be fulfilled only if the civil registry services operate throughout the territory of Morocco and are truly accessible" (2008, 165).

Yet fraud can too easily take place if the overseas marriage was never registered in Morocco, and there is nothing legally binding that forces people to register their marriages. In Nejma's case, she never registered her American marriage in Morocco, and there was no legal cooperation between the two countries that would have informed Moroccan authorities of her marriage. Additionally, the civil registry services and courts in different jurisdictions are often disconnected from one another and follow different procedures, which has also been a problem in achieving a consistent application of the mudawana. Although the courts granted Nejma her divorce and then demanded Rachid pay her support, he was unable to pursue his counterclaim of marriage fraud plus compensation for the harm done to him as a result, which is also a feature of the new mudawana that did not work for him (Article 66).

An additional problem, which I saw frequently during my first fieldwork with a women's NGO in Fes in the early 2000s, is that spouses residing in Europe frequently lie, not only about previous marriages but also about their sources of income (Newcomb 2009). Many of those who came to the NGO in search of legal advice were women whose immigrant husbands were divorcing them but claiming unemployment so that they would not have to pay their wives. There were numerous cases where husbands somehow managed to abandon their wives on family trips back to Morocco, returning to Europe with their wives' passports so that the latter could not travel. Women also came to the NGO hoping to recover jewelry and other valuables they had left in their houses in Europe, and which their husbands now failed to return to them. Others, like Hanane, wondered whether they had squandered their marriageable status as virgins to men who were just looking for a sexual partner while visiting Morocco.

Rachid's short-lived marriage to Nejma owed its very existence to globalization. The independent migration of Moroccan women for economic reasons, the couple's communication via the internet, Rachid's rootless existence as an economic migrant to Spain, Nejma's emphasis on acquiring goods for material consumption, and the increased power of women to divorce men are all aspects of a marriage story that would not have occurred half a century ago. Certainly, the ease with which Nejma was able to get a divorce demonstrates the success of at least one portion of the mudawana: the ability of women to petition for judicial divorce. Since the 2004 mudawana revisions added "discord" as a premise on which women can petition for divorce, divorce petitions have risen dramatically, with 65 percent of them being brought by women (Carlisle 2013). Recent studies have shown that although women often have to forgo monetary awards, they are being granted virtually all of the shiqaq divorces they have initiated (Rosen 2016).

However, these factors exist alongside more traditional features of Moroccan culture that have not changed: the rigid expectation that women remain virgins until marriage; the fact that many look down on the independent and mobile "modern" Moroccan woman; the lack of legal rights or sexual health knowledge imparted to unmarried Moroccans; and the overall sense that traditional, arranged marriages are stronger and more certain than those contracted between autonomous individuals.

Traditionally, marriages were an affair of families rather than individuals: it is the families who often negotiate the marriage contract to ensure compatibility and satisfactory financial arrangements. Women have greater bargaining power before marriage if they choose to negotiate in the marriage contract itself whether they will continue education or work, or the financial burden a prospective husband would incur upon taking another wife. Unfortunately, most Moroccan women do not make specific demands in their contracts and use a standard marriage contract. After marriage, the advantage typically goes to the man, who can divorce with greater ease and less stigma (Assaad and Krafft 2014, 2).

Globalization has changed the circumstances under which Moroccan marriages take place, with marriages increasingly outside one's social class, city, and, frequently, nation. It also reflects an increased tendency toward individualism: as nuclear marriages become the ideal, replacing marriages with residence in the extended family unit, families have less control over marriages and their outcomes. And is it realistic or fair to blame women for the increased amount of suspicion with which many Moroccans view "modern" marriage? The institution of marriage in Morocco has experienced profound shifts over the past few generations, in terms of potential marriage partners, age at first marriage, financial and living arrangements, expectations for both men and women, and the number of children marriages produce. Additionally, the large number of Moroccans residing abroad has meant that many marriages are transnational, a situation that brings with it its own particular set of problems and issues.

As noted, some authors have referred to Morocco's tendency to valorize the traditions of the past while embracing contradictory aspects of modernity as exemplifying its "schizophrenic" identity. Moroccans will celebrate cosmopolitanism and advancements in women's rights that adhere to internationalist standards while also describing a longing and nostalgia for the more traditional, supposedly subservient women of the past. Gender and marriage expectations demonstrate this quite glaringly, as they suggest women should be full, autonomous participants in the global economy, yet demonize them for material consumption or for actions that go against patriarchal constraints on women's behavior, such as premarital sexual activity. Attempting to take into account local notions for behavior alongside global messages is, perhaps, nothing new for Morocco. In the words of Loubna Skalli, "In a country like Morocco, cultural 'hybridity' is an inherent characteristic that predates colonialism, though it has been exacerbated by its direct imperialist legacy" (2006, 2).

Most studies of Moroccan marriage practices focus on women, but men are affected by these conflicting expectations as well. Underemployed, frequently unable to marry until well into their thirties, and grappling with multiple conflicting messages about the nature and purpose of twenty-first-century marriage, men like Rachid experience a crisis of masculinity when attempting to operate among conflicting registers: old patriarchal frameworks, traditional marriage expectations, and new, globalization-related realities. While men have been able to take advantage of the legal system for years when seeking divorce, the new mudawana now makes it easy for women to do the same. Equality and fairness are admirable goals of laws that are part of a system where competitive advantage, deception, different standards in different courtrooms, and a lack of communication with other regions and foreign legal systems now allow women to pursue their own economic advantages in ways that men always have. Rachid was now experiencing what Lawrence Rosen describes as "a kind of legal limbo . . . as individuals, trapped in procedures that are unclear or internally contradictory, are left with no clear resolution to their problems" (2000, 10).

Notes

1. Traditionally the groom's family gives money to the bride and her family, and in exchange, the bride's family is expected to provide furnishings for a house. This *sadaq* is expected to go to the bride but in some cases may be taken by the bride's family.

2. Alimony was a new condition that the revised 2004 mudawana now made possible; previously, a man had to support his ex-wife only if there were children involved.

3. See "UN CEDAW and CRC Recommendations" 2016 for more on specific requirements for the age of first marriage. Unfortunately, the age of marriage requirement can easily be over-

ruled by a judge, and approximately 10–11 percent of marriages every year are still between adult men and underage girls.

4. Some European countries, among them France and Belgium, do respect aspects of the personal status codes for Moroccan marriages (Rosen 2000, 13).

5. For more on the history of the Moroccan women's rights movement, as well as how local Moroccan NGOs have translated transnational women's rights agendas into local discourse, see Evrard 2014; on the divide between women's secular and Islamist NGOs, see Elliott 2015.

6. A survey of highly educated graduate students in Rabat revealed that most had mixed feelings about the revisions, with many of them expressing outright their sense that the laws transgressed Islam, disadvantaged men, or gave women too many rights (Deiana 2009). In her long-term fieldwork conducted in rural areas of southern Morocco, Elliott (2015) also found that mudawana reforms were vehemently rejected by both men and women.

7. A survey conducted in Rabat between 2006 and 2008 by the Emergency Contraception in Africa (ECAF) research team among respondents over eighteen who had already been sexually active, including twenty-three health professionals, found that over 90 percent felt that women should uphold their virginity at all costs before marriage, even though many of the female respondents had not done so (Bakass and Ferrand 2013).

8. See, for example, Skalli 2006; Allali and Hamdani 2006.

9. For more on Moroccan women employed in the Spanish agricultural sector, see Mannon, Petrzelka, and Glass 2012.

2

REPRODUCE

Changing Conceptions of Reproduction and Infertility

SUMMER 2009. AS I WAITED at the taxi stand in the Ville Nouvelle for Rokiya and Hanane, I stepped back from the sidewalk to watch the slice of Fes life streaming by me. Several female college students, dressed in jeans and fitted shirts, laughed together, and professional men and women strode by briskly, clutching leather briefcases. A large family in djellabas descended from a dusty bus, heading in the direction of Mohammed V Avenue's doctors' offices and banks. Cars sped down to the roundabout, punctuating the air with honking horns and exhaust fumes. I waited near the park for almost twenty minutes before a red taxi pulled up beside me.

"Get in," Rokiya told me, and I crammed myself into the small, seat belt–less backseat with the two women. The taxi driver slipped into a narrow space between cars and merged into the stream of traffic, and we were off to the medina. Rokiya, a medina resident her whole life, was taking Hanane to an *m'sada*, a traditional masseuse who specialized in infertility. Hanane sat quietly, wearing a nondescript beige djellaba, her dark brown hair pulled back into a ponytail, wisps of gray just beginning to appear at her temples. She had just turned thirty-seven.

"Did you bring your pills, in case she asks what you're taking?" Rokiya inquired. From the bag, Hanane pulled out a few boxes of pills. I asked her what they were for.

"This is to help the eggs grow," she explained, holding up a box of Clomid, a fertility drug that stimulates ovulation. I did not recognize the other medicine, but she told me, "The other is for the cold [*l'brd*]. I take this for the cold along with *l'achoub* [herbs]."

Standard pharmaceutical therapies for fertility combined with herbs prescribed by a traditional healer crystallize the dual systems of health care found in Morocco: allopathic and holistic or traditional. Many Moroccans believe that too much cold entering the body can be a cause of infertility. The traditional masseuse we were visiting would stimulate Hanane's uterus, "heating" it up to create optimal conditions for conception. The presence of both an allopathic and an indigenous system of beliefs means that Moroccans will pick and choose from among different therapies, often depending on their socioeconomic circumstances. Although the latest assisted reproductive technologies (ARTS) are available in Morocco, they are not always financially accessible, and Hanane had reached the limits of what she could afford from Western medicine. The indigenous system, a combination of local beliefs, Prophetic, and Galenic medicine, relies on a sense that cold and heat are out of balance in the body. Galenic or humoral medicine, which originated in ancient Greece, is based on the idea that the four humors of the body are out of balance. In Morocco, derivatives of this system are still found in beliefs about the power of heat and cold to cause sickness, and Moroccans have infused this tradition with Prophetic medicine, which loosely means practicing medicine according to the example of the Prophet Muhammad. In Morocco, Prophetic medicine also includes the idea that individuals may be attacked by negative spiritual influences, necessitating religious curing or healing in the process.[1]

We arrived at the top of the medina and exited the taxi, walking into Bab Guissa, one of the large open doorways in the ancient medina's crenellated walls. As we descended, Rokiya led us expertly down side streets and alleys that she had known since childhood. It was quiet here, in a residential section, and as in most of the medina, the passageways are too narrow for cars. Rokiya had a greeting for almost everyone we walked by: a tiny schoolgirl with an oversized backpack, an old beggar sitting cross-legged against a wall, and a mother and daughter lugging a bag of vegetables back to their house.

Hanane was in her second marriage. Her first, to a Moroccan migrant in France, had ended almost as soon as it had begun (see chapter 1). She moved on with her life, and after a few years she married again, to a man in his fifties. This was a pattern I noticed frequently with women: usually younger women married men many years their senior, and if it was a second marriage, or if the woman was already in her thirties, it was not uncommon for her to marry someone in his fifties or older. Statistics confirm that Moroccan men are frequently older than their wives, on average eight years older than their spouses (Assaad and Krafft 2014, 6).

After two years of marriage without children, Hanane became worried that she might not be able to have children. Earlier that year, she had finally succeeded in getting pregnant, and a medical doctor had given her injections to help "hold the baby in." But she had a miscarriage.

"They didn't tell her," Rokiya whispered to me confidentially, "that she shouldn't sleep with the husband, and she did, and she lost the baby." Actually, Hanane had gone for testing, and the doctors had not been able to determine a specific reason for the infertility.

"They told me that after age thirty-five, each month I might not have eggs, and that I needed treatments to heat up the uterus so the eggs will come out," she explained. I thought it was interesting that physicians, too, spoke in terms of heat and cold in explaining the effectiveness of ARTs. For now, Hanane had been taking the Clomid to stimulate ovulation, but beyond that, she could not afford more costly therapies. At around $4,000 at that time in Morocco, one cycle of in vitro fertilization (IVF) was beyond her means. There was the added complication that her husband refused to be tested to see if he might be responsible.

"I would try it [IVF] if I were rich," Hanane said. "But I don't know if it's worth it. I know people who have had more luck with herbs. And I have a cousin who did IVF three times and still has no children."

Today she had her period, an essential condition, Rokiya said, for the treatment she would receive.

"You don't want to do the massage if there's a person in there," Rokiya explained. The massage with the m'sada is supposed to take place early in the morning, ideally before the patient or the practitioner have had breakfast. But it was already late morning. Down a small, cobblestone alley, Rokiya knocked at a nondescript metal door, and a young girl opened it for us. This was the house of the "famous" m'sada, Rokiya said. Inside, the house had one central courtyard with high ceilings and old, chipped tile floors. A smaller room off the courtyard was where the m'sada, Lalla Maryam, saw her patients. After we waited a few minutes on a narrow bench, Lalla Maryam came down to us. A thin woman in her fifties with tired eyes, she told us that her blood pressure had been high and she was not feeling well.

"It's too late," she said. "I've been sick for fifteen days. But I'll be better tomorrow. Come back tomorrow morning at eight."

Hanane looked disappointed, but Rokiya knew another m'sada nearby who might take us.

"She's not as famous as Lalla Maryam, but this one helped my sister," she said to Hanane. "My sister was like you: married two years and no baby. Now she has a girl." Rokiya herself had experienced infertility: six years of marriage with no child. The medical doctors told her she had blocked fallopian tubes, and she was scheduled for an operation, but a combination of herbs and a visit to a m'sada fixed her first. Just before the operation, she found out she was pregnant, and her son was now almost three.

"Everything is possible with (nia) [intention]," she told me. "Nia" involved having an Islamically oriented mind-set about one's goals, focused toward the divine. Both women agreed that if one person in the couple did not have proper intentions, a lack of nia could be another cause of infertility, something that I heard echoed by other women as well.

We wound our way through more alleys, passing donkeys laden with merchandise, vegetables, and enormous water bottles. Conflicting smells filled my nose as we walked further: dried manure, hot bread from an oven, the sweet smell of mint and hot tea. Rokiya continued to ask directions, until finally a young boy led us through smaller and smaller alleys that ended in a doorway. A dark-skinned woman answered, her hair pulled back in a bandanna. She was dressed in the pajamas women often wore for housework. It seemed unclear whether there was a m'sada here after all, but after some back and forth questioning (with Rokiya establishing her connections to their area of the medina, describing where her family lived and finding people they knew in common), the woman decided to let us in. An older woman called down to us from a high window, and we went up two flights of ancient, narrow stairs, where Fatima Zahra, her mother, and her adult daughter were all doing housework, a table covered with skinned fava beans in front of them.

"My mother doesn't do this professionally, just for family," the daughter of Fatima Zahra told us. She led us into a small sleeping room, and pulled a narrow mattress down from a stack of mattresses and onto the floor. A bowl of olive oil was found, and Hanane took off her djellaba, underneath which she wore a long, tank-style undershirt and woolen leggings, and lay down on the mattress. Fatima Zahra began rubbing Hanane's stomach as if she were kneading a hunk of bread dough, and her thorough manipulations must have been painful, judging by the grimace on Hanane's face. Over the next fifteen minutes, Fatima Zahra ground her fist into Hanane's belly button; turned her over to massage her back (where she said the uterus was); tied a scarf very tightly around her midsection; and made her spread her legs and push her belly forward on the floor. After it was over, she ordered Hanane to buy a special suppository from an herbalist, to drink lavender water for three days, and perhaps to come back again tomorrow for another massage. Hanane winced as she got up slowly, pulling her djellaba over her head. As we left, Rokiya pressed thirty dirhams (about four dollars) into the hands of Fatima Zahra, who made a show of trying to refuse it, still protesting as Rokiya let go of the money and slipped out the door, with Hanane and myself trailing her.

"Did that hurt?" I asked Hanane, who nodded quietly. We made plans to meet the next day in the early morning to return to Lalla Maryam.

The next morning, we met earlier at Bab Guissa and wound our way through the alleys to the narrow, dark alley where Lalla Maryam lived. This time the famous m'sada was feeling better, and she said her blood pressure issues were not bothering her today. A descendant of the Prophet, a *cherifa*, Lalla Maryam had inherited *baraka* from her father. Baraka consisted of the inherited spiritual gifts or powers necessary to do this sort of work, and she had also trained with an uncle who did some kind of massages, "though men don't really do them anymore," she explained. Also, her father had not passed his abilities on to his sons, just to his daughter, and he had stipulated that the baraka to do massages would stop with her. None of her children had inherited her abilities. She married a *fqih*, a Qur'anic healer, when she was fourteen, and began to conduct massage sessions shortly after that.[2]

"I'm close with both the doctors and herbalists," Lalla Maryam told me. She handed me a sheaf of papers that showed test results for a man named Abdulaziz. Skimming over them, I saw that the results said he had no living sperm. She began to talk about his diagnosis, and how she concurred with his doctor that even herbs would be of little help to him. It seemed important to her to show me that she was conversant with medical therapies in addition to the traditional techniques. She did not do massages for men, but they did come to her for medical advice.

"I consult with people. I read their lab tests, and the things their doctors have written. Most people don't know what their test results mean, so I interpret for them. In a case like this, I told this man there's no hope for him, and he should stop spending money on treatments, either medical treatments or herbs."

"Do you have success where doctors don't?" I asked her. She laughed confidently.

"I have helped more people than I can count. Poor, rich, they all come to me. If doctors could heal all women, I'd be out of business. But there are different types of infertility. Just as the doctors can cure some things but not all, I am the same. I can help people the doctors can't help. At the heart of it is nia [intention]." Again, the idea of nia, the combination of belief and biology, was invoked.

Lalla Maryam took us into the small room off her central courtyard. A curtain hanging over the doorway darkened the room, and we sat on the low sofas lining the walls. She consulted with Hanane about her treatments so far, and Hanane told her about the miscarriage, the subsequent tests at the doctor's, and the massage the day before. Lalla Maryam was critical of the other m'sada's techniques and said she should never use the suppositories the other woman had recommended.

"They can cause infections, you shouldn't do them," she admonished her. "If I prescribe herbs, they will go in the food. Don't take herbs unless I tell you to. Did you bring your test results from the doctor?" Hanane did not have them, but she pulled the same boxes of pills out of her bag that she had showed me, which Lalla Maryam also seemed knowledgeable about. She began asking about the Clomid.

"Do you have your period now? Did you start these pills on the third day? Good." Lalla Maryam was familiar with the protocol for taking this drug. While she talked, a young woman brought in a clay dish of hot coals over a small gas tank, and Lalla Maryam set a big piece of wood on the coals. Dipping her hands in a bowl of olive oil, she massaged Hanane's abdomen more gently than the m'sada had done yesterday, feeling around carefully for her uterus and ovaries. She had the authoritative demeanor of a gynecologist even though we were in a room in the medina.

"Everything is in its place," she announced. She also rubbed Hanane's lower back and used the same technique with a belt that Fatima Zahra had employed yesterday with a scarf, though somewhat less vigorously, and there was only one moment when Hanane flinched. Lalla Maryam took the now-fragrant piece of wood off the hot coals, tapping it on Hanane's hands and back. After the wood had cooled down slightly, she also tapped her belly with it.

"This will help against the cold," she said, "and it will open her up to make her receptive to children. Everything looks good. *In sha allah* [God willing], this will be a good month for you."

Lalla Maryam announced that she agreed with the doctors, and she could not determine a reason for Hanane's infertility. Perhaps someone had inflicted sorcery, thus "tying" her up (*thqaf*). There were two ways to diagnose the sorcery, she explained. The first was to get water from seven mosques, pour it over herself into a basin, then take the dirty water and sprinkle it on a tree. If the tree showed new growth, she was okay. The other solution was to get forty spices from an herbalist (she had a specific recommendation for one she worked with), mix them up in a blender, and bring them back to her. Lalla Maryam would then recite Qur'anic healing verses, *ruqyah shariah*, over them. She would not accept any payment for doing so because this was the only way the baraka would work.

By the time we left, there were several more clients waiting for Lalla Maryam in the main courtyard: a pretty young woman by herself and a family. Knowing exactly what to do, the young woman came in and immediately laid on the mattress as we walked out.

Hanane seemed happier than she had the day before, and her face was bright with optimism. That summer, she continued to pursue traditional treatments, including the Qur'anic healing Lalla Maryam had suggested, in case some jealous person had "tied" her ability to have children. A year later, she still had not been able to conceive. Her husband had no plans to leave her and insisted that he accepted a marriage without children, but she still continued to visit healers, having exhausted her financial resources where medical doctors were concerned. She reported that she and her husband had visited a doctor in Fes together, and that doctor had emphasized to them that a marriage without children was perfectly respectable.

"She [the doctor] told him, 'You knew when you married her that she wasn't a girl of twenty.' And she told us to keep trying. You never know when it will work. Marriage today is different. He knows that. Children are expensive anyway, you can't afford to have a lot of them like our grandmothers did." Disappointed but not completely resigned, Hanane continued to hold out hope that the healers offered her the best possible chances for success.

GLOBAL DISCOURSES ABOUT FAMILY FORMATION

Hanane Benjelloun's story suggests a number of themes related to contemporary Moroccan marriages, infertility and reproduction, and a globalized medical system that is, to some extent, largely unaffordable for the majority of the population.[3] Globalization has brought new discourses about marriage, family formation, reproduction, and infertility to Morocco, as well as many of the same biomedical treatments that are available in Western countries. Most cannot afford the Western medical therapies, and even the small minority who have the money for the most expensive therapies, such as IVF, often will attempt to enhance their chances of conception by continuing to draw on traditional practices their mothers and grandmothers used. The desire to have children to complete a family is a strong one, but global models of companionate marriages without children are making the possibility of remaining childless more acceptable for those who are unable to have them. Traditionally, Moroccan marriages were extended family affairs, arranged as alliances between families. After marriage, brides usually went to live with their in-laws, but today that pattern is changing. Most couples prefer to have more choice in a marriage partner and wish to live independently after marriage.

Even the few women I knew with the financial resources to pursue assisted reproductive technologies such as IVF did not put much faith in them and continued to pursue complementary treatments from traditional therapists. Physicians, meanwhile, described their roles almost as counselors whose job was to lift the veil of misinformation while informing couples that the strength of their marriage should not be measured by whether or not they had children. In previous generations, the extended family would often encourage couples to divorce in cases of infertility, or advise husbands to take a second wife. Now the extended family seemed to have less influence on the outcome of marriage, and while most women were not indifferent to the prospect of childlessness, many, like Hanane, found it worth mentioning that their doctor had counseled them to remain together despite infertility.

New professional roles for women have led to a delay in the age of marriage and childbearing, which has contributed to a decline in fertility (Althaus 1994, 1997). In addition, the Moroccan government's 2004 revision of the mudawana personal status codes governing a woman's rights in marriage and divorce has affected popular attitudes toward marriage. The mudawana, one of the few areas of Moroccan law derived from the principles of shari'a, was revised to make the marital relationship more egalitarian, to guarantee financial support in the event of a divorce, and to extend the grounds for which women can ask for a divorce. When I conducted the research for this chapter, five years after the laws were changed, there was a shared perception among all the Moroccans I talked to that divorces were more difficult to obtain, particularly for the husband, with more financial accountability demanded on his part.

"Because the laws make it harder for men to divorce their wives," a young male physician told me, "it gives us more reason to tell a couple to stay together even if they can't have children." For urbanized middle- and upper-class Moroccans, this shift reflects the loss of control of extended kin networks over the marital relationship while highlighting the increased significance, and authority, of extrafamilial discourses of law and biomedicine. The story that Naima, a woman in her sixties, told me about her cousin Rachida's infertility forty years earlier is representative of attitudes of the past toward marriage and infertility.

"They tried everything they could, but at that time, they didn't have the doctor's treatments like they do now," Naima told me. "I remember my aunt taking her everywhere—to visit the saints, the herbalists. Her in-laws pushed [her husband] to take another wife or divorce her. He wouldn't divorce her, but he did marry someone else, and they had children. He still gave Rachida money, but he didn't stay with her much. It was important to her dignity that she was married, even if she hardly ever saw her husband. Her sister gave her one of her children to raise. Amina [the sister's child] thought of her as her own mother. I don't think she knew until she grew up that Rachida wasn't her mother."

Rachida's husband died in the 1980s; she never remarried but had maintained close ties to her sister's family. In this more traditional model, the ex-

tended family intervened to advise the couple about the treatment of infertility, to counsel for divorce or polygamy, and to supply the infertile woman with
a child she could raise as a surrogate.[4] This was another traditional solution to
the problem of infertility. Although the woman raised another family member's child, she was still considered an aunt. Because adopted children do not
have the same legal status as biological children, adoption has a mixed reputation in Moroccan society. One way around this, more common in the past
than today, was for a childless couple to make arrangements to take someone
else's baby and register the child legally as their own, not telling the child that
he/she was adopted. Occasionally the truth comes out when the presumptive
parent dies and the child tries to claim an inheritance, only to find that another family member who knows the secret suddenly informs everyone the
child was adopted.[5]

To study social life is also to attend to the ways that society reproduces
itself. "Reproduction," write Faye Ginsburg and Rayna Rapp, "is inextricably
bound up with the production of culture" (1995, 2). Over the past thirty years,
as in many other Global South countries, Morocco has witnessed a dramatic
decline in its birthrate, accompanied by other political and economic changes
affecting women's roles in the public sphere. In 1980, Morocco averaged 6.6
births per woman, but by 2004 this had declined to less than three births per
woman (Ayad and Roudi 2006).

Several interrelated processes of globalization can be found in Hanane's
story, which was not unusual in the range of experiences for women that I
knew in Fes. To begin with, since the 1970s, the government has encouraged
smaller family sizes, a process I explore in more detail below. Recent changes
to the marriage laws, which came about in part due to pressure from Moroccan activists involved in transnational networking, have affected marriages
since 2004. Had Hanane's first marriage taken place after 2004, it is more
likely she would have been able to hold her first husband accountable for marrying and then abandoning her, regardless of his supposed inability to support
her. These changes to the marriage laws, in addition to the introduction of
ARTs, have resulted in profound social shifts in cultural ideals concerning
marriage and family, a decline in kinship-centered marriage practices, and a
redirecting of the locus of control over women's bodies from the family to the
nation-state and biomedicine. Since the ways in which societies receive and
interpret new technologies are both culturally distinctive and indicative of
social relations, I focus specifically here on changing cultural understandings
of infertility, and how these understandings relate to ideas about marriage.

As a global health concern, infertility affects between 8 percent and
14 percent of all couples worldwide, although in the Global South, the numbers

are often higher due to preventable infertility resulting from untreated secondary infections (Sciarra 1994). In Morocco, 54.5 percent of infertility cases result from infection (Zhiri and Benyahia 1987). As Marcia Inhorn has noted, women tend to "bear the major burden of infertility, in terms of blame for the reproductive failing; emotional responses of anxiety, frustration, grief, and fear; marital consequences, including duress, abuse, divorce, polygamous remarriage, or abandonment; and social stigma and community ostracism" (2007, 185).

While Moroccan women still experience infertility as a devastating condition, it has become a less precarious one in terms of its potential to destroy a woman's entire sense of well-being, social position, and economic security. Divorce due to infertility frequently took place at the urging of the kin group, since, as with other patriarchal societies of the Middle East and North Africa (Inhorn 2005; Charrad 2001), a woman's primary role within family life has been defined by her ability to bear children to continue the patriarchal family line.[6] Yet now, because divorce in Morocco potentially requires more extensive financial obligations on the part of the husband (and rumored imprisonment should he fail to have sufficient resources), couples are less likely to divorce and, in some cases, to marry in the first place. New legal reforms instituted by the nation-state have thus come to affect decisions about whether a marriage should be terminated.

Additionally, the introduction of ARTs has led to the increased significance of the physician in marital relationships. Control over the marital relationship, once the domain of kin groups, now extends outward to include new forms of biopower and legal discourses. Scholars have argued that legal and biomedical discourses represent the hegemonic control over the intimate domain of family life by the nation-state and biomedicine, in particular allowing biomedicine, controlled by male physicians, to force a patriarchal agenda on women by emphasizing only women's reproductive identity (Arditti, Klein, and Minden 1984, Corea 1985; Spallone and Steinberg 1987). Yet many Moroccan women I interviewed in 2009 and 2010 saw the new technologies as empowering, giving women greater bargaining power in marriage and divorce and encouraging a vision of a marital relationship in which children are not necessary to its survival.

"What's good about the doctors now is that they can tell you if it's the woman or the man who has the problem," one woman, Fatima, told me. Fatima had children of her own, but her sister had been unable to conceive. Fatima's sister, now in her late forties, was still married to her husband. "In the past it was always the woman's fault. At least now people know that it can come from the man too." As we will see below, these discourses displace the authority of patriarchal kin groups and often support the maintenance of the marital relationship, even those in which there are no children.

CHANGING LAWS, CHANGING EXPECTATIONS

When Morocco revised its personal status codes, the mudawana, in 2004, the reforms were widely considered to be among the most progressive in the Middle East and North Africa. As described in the previous chapter, data from studies conducted since the laws' revision indicates that actual implementation has fallen far short of ideals.[7] Not everyone in Moroccan society recognizes the greater vision for women's autonomy that the laws seem to promote.[8] Yet rumors about the revised laws giving more control to women have been widespread since 2004, and among middle- and upper-class residents of Fes, those rumors were felt to possess no small power over the marital relationship itself.

Within a year of the 2004 revisions, the incidence of divorce plummeted 40 percent. In 1998, for example, there were 50,763 registered cases of divorce, while in 2007 there were only 27,904 (Ministry of Justice 2007). However, in recent years, the number of divorces has gone up again, from 55,255 cases in 2009 to 56,198 in 2011 ("Moroccan Women No Longer Abashed" 2013). Of the 64,729 petitions for divorce in 2011, 38,435 were initiated by the wife. These numbers reveal a sentiment expressed by many of the people I interviewed, which was that women had now turned the tables on men and that men no longer had the unilateral ability to end a marriage that they once did.[9]

There was also a widespread sense among people in Fes that ARTs gave women greater advantage because it could not immediately be presumed that they were the party at fault. A second theme also emerged, which was that many Moroccans believed that the revised mudawana protected infertile women from being suddenly divorced by their husbands.

"In the old days, the man would divorce her, or he might take a second [wife]," one man told me. "But not now. Now the husband would pay a steep penalty, so the couple will stay together. She could take his house!" This opinion, though reiterated by many, was based on misinformation: according to the new laws, the wife does not have the right to half the husband's assets unless she has stipulated this beforehand in the marriage contract. Nevertheless, perception of the husband's potential financial loss meant that many felt that the couple would stay together and try to work out a childless marriage. It also meant that they would continue to seek medical intervention.

"There are so many things the doctors can do now," said Hanane's mother, Latifa. "They give injections, make test tube babies [atfal anabib].[10] Or the woman can see a m'sada. Or if she has problems with the cold [l'brd] seizing her uterus she should visit an herbalist.[11] But the husband will be patient. Divorce isn't a good thing. People don't rush into it like they did before."[12] She was certain Hanane and her husband would stay together. "They love each other. They support each other," she explained. Indeed, Hanane's husband did not seem to mind if she was not able to have children. "He likes a quiet life," Latifa explained. "It bothers Hanane more than it does him. I think babies would be a shock to him at his age."

Some Moroccans told me that infertility could be caused by incompatibility, and that couples could remarry others and have better luck. There was a notable division of opinion among my interlocutors according to age, with older Moroccans (those over fifty) asserting that infertility defeated the very purposes of marriage and necessitated remarriage to produce children. Younger Moroccans were more circumspect, and gave two reasons an infertile couple should remain together: the high cost of divorce as well as the idea that the central purpose of marriage could be companionship rather than procreation. Marriage without children was increasingly viewed as acceptable, particularly when women married later in life, which in itself may be a new practice. Women in Latifa's generation told me that in the past, older women would never have married for companionship. "If they didn't marry young, they did not marry at all," Latifa said.

Marriage is still widely desired, yet the age for marriage is rising. The average age for first marriage in 2004 was 31.2 for men and 26.3 for women (Boudarbat and Ajbilou 2007). In part this is due to economic expectations associated with marriage. High levels of unemployment mean that many men cannot live independently of their families, and brides expect their future spouse to provide an apartment, rather than living with their husband's family, which was the preferred arrangement in the past.

"In the old days," said Mourad, "the wife would be happy with the bride price [sadaq] and they would move in with his family. Marriage was simple, you said a *sura al-fatiha* [a verse from the Qur'an], and off you went. Girls today expect everything, sometimes even the furnishings in the apartment.[13] And if there is a divorce, watch out. Your wife can take everything. Marriage is too expensive; nobody can afford it now."

Mourad's comments show the fear many men held that the new law entailed more legal and financial responsibilities than before. Yet changing expectations for women's roles in society are also responsible for the higher age at first marriage. Education and a career have become increasingly important for many middle- and upper-class women. However, I also met many women in their forties and up who had children first and later returned to a career.[14] Among the younger generation, though, young women who were on a professional track now waited until their late twenties to marry.

Later ages at marriage have contributed to a lowered birthrate and also to a decline in fertility. Currently the fertility rate in Morocco, estimated at 2.2 live births per woman, is among the lowest in the Middle East and North Africa (*CIA World Factbook* 2017). Yet the fertility transition began about forty years ago, when from 1974 to 1977 the number of births per woman dropped from 7.4 to 5.9, a sharp decline of 5.5 percent per year (D'Addato 2003). Falling phosphate prices on the world market and a war in the Western Sahara led to reduced nontax revenue, so the government raised taxes on households by more than 50 percent from 1972 to 1975. With encouragement (and pressure) from the nation-state, women entered the labor market in droves. During the 1980s, women's educational levels increased, as did rural-to-urban and access to birth control. With Morocco's participation in structural adjustment programs limiting government contributions to social programs, more Moroccans, including women, had to work to make up for falling incomes. Fertility rates fell even further as a result (D'Addato 2003). During this period, the Moroccan government also embarked on an extensive (and highly successful) family planning program. Urbanization is also a significant factor in reduced fertility (urban dwellers now represent 58 percent of the population). D'Addato writes: "From a demographic viewpoint, urbanization implies the concentration of the population in urban areas; taking a sociological point of view, it implies the diffusion of 'urban behaviors,' characterized by individualism, isolation, anonymity, and competition, all of which are features that lead to a reduction in family size and to a weaker patriarchal system" (522).

The change in expectations for marriage reflects these societal transformations, as well as the fact that many women in Moroccan society have more educational and employment opportunities and, as a result, income of their own. The effects on the influence of the extended family are apparent. Ideally, couples now start a new household after marriage, whereas thirty years ago they would have resided with the husband's family. This can have positive effects for women who are no longer under the fabled dictatorial command of a mother-in-law who perceived the new bride as an interloper.[15] Women's importance to the family had been defined largely by their ability to produce offspring, ideally male children to continue the patriline.

The extended family is, without a doubt, still important in marriage negotiations and everyday life, particularly when they live in the same city as the married couple. Parents still frequently intervene in demanding that the future husband pay a high bride price as "insurance" protecting their daughters. Yet the kin group's previously all-important role in married life has declined. Expectations for marriage are different. Although some marriages are still arranged, women believe in love marriages and often intend to choose their husbands. The global circulation of discourses promoting companionate marriage contributes in no small part to this ideal. Media images, from both Moroccan television networks and other Arab networks viewed by satellite that are now ubiquitous in middle-class homes, emphasize the nuclear family in both programs and advertising. Music videos, particularly from countries such as Egypt and Lebanon, project fantasy narratives of romantic love in which men court beautiful women and live out visions of contented nuclear domesticity (sometimes with a young child) in palatial abodes. Within Morocco, popular television commercials for common household items such as yogurt and cream cheese advertise a vision of domesticity that often includes an attractive young couple with one or two children. Occasionally, during holidays, advertisements for products such as cooking oil or tea emphasize the extended family coming together over a meal, but the ideal family is almost always depicted as nuclear. These visual exemplars of what Arjun Appadurai (1996) has termed "mediascapes" create and confirm a narrative in which Moroccans imagine themselves as aspiring to a vision of both companionate marriage and smaller family sizes consistent with nation-state interests.

Although kin continue to influence marital decisions, and men and women still occupy separate spheres socially (despite the sizable presence of women in the public sphere), the emphasis on companionate marriage and nuclear households has meant that couples are often able to build relationships independently of their families. Malika, a lawyer in her thirties, had tried unsuccessfully to have children with her husband of ten years, but they had no plans to separate: "His mother suggested once that he should think about divorcing me. But he told her no, and asked her to be happy with her other grandchildren. *Bien sur*, of course things are strained in my relationship with her now. But he has always stood by me. There is an understanding between us that we built a long time ago, and which goes beyond children. We married because of love and understanding. Of course I would like children, and I think about it often. But it wasn't my fate [*mektub*], and he still loves me."

Despite changes in attitudes among the middle and upper classes toward acceptance that women can be valued for other roles besides motherhood, adoption was still not a viable option for most. As previously mentioned, forms of adoption in which an adopted child is considered legally and socially as significant as a blood relative are prohibited in Islam (Sonbol 1995). Although a form of foster parentage of orphans, *kafala*, is common, and cited in Islam as a good deed, such children are never considered as true sons or daughters, and foster children do not have the same rights of identity or inheritance. Thus, among the childless couples I interviewed, most said they preferred to remain without children entirely, although a few mentioned that they would consider fostering an orphan if they did not achieve success with the help of biomedicine.

BIOMEDICAL TECHNOSCAPES

As other anthropologists have noted (Inhorn 2007, 5), around the world, women's health is frequently defined by the biomedical establishment rather than by women themselves. Women's bodies are increasingly perceived as needing medical intervention, and normal life processes such as puberty, childbirth, and menopause become conditions to be managed by biomedicine (14). In Morocco, this represents a shift from prior patterns of health care, since before colonialism, female practitioners managed most matters related to birth and reproductive health (Amster 2013, 144). Colonialism first introduced biomedicine to Morocco, with the French elevating biomedical knowledge while dismissing local knowledge.[16] Moroccan women were frequently the most prominent targets of French medical authorities, since women relied on several intersecting traditions influential in the country: Galenic medicine, as well as "saintly healing, and 'Prophetic medicine,'" derived from the example of the Prophet (Amster 2013, 143). In the contemporary management of birth and reproduction, technology attempts to surpass female authority, becoming the most necessary and powerful intervention a woman can have. One might think that medical technology results in safer births for women, but in countries like Morocco, because medical care is unevenly distributed, particularly in rural areas, maternal mortality rates can be quite high. Unfortunately, the French discredited traditional midwives, putting the one female-centric health practitioner out of business while failing to provide safe birth alternatives, a situation that has not quite been remedied by the Moroccan government.

There is no doubt that the encouragement of doctors and the presence of ARTs give hope to couples that at some point they will be able to conceive with medical intervention. With one treatment cycle of IVF costing about 35,000 Moroccan dirhams (about US$4,400) in 2009, ARTs are costly and available only to those with sufficient capital. Nevertheless, I met many women who, despite limited means, did everything within reason to pursue the treatments. Malika, for example, had been through two failed IVF cycles and had dipped into her family's resources to pay for them. Even though she was a lawyer, she still found the IVF to be expensive. Her mother had sold a valuable antique gold wedding belt to help her.

One of the hallmarks of globalization has been the rapid flow of technologies across previously impermeable boundaries, resulting in the creation of what Appadurai (1996) has termed "technoscapes." The "odd distribution of technologies" that constitutes Appadurai's vision of a technoscape is visible in the distinctively local characteristics that IVF takes on in the Moroccan context. IVF was first successfully practiced in 1978 in England, and the first "test tube baby" born in Morocco came in 1990. Currently, approximately 2,500 successful pregnancies are accomplished each year ("2500 fécondations in vitro réalisées" n.d.). Therapies such as IVF have shifted the landscape of infertility in Morocco by importing a new idea of reproduction that takes place outside the body, while at the same time IVF is interpreted according to Moroccan cultural principles that accord with Islam. The use of donor gametes, for example, is forbidden due to the belief that the mixing of sperm and egg for an unrelated man and woman constitutes a form of adultery and a threat to the stability of the patriline.[17]

Most of the women who went to fertility doctors knew that some forms of ARTs were forbidden in Islam and felt that their doctors had explained which therapies were religiously permissible and why. Moroccan physicians are even consulted by migrants to Europe. One study from the Netherlands showed that Moroccans experiencing infertility did not believe doctors in Europe understood Islam and would return to Morocco to consult a physician (as opposed to an imam) about what was allowed (Korfker et al. 2014, 6).

Doctors are also intent on changing the cultural message that women were always to blame for the failure to procreate. "Women did not have a chance in the past because infertility was assumed to be their fault," Dr. Alami, a male physician in his sixties, told me. "Now that we can test both people in the couple, although men sometimes refuse, we show them that it is frequently the problem of the man." He added that more couples stayed together because of this. A Moroccan magazine article on the topic asserts that "according to statistics, men are implicated in 50% of reproductive problems. The equality of the sexes is therefore present at this level" ("2500 fécondations in vitro réalisées," n.d.). Inter-cytoplasmic sperm injection (ICSI), a male-directed therapy that identifies viable sperm and then injects them into the oocyte, has been practiced in Morocco since the mid-1990s.

Many Moroccans told me that advances in medical technology enhanced the stability of marriage for women, since, according to one woman, it was now known that there were scientific reasons for infertility. Although some still believed in the concept of the evil eye, or the idea that infertility might have been caused by sorcery, most agreed that physicians potentially held the technology to "unblock" whatever force was obstructing conception. Increasing cognizance of reproductive principles led some to describe obstacles to conception in biomedical terms.

"Sometimes the man's water [sperm] is without life," said Rokiya. "And other times the eggs are damaged, or there is something blocking the water from reaching them." These were a few of the afflictions that medical technology could solve, even though some people believed that secondary causes were magico-religious in nature. Holding both beliefs simultaneously was not uncommon.[18]

Regarding sorcery, a few women told me that they were only hedging their bets: they did not necessarily believe that someone had cursed them but were willing to try any therapies, even traditional ones.

"It was my mother and aunt who suggested I see an herbalist," Malika, the lawyer, said. "My aunt also took me to a fqih." The fqihs asserted that the recitation of the Qur'an or creation of amulets could expel the negative influences of sorcery from the body. Although Malika stated that she did not believe these would work, she humored her family members and tried the prescriptions of the traditional healers, observing, "Some women have had luck with the herbs, and others have had no luck with the doctors, so who knows which might work in the end?" Faith in IVF was equated with belief in sorcery because both held empirically low outcomes. One woman, Fadwa, who tried for almost nine years after the birth of her first child to conceive a second, reported that she had seen "all the doctors," and they could not find anything wrong with her. She attributed her eventual success to the prescriptions of an herbalist. "The herbalist had to find the right things to heat up my uterus," she explained. Just as Lalla Maryam did, herbalists in Fes described illnesses using a combination of medical terminology and local understandings of the cold (l'brd). Interestingly, doctors also said they played on local medical metaphors, such as the concept of l'brd, in explaining biomedical therapies for infertility as well.

"People understand reproduction within these traditional frameworks," said Dr. Alami, "so when we explain to them what's wrong, we try to use whatever they know to help them understand."

DOCTOR, COUNSELOR, JUDGE

While women's changing social roles and new legal discourses affect Moroccan conceptualizations of the marital relationship, the authority of physicians has also been elevated. Doctors are increasingly prominent as arbitrators in the marital relationship, particularly among couples who are middle and upper class. Although Moroccans were sometimes cynical about the success rates for assisted reproductive technology, the prospect of future success and a doctor's encouragement frequently convinced couples to stay in a relationship much longer than they might have otherwise.

Although some people who did not conceive told me that the doctors were charlatans who had just stolen their money, for the most part there was a deep respect for those physicians who held the keys to unlock the mysteries of conception. The doctors who specialized in reproductive health all perceived their own roles as extending beyond offering medical advice to taking sides in divorce disputes or even acting as marriage counselors.

"Women have become wise to the tests that men can do to see if it's their fault [that they can't have children]," one woman told me. "Some men will submit to the test, but others are afraid. So if the husband doesn't want to get the test now, she can threaten him with divorce. It places the man in a bad position because if he ends the marriage, he will have to support her, but he will also have to prove that the infertility is not his fault, so the judge will require him to take the test."

The "test" that she refers to bears witness to the presence of biomedicine as a factor in divorce negotiations. Divorce now requires greater evidence from the husband in the event that he desires its dissolution, and medical professionals are frequently called on to issue expert opinions in divorce cases. A doctor may validate infertility test readings, state a husband's refusal to get tested, or announce which therapies had been attempted.

"Infertility alone is not sufficient reason for divorce," I was told by Dr. Belarbi, a prominent gynecologist in Fes. "Sometimes I have to tell couples to remain patient, and to keep trying. Sometimes the problems aren't even medical—like the woman I just saw whose husband is in the army. She sees him rarely; how do they expect to have children? I told her that they need to live closer to one another, but I also educated her about her menstrual cycle and when she is likely to be fertile."

Dr. Belarbi, herself the mother of two grown children, has been practicing in Fes for over twenty-five years, and commented on what she saw as tremendous societal changes in the status of her female patients during that time.

"I see all types, all social classes," she told me. "Poor people come for consultations, even from the countryside, even if they can't afford the treatment." Increasingly she was seeing a new category of patients: women achieving higher levels of education, and postponing marriage and childbirth, many until they are in their forties.

"Very educated women are marrying when they're older. I didn't used to see this when I first worked in Fes. They get married and they can't have children, because they're forty-five or forty-six. It's very hard for them to have babies when they're this age, but I don't want to cut their hopes." So she would begin a long relationship in which the couples' files became thicker and thicker as they continued to fail to respond to treatments. Frequently the husband was even older than the wife.

Dr. Belarbi insists that couples see her together, and that both submit to testing. Anecdotally, she said, women were increasingly using a husband's infertility as leverage for a divorce.

"It's her right," she says. "A woman has a right to children as well. But this wasn't something you saw a long time ago. Before ICSI and IVF, there were fewer options. If the couple couldn't conceive, it was generally the wife who was abandoned."

Dr. Belarbi seemed resistant to using her medical expertise to assist a man's claim to divorce. "Men have always been able to get divorces easily. The stigma has been on women asking for them. The tests we now have for men give women more rights—the right to know if it's not their fault, and to leave the marriage if having children is so important to them." But she also felt it was her role to dispense advice to the couple about marriage. She told me:

> Men are always coming to me, saying they want me to write a letter to the judge [who prevails over a divorce case] saying their wife can't have children. But I won't do this. I will write a letter saying that this couple has undergone this or that treatment, but I always say that there is still hope. I am never going to give a man a paper saying, "This woman can't get pregnant." If they are young, I tell them they must keep trying. If not, I tell him that he must give her her support, that he married her not just because he wanted children but because he loved the woman herself. This [infertility] is no longer a good excuse to divorce someone, but also, the men now don't want to divorce because they will have to pay a lot.
>
> As a doctor, I know these couples well, and I play a lot of roles. Sometimes I'm like a lawyer, sometimes a judge or intermediary. Since I'm educated I see my role as trying to correct society. I'm not going to hurt either of them, the wife or the husband, even though sometimes their families come to me and try to argue that I should write for them this paper.

Dr. Belarbi's comments reflect not only the continued importance of reproduction in Moroccan society but also her belief in the authority the physician has over the marital relationship, particularly in conflicts with kin groups. She was not swayed by attempts on the part of family members to intercede for a man seeking medical evidence of his wife's failure to conceive. "I tell them it's none of their business, this is between the couple."

Margaret Sandelowski has written that infertility exemplifies both "the premium placed on genetic kinship and on women bearing children and of a general faith in physicians and medical technology to resolve a wide range of problems, including ones that are not clearly in the medical domain" (1991, 31). While for many Moroccans, kinship remains essential to family formation, the role of extended kin has declined. Thus, the ideal marital relationship reduces claims of the extended family to offspring, with medical discourses carrying increasing weight. As the domain of marriage has become even more intimate and private, an affair of couples rather than families, the physician becomes the stranger who has entered the marital relationship and is given the authority to interfere.

Yet despite this critique of the authority of biomedicine, in Morocco many people believe that legal and biomedical discourses regarding infertility (which were widely believed to have emanated from outside Morocco) give women an advantage, not only over their husbands but also over the prior interests of families and kin groups. Dr. Belarbi's words are a good example of this. Her status as an elite, educated physician counseling her patients on their marriages lends authoritative weight to discourses that privilege the notion that infertility is not sufficient grounds for divorce. In fact, she even stated that she sees her position as an important one to "correct" society's outdated notions of the wife as reproducer, easily discarded should she fail to produce heirs. Finally, the doctor's role is to "offer hope" and encourage couples to continue to try as many different treatments as possible until they have exhausted all their resources.

Conclusion

Dr. Belarbi's position aligns with nation-state interests in promoting an image of Moroccan female modernity consistent with ideals for women's rights in the West. In this vision, the Moroccan woman plays multiple societal roles, including one as a productive part of the nation's economy, and is not limited solely to her childbearing ability. A Moroccan government website that was accessible for a few years in the early 2000s, around the time mudawana reform was proposed, stated that Moroccan women of the twenty-first century want to "live with their time and be free of social dichotomies and various kinds of negligence which have been condemned by the United Nations conventions on the banning of all forms of discrimination against women" (Newcomb 2009, 25). These interests are reflected not only in the 2004 revisions to the mudawana but also in Morocco agreeing recently to sign on to the full version of the Convention on the Elimination of All Forms of Discrimination against Women, which they had previously rejected ("Morocco Withdraws Reservations to CEDAW" 2008).

These state-sanctioned visions of more egalitarian gender relations may not mirror existing conditions in the population but are nonetheless influencing middle- and upper-class Moroccans. In the case of infertility, social, bio-medical, and legal influences have aligned to help women maintain a marriage without children where they previously might have faced divorce, and have enhanced their ability to leave those marriages as well. Thus, in addition to the greater number of women marrying at a later age, there are now more ex-amples of companionate marriages without children, in which couples resist the advice of kin that childbearing must take precedence.

Assisted reproductive technologies contradictorily affirm both the desire for procreation and the continuation of childless marriages. The invasive, highly medicalized, and time-consuming nature of these treatments inserts the physician into the marital relationship as the authority figure who enables reproduction and whose elite status and technological expertise grant the physician the de facto right to advise couples about the very marriage itself. Traditional healers like Lalla Maryam, and also the herbalists I interviewed—one who ran a family business in the medina, and the other a man in the Ville Nouvelle whose spare office had no visible herbs and resembled a doctor's office—also advise couples and invoke their own medical authority in the ways they offer consultations and in their professed success rates. The in-volvement of medical professionals in marital issues that can make or break marriages coincides with liberalized marriage laws that have made divorce prohibitively expensive.

This is not to say, however, that these new legal and biomedical discourses uniformly favor women. Moroccan judges may ignore the mudawana in their rulings, and the most expensive ARTs do not reach most Moroccans due to their prohibitive costs. The resilience of local practices thus coexists with a changing dynamic about how infertility is viewed socially. While still a condi-tion that brings great unhappiness to those it affects, infertility is no longer the private affair of the patriarchal family, as it once was. Across all social classes, people still turn to traditional therapies for infertility. As the example of Lalla Maryam indicates, traditional practitioners further legitimize their own work through biomedicine by both demonstrating their medical knowledge of re-production and presenting their therapeutic techniques as complementary to biomedical therapies.[19]

Finally, the social importance of marriage for women cannot be underes-timated. Many Moroccans, particularly in situations involving women with low levels of education or professional employment, still consider a marriage without children to be devastating. Nevertheless, for a good number of middle- and upper-class Moroccans who will do whatever is within their means to avail themselves of new therapies, the confluence of legal reform, so-cial change, and ARTs affirms new possibilities for marriage as well.

Notes

1. See Amster 2013 and Greenwood 1981 for more on these traditional systems.

2. For an excellent study of the place of contemporary f'qihs in Moroccan society, see Spadola 2013.

3. Hanane was the woman I knew best among the eight women I formally interviewed during the summer of 2009 on the topic of infertility, introduced to me both through my existing social networks and through Rokiya, who, although not a health practitioner herself, was somewhat of a "broker" who introduced other women to the traditional healers. Although all were residents of Fes, these women came from different social classes, ranging from lower middle to upper middle. I also interviewed medical practitioners in the city of Fes, evenly divided among medical doctors and traditional healers such as herbalists, midwives, and massage practitioners. I additionally held informal conversations with both men and women about their own perceptions of marriage and infertility, which were often based on experiences their friends and family members had been through.

4. This practice of "giving" children to women who could not have their own has been documented by Jamila Bargach (2001).

5. On this topic, see Bargach 2002 and 2001.

6. A 1987 study of infertile couples in Morocco revealed that one-third of them had been in a marriage that had previously ended in divorce due to infertility (Zhiri and Benyahia 1987).

7. For more on the difficulties Morocco has experienced in implementing the new laws, see *Rapports annuels sur l'application du code de famille*, published by the Ligue démocratique des droits des femmes (various years), and Gomez-Rivas 2008.

8. In fact, the wording of portions of the mudawana maintains an emphasis on patriarchy, giving preference to men in matters such as legal representation of children (Elliott 2009, 218). Further, accurate information about the revised laws has not yet been effectively disseminated throughout the population, and women, particularly those who are poor or illiterate, are often at the mercy of judges who may choose to rule against the law and face no oversight.

9. Again, it should be noted that this is largely a matter of perception and misunderstanding, and as I show in the previous chapter, Moroccans are often misinformed about the laws' content as well as their reach. A common fear, which I saw echoed in a documentary that appeared on national television about husbands who had supposedly been turned out of their homes, was that the wife would divorce her husband and take everything, though I never encountered any actual cases in my fieldwork of this happening.

10. Biomedical treatments are prohibitively expensive, so while women across all social classes may visit a physician who specializes in infertility, many are not able to pursue the costly treatments. Given adequate financial resources, however, many Moroccans also continue to try indefinitely to pursue the therapies needed to have children, the "never enough" quality of ARTs that Sandelowski (1991) has written about.

11. The idea of the "cold" (l'brd) attacking the uterus and preventing conception is still a commonly held belief derived from a form of Galenic humoral medicine widespread in Moroccan traditional medicine. For more on this, see Greenwood 1981.

12. Latifa's emphasis on therapies focusing on the female body may have been due to her daughter's situation: in this case, tests indicated that the husband was fertile, so Hanane had been the target of most treatments.

13. Tradition often dictated that the woman's family would furnish the apartment provided by the husband, though in some cases men were now required to provide both the apartment and the furnishings.

14. One physician I interviewed married at nineteen and had children while continuing her studies, a stipulation her parents had demanded for her in her wedding contract. She was now in her late forties and a respected physician in Fes.

15. In some cases, the absence of an extended family when nuclear families move to urban areas on their own can mean that women cannot rely on support of or intervention by members of their extended family in the event of a dispute or violent treatment by a spouse.

16. For an excellent account of the dissemination of French colonial ideas about modernity and the body through medicine, see Amster 2013.

17. See Inhorn 2006 for an extensive survey of Sunni and Shi'i attitudes toward IVF and the use of donor gametes.

18. The evil eye and sorcery, in other words, were much like Evans-Pritchard's famous analysis of witchcraft among the Azande: a roof might fall in because it had been damaged by termites, but what caused it to fall at a specific moment could be blamed on sorcery.

19. This is not new; as Ellen Amster has shown, Moroccan midwives in the 1950s frequently sent their difficult cases to French hospitals (2013, 200).

LABOR

Migration and the Informal Market

KHALED BENJELLOUN PENSIVELY SIPPED A glass of hot tea in the café where he spent his days. "Work in Morocco," he said, "is all about connections or luck." Khaled, unemployed ever since I'd known him, was not without family connections, but he certainly seemed to be out of luck. The café, he assured me, was an important site for networking and for hearing about what opportunities might be out there, but he was interested in very few of them. The problem with connections, he said, was that they might find you a job, but it would not be the kind of job you wanted. There were no good jobs available.

"He's just not interested in working," another Moroccan told me, speaking of Khaled. Some said Khaled could not work, that he was constitutionally unable to hold down a job doing anything after so many years of unemployment. But Khaled disagreed.

"I could have pictured myself in an office somewhere," he said vaguely, when I asked him what he had hoped to do when he was in college. "In a government job, like our constitution promises us. But those days are gone. The government did not live up to its promises." He was referring, incorrectly, to a set of decrees from long ago that supposedly guaranteed a job to all who graduated from Moroccan universities. At one point during the 1970s, when the state was the nation's largest employer, this might have been an easier promise to fulfill. Yet after the structural adjustment years of the 1980s, government jobs were reduced to a small fraction of those that had once been available. And even though his father had been a government employee and his family had more resources than many others in the middle class, Khaled insisted that the Benjelloun connections were now so diffused that none of them could be transformed into adequate employment.

"Who do we know in the local government?" Khaled asked. "Only people who used their contacts to help their own children find work." Family networks, he said, could be helpful if he had his own business and was seeking clients, or if he needed something at a good price at a business owned by someone in the family. But connections that turned into work, he said, generally benefited only the most immediate relatives.

Many Moroccans criticized Khaled and others like him for choosing the wrong degree, or for not being willing to take any employment he could find. What did he expect, majoring in English? If he did not want to tag along with groups of tourists, or work in a hotel, where did he think his skills would make him employable? The smart degrees were now business and engineering, people said, as if Khaled should have known that when he attended university in the 1990s. The country needed more people with "practical" skills, others said. Yet I have met many unemployed Moroccans who did take out loans to attend a private business college, or who studied engineering, and many of them were also wondering where the jobs were. Rather, if there were jobs available, they said, they were given to those who had degrees from Europe or North America.

The Benjelloun family's experiences represent the circuitous and often frustrating paths by which middle-class urban dwellers negotiate the labor market in an era of globalization. Reflecting larger trends in Morocco, their experiences run the gamut from migration to microcredit, and from the informal economy to the public sector. Khaled's brother Rachid did not go to college but has worked in Spain for over a decade. Their sister Hanane is employed in a coveted public sector position as a teacher, in a job that, while low paid, offers decent benefits. Ilham, a stay-at-home mother, represents the majority of Moroccan women who work at home. Finally, the oldest brother, Mourad, is a small-scale entrepreneur with a business selling used clothes, work that provides consistent income to support his family.

Despite the busy, bustling appearance of Morocco's second-largest city, despite promises that structural adjustment and privatization would lead to an era of well-compensated work for private corporations, most jobs in Fes, as in the rest of the country, are located in the informal economy. Untaxed and unregulated by the state, these jobs are created not by corporations investing in Morocco's human potential but by individuals improvising with minimal resources. For poorer Moroccans working in the informal economy, microcredit loans have been available since the 1990s, but rather than lifting people out of poverty and into a new social class, they tend to support basic family survival and often lead to participation in multiple microcredit schemes that keep the borrower eternally in debt.[1] For those members of the middle class with aspirations toward entrepreneurship, loans do not lead to job creation for others, but rather allow borrowers to create opportunities for themselves. There is a further disconnect between education and employment. While government officials debate whether the current system adequately trains people for twenty-first-century jobs, recent graduates wonder what jobs they might be referring to. The good jobs all seem to go to those educated abroad who have family connections in prominent firms, while the rest of the educated labor force languishes in unpaid internship after unpaid internship. As Khaled told me, finding work continues to be about connections and luck.

How do Moroccans find their livelihoods in an era where the path to employment is murky and often indirect, and where there are no guarantees that any particular educational track will lead to employment? During the period following colonialism, education and employment were largely controlled by the government. But now the Moroccan market is dependent on trade and investment with public entities such as the European Union as well as private interests from Europe and the wealthy Gulf states. For citizens in their twenties, thirties, and forties, the economic landscape is quite different from the one confronted by previous generations, and while the standard of living has improved for most Moroccans, jobs are more competitive. Moroccans in their fifties and older benefited from a public sector that employed a large percentage of the population. Urban populations in the past were also much smaller, as globalization has led to mass migrations to the cities from the countryside, where many migrants had been employed in agriculture. There are now far fewer jobs in agriculture or in the public sector. Unemployment remains high among educated youth, and personal connections are still the surest path to a job. The actual work Moroccans find themselves doing, whether in the informal economy, in the public sector, in private enterprise, or outside of the country, is intimately linked to globalization. Investment and privatization, meant to take the financial burden off the state, have created new construction, shopping malls, luxury ports, and housing developments, but they have not fulfilled their promise of providing gainful employment for the population.

Migration

There are a number of ways Moroccans migrate to Europe; the most common is to pay a smuggler several thousand dollars to be stowed away on a raft from northern Morocco to Spain. Rachid Benjelloun, however, was one of the lucky ones who managed to get a visa in the early years of the new millennium to attend a family wedding in France. At the time he had a job in his uncle's real estate office in Fes. Although Rachid was not paid very much, his uncle reported a higher income on Rachid's salary statements for several months, giving the impression that his income was higher than it actually was. Knowing he would not get a visa on the merits of his own income, his family helped him plan in advance, depositing extra money in his bank account over a period of several months so that when he applied for the visa, he could show the consular officials proof of sufficient income and wealth that would make him unlikely to emigrate. The consulate also required evidence of property or other ties to Morocco, so the title of a dilapidated apartment in the medina belonging to Rachid's mother was transferred to his name, also well in advance of the visa application.

With the visa successfully in hand, Rachid went to France for the wedding and did not come back. One of his cousins was working on a farm near Valencia, Spain, and found agricultural work for Rachid. Because he spoke no Spanish, was undocumented, and had no high school diploma from Morocco, there was little else he could do, but for the next few years he worked hard in jobs on a series of short-term contracts, in fields ranging from farming to construction. He learned enough Spanish to get by and was able to take advantage of a government program that granted amnesty to foreigners able to prove they had been in the country before a certain date, and he successfully applied for permanent residence.

When the economic downturn of 2008 came, Rachid's work dried up. Around the same time, Spanish farm owners began to prefer a feminized workforce that included Moroccan women but not Moroccan men. The women, who came on short-term contracts, were more pliable and less likely to overstay their visas, especially when they left children back at home (Mannon, Petrzelka, and Glass 2012). Rachid continued to work when he could, but he made much less than he used to, and he was not able to send money back to his family. Now, most of what he earned was directed toward survival. He moved to Madrid, hoping to find more opportunities there, and lived in an apartment with several other migrants who were also sporadically employed. For a while he found employment on three- to six-month contracts doing everything from cleaning industrial buildings to working as a security guard. He returned to Morocco more frequently, helping his brother Mourad with his clothing business, but Mourad, who only made enough to support his own family, was not able to pay Rachid a regular salary. Rachid returned to Spain to keep his residency activated, working wherever he could.

In contrast to his brother Khaled, perpetually unemployed and dissatisfied, Rachid took his situation in stride, always believing an opportunity was just around the corner. Unlike Khaled, he continued to actively seek work, and did not feel that anything was beneath him. If his cousin in Fes who owned a catering business, for example, needed an assistant to load and unload trucks or help with setup, Rachid would go, even if an afternoon of labor netted only fifty dirhams (approximately five dollars).

"You never know what might turn into something else in the long run," Rachid said, although the cousin also had his own more immediate (and un-employed) family members to whom he was more likely to offer work. As long as he was busy, Rachid was optimistic that things would get better. A friend of the family was opening a hotel in Tangier, and Rachid planned to go there next to see if they could use someone with passable Spanish and a little English, even if he might use those skills only as a waiter in the hotel restaurant.

"I didn't finish school. I don't feel the government owes me a job," he re-sponded when I asked him who was responsible for the lack of jobs. "It's up to each person to find his *rizq* [daily bread]. As long as I am not too old to keep moving around like this, I will keep searching." However, Rachid sometimes expressed regret that he did not have sufficient capital or a steady income to get married. A brief marriage to a Moroccan in the United States had ended in divorce a few years earlier, and although family members often tried to set him up with available young women, Rachid never pursued these opportunities beyond an initial meeting. Khaled, it seemed likely, would never marry, but his mother, Latifa, often spoke of Rachid as a possible candidate, and in an in-teresting reversal of gender expectations, she told me she was actively search-ing for an employed woman who might want to marry a good man without expectations of a regular income. She longed to see all her children married, with families of their own.

"He has his residency in Spain. And the economy is getting better," Latifa said hopefully. "He might marry someone who is divorced, or who waited too long to marry because she went to university and then worked." I wondered if the educational discrepancy between Rachid and a potential career-minded spouse might be unbridgeable. The only cases I saw of disparate educational levels were educated men seeking a less-educated spouse who would be dedi-cated to keeping house and raising children.

Almost every family I met in Morocco seems to have at least one family member who has migrated. Rachid is an example of the one in four Moroc-cans who left for Europe between 1981 and 2009 and has since returned home (de Haas 2014). From 1972 to 2010, the number of Moroccan migrants in Europe climbed from 300,000 to over 2.5 million, an estimate that does not include immigrants who entered Europe illegally. Roughly 85 percent of the Moroccan population residing abroad lives in European Union countries

(Ennaji 2014, 36). Although the worldwide economic downturn of 2008 did result in a temporary dip in remittances, by 2012, remittances comprised a staggering $6.9 billion contribution to the Moroccan economy. Each year, money sent home by Moroccans represents between 7 and 9 percent of the country's GDP ("Workers' Remittances," 2016). Migration remains an important employment strategy not only for individuals hoping to support themselves and their families, but also for the government, for which migrants remain a significant source of income in the Moroccan economy.[2] At the same time, as David McMurray writes, emigration "works to relieve some of the social discontent caused by high unemployment," while the wages of migrants hold "down the cost of living by covering consumption costs within the emigrant households at the local level" (2001, 131). In other words, migration is both an acceptable safety valve to relieve the discontent of the unemployed and a strategy to increase family consumption in the Moroccan economy.

When he was receiving a steady income from his work in Spain, Rachid faithfully sent home wages to his mother and to other family members who needed assistance. Money exchanged among family members was not closely accounted for. Although by 2015 Mourad's used clothing business was running smoothly, there were years when he was underemployed, and Rachid quietly assisted him. While Latifa received a small pension from the government because of her late husband's employment, she also benefited from Rachid's support, as did Khaled. Money could be sent quickly from Spain via services such as Western Union, and if money was needed to cover household repairs or medical expenses, Latifa would often call on Rachid to help out. Family members took care of one another without comment or complaint, making sure that everyone had food, clothes, school fees, or other necessities.

Some scholars have argued that the family serves as a "bank" that funds migration, and that remittances amount to the migrant paying back the bank (Bougha-Hagbe 2004, 4), but this characterization seems too mechanistic and utilitarian to apply in the case of families like the Benjellouns, who support one another without any immediate expectation of repayment. Everyone knew that even though a family member might be flush with cash at one moment, later he might be without a job. Additionally, even with someone like Khaled, who did not work at all and never contributed income to the family, nobody grumbled about supporting him. Khaled ran errands for Latifa and was always willing to help his other siblings when they needed a hand, and in return they gave him daily pocket money for the café. Mourad also gave him desirable name brand clothes from his stock. The sisters, Ilham and Hanane, did not give money back to the family but were close to their mother, who would stay with each of them for long periods of time. They supported her by taking her to doctor's visits and on vacations. Ilham, as a homemaker, had no income of her own, but Latifa frequently stayed with Ilham and helped her with the children and housework. Hanane received a teacher's salary, but everyone knew she spent much of her disposable income on infertility treatments, so nobody seemed to expect her to contribute to the family finances.

Studies of migration in Morocco have shown that most remittances are used to increase family consumption, but that, beyond household consumption, migrants—even those who are entrepreneurs—are more likely to invest remittances in real estate or construction than to start new business ventures (Bougha-Hagbe 2004, 4). McMurray (2001) notes that longtime migrants from the northern city of Nador contributed to a construction boom in the city, adding to their buildings little by little so that they would not be taxed by the authorities. (It was, in fact, a successful migrant from northern Morocco who caused the local scandal described in chapter 5 by attempting to purchase real estate to open a bakery in the Benjelloun neighborhood.) While Rachid did not make enough money to invest in real estate, in many other Moroccan families, the migrant would buy a modest apartment to use when he or she returned for a visit to Morocco. Some bought apartments outside Fes, particularly in locations closer to the ocean, where they could bring their families during Europe's August holidays. Since Mohammed VI became king in 1999, the formerly almost untouched northern coast of Morocco has seen considerable development and has become a popular place for migrants to invest.

When they return to Morocco for visits, migrants bring with them not only money but also new ideas, cultural practices, and products from Europe.[3] Since the late 1990s, satellite media and the internet have additionally exposed Moroccans to the latest cultural exports, and consumption has increased as a result. Families often ask migrants to bring home fashion, music, technology, and other merchandise available only in Europe. Increased economic contact with China has also led to a tremendous black market of Chinese-made counterfeit goods, ranging from Dolce & Gabbana T-shirts to pirated Microsoft software. Many Moroccans, though, told me they rely on family members abroad to bring back the "real thing."

"A few years ago, my sister Ilham was crazy about a Dior purse she had seen in the window of a store in Casablanca," Rachid told me. I knew the purse, a shiny black leather bag she often carried when she attended weddings or other special social events. "She usually doesn't ask for much, so when she asked me for this, I saved up money to get it for her, even though it was expensive. It was still less than it cost in Casablanca. She was thrilled, and she uses it only on special occasions." Although many Fassis still measure personal wealth in traditional accoutrements worn at weddings, such as gold belts, jewelry, and silk caftans, name brand items from Europe also carry considerable status, especially since they are harder to find and more expensive in Morocco. Traditional status symbols, produced close to home and purchased directly from artisans, coexist with the symbols of global capital, made for a pittance in the factories of Asia and sold at a high price.

Migration is one of the most obvious ways that work and the Moroccan economy have become closely tied to global processes. Throughout every stage of life, in seeking to make a living, individuals face constraints from both local circumstances and the world market. But what about those who, unlike Rachid, have actually completed degrees in higher education?

EDUCATION

The path toward a career for many begins with a successful performance on the baccalaureate high school exit exams, which guarantees students a spot in one of Morocco's fourteen public universities. The exit exams are challenging, and not all students pass: in 2014, for example, 44 percent (141,984) of the students who took the exam succeeded ("Meet Houda" 2014). Higher scores admit students into more lucrative STEM fields such as engineering, but a lower score, while guaranteeing a spot in a university, restricts one's choices to fields with fewer job prospects, such as English or history. For the remainder who do poorly on the exams and are ineligible to attend a public university, there are other options, such as private universities that focus on practical training in fields such as business management and computer science. But what is the value of these degrees, and are they a guarantee of employment?

In 2013, King Mohammed VI called for educational reform, in response not only to criticisms of educational quality but also to the fact that unemployment among university graduates remains a pressing problem throughout the country. The World Bank places Morocco's educational system at the very bottom of the Arab world, and has characterized its educational reforms (undertaken with large World Bank loans) as only partial (Boutieri 2014). Modeled after the educational system of the colonizing French, in the postcolonial era the Moroccan educational system simultaneously attempted to pursue what Charis Boutieri has described as two potentially contradictory aims: to produce "an evolving labor force to meet so-called global but predominantly French needs," and simultaneously to promote "Arabo-Muslim official culture, and consequently the monarchical state's socio-cultural legitimacy, through the creation and safeguarding of a specific version of the past" (2014, 3). One by-product of this was the language Arabization project undertaken in the 1980s, during which the language of educational instruction was abruptly switched from French to Modern Standard Arabic (MSA). Both languages place students at a disadvantage when their family language at home is vernacular Moroccan Arabic (darija) or Berber (Tamazight). At the university level, much of the instruction still takes place in French, and current linguistic debates in Morocco concern whether the language of instruction should remain MSA rather than mother tongues such as darija or Tamazight. As Boutieri notes, much of the economic investment in the country involves multinational corporations such as Renault, which would necessitate skilled workers being able to speak fluent French, thus reproducing already existing global structural inequalities (Boutieri 2014, 3).

Until the 1980s, most educated Moroccans expected to be employed by the nation-state, in jobs that came with benefits such as health insurance and retirement pensions. Although Morocco was never completely dominated by state-owned enterprises, after colonialism most industries inherited from the French, such as the phosphate industry, were government-run (Najem 2001). The private sector remained weak despite official encouragement throughout the 1970s. Yet during the 1980s, structural adjustment reforms led to a decrease in state sector employment, since this was a mandatory condition for Morocco receiving IMF loans. While during the 1970s a rapidly growing educated class was virtually guaranteed a job in the public sector, by the 1980s this was no longer true. By 1983, jobs in the public sector had fallen from a previous high of 50,000 to 5,000 (Akesbi 2003).

Unemployment has disproportionately affected university graduates. In 1982, before structural adjustment, unemployment among university graduates averaged 6.5 percent, a figure that rose to 26 percent in 1991 and 40 percent in 2002 (El Aoufi and Bensaïd 2008). Since the early 1990s, unemployed university graduates have protested regularly in front of Parliament in Rabat, demanding that the government provide them with public sector jobs. They base their claims on both a constitutional article suggesting that "all citizens shall have equal rights in seeking education and employment" and on ministerial decrees stating that university graduates shall directly enter the public sector (Bogaert 2011, 252). While private sector jobs do exist, most of the demonstrators do not believe them to be adequate to their level of education. The protests have resulted in some successes: after months or years of protests, many are given government jobs, only to be replaced by new groups of recent graduate protesters (242).

Another pattern is that recent graduates will work in unpaid internships for a year or so, after which they are replaced by the next group of new graduates. Zahra, a twenty-seven-year-old cousin of the Benjelloun siblings, not only attended university but also received a master's degree in chemistry, finishing at the top of her class. After graduating, she worked for one year in

Casablanca as a lab technician at a pharmaceutical company. After her year was finished, however, the company let her go. She told me that there were many others like her at the company, and none of them, except for a new employee whose degree was from France, were retained. Zahra briefly took part in the February 20th Movement in 2011, which enveloped not only those who sought government reform but also many unemployed graduates, but after a few months she moved back to Fes to live with her parents. She had also participated in some of the demonstrations of unemployed graduates outside Parliament, but as her brother Faris said, "For that to work you have to take beatings, and sometimes stay there for years. Our family didn't like to think about her in that situation, and our father wasn't going to pay for her to live in Rabat and lie down in front of Parliament every day." From Fes, Zahra continued to seek jobs and send out her resumé, but she has not been employed in several years.

"I often want to give up because I don't know anyone in my field, except at the place where I used to work, and the people I went to school with," she told me. Her professors, she said, had few connections in industry, and those who did shared available opportunities with favorite students or family connections. Her fellow graduates were either unemployed or working in fields that had nothing to do with chemistry. "It's not a system of merit. If it were, I would have a job now."

This pattern was common for other graduates as well, in fields ranging from engineering to computer science, and it was disheartening to see that so many firms, especially the prestigious multinational companies, albeit with Moroccan managers in place, benefited from skilled but underpaid or unpaid labor. In the Moroccan media, people complained that the educational system was not adequately preparing students for the jobs that existed. But where were those jobs? Earlier this may have been true, but over the years I have seen many examples of skilled graduates who seemed to pursue the "right" fields, worked for free, and then were dismissed to make room for the next crop of free laborers. For permanent hires, private companies tend to select those with more prestigious degrees from overseas.

The lives of the Benjelloun siblings reflect these trends. Only Hanane has found work in the field she studied at university. Hanane, Mourad, and Khaled all have university degrees, while Ilham and Rachid do not. All are now in their thirties and forties, and none of those who attended college was able to find employment immediately out of university. After graduating with a degree in education, Hanane worked as an assistant in a private school for a few years in a low-paying job with no benefits before she obtained a teaching job in a public school. Someone with an excellent score on a national exam for teachers will have a good chance of a job offer. The majority of those with an education degree, however, have scores that are merely acceptable, and they compete for a limited number of jobs throughout the country. Those with connections at the Ministry of Education may receive placements before those with no connections. Hanane did well on the exam, but she also had a family connection, a cousin who had just started working in the ministry in Rabat, so the year she took the exam she was also placed in a job.

Currently, the outlook for teachers is grim. In January 2016, thousands of teachers and teachers-in-training participated in protests after the government announced that it was cutting teacher training pay in half, from 2,500 to 1,200 dirhams per month (about $121), and that of the 10,000 teachers currently training, only 7,000 would be awarded employment ("Morocco's Teacher Protests Trigger Political Crisis" 2016). The government explained that they expected many graduates would be able to find lucrative jobs teaching in Gulf countries, but for many this was yet another example of the government promising work that never materialized. After the strikes, the government backed down and compromised with the current crop of teachers by agreeing to create more jobs. Nevertheless, the state refused to change the lowered stipend.

THE INFORMAL SECTOR

Several kilometers from the center of Fes's Ville Nouvelle, Hay Zahra is a busy neighborhood marked by a traffic roundabout that sends cars toward the autoroute and other suburbs of the new city. About two blocks from the traffic circle there is a bus stop where three different local bus lines meet, and across the street is a taxi stand. During rush hour, the neighborhood projects a cacophony of sounds, a chorus of honking horns and grinding diesel bus gears, pedestrians shouting at one another, and everyone rushing to their final destinations. The street is lined with stores, ranging from bicycle, computer, and cell phone repair shops to butcher shops and stores stuffed to the brim with plastic buckets, dish drainers, bowls, cheap silverware, and tablecloths. Fruit and vegetable vendors sell dirt-stained carrots, potatoes, and onions laid on bedsheets covering the sidewalk, while women offer mountains of honey-coated *shabakia* pastries and stacks of dimpled *bghrir* pancakes fried in the early hours. Close to the bus stop, a food cart features hot *sfinj* doughnuts that people can buy as they climb onto a bus bound for the city center and their work. The entire scene contrasts with the sterility of the modern supermarkets, demonstrating that while mega-markets may have ruined small businesses, in these outer neighborhoods there remains a thriving and vibrant trade for those less concerned with status.

In one narrow alley, Mourad Benjelloun has his own small shop, crammed between two buildings, yet covered with a roof. Clothes for men, women, and children are hung to the ceiling along the narrow walls, ranging from name brands (and a few counterfeits) such as Adidas and Nike to nondescript Chinese-made clothes. Like the stores surrounding him, his shop is busy, and although only two or three people can stand inside at once, he does a lively trade throughout the day. His merchandise has traveled from Spain via the duty free zones of Ceuta and Melilla in the north. There is nothing aesthetically appealing about the small space, but Mourad arranges the clothes carefully to display brand names mixed among anonymous but functional pieces. People come seeking both: the caché of Dolce & Gabbana T-shirts appeals to the neighborhood's teenagers, while their mothers come to purchase woolen leggings to wear under their djellabas during the winter.

Mourad earned his degree in accounting. After graduating, he was unemployed for a few years before he found a job with a multinational corporation in Mohammedia, near Casablanca. He worked there for almost ten years but was unable to keep up with new technologies at work and was fired. In 2000, when the internet was still taking off in Morocco, he applied to a "young entrepreneurs" program and received a loan to buy secondhand computers and rent a space in the Ville Nouvelle in Fes, where he opened a cyber café. He was able to keep his business open for two years before going bankrupt, since cyber cafés had become a dime a dozen by that point. The price to use the internet for an hour had gone down to only about fifty cents, which was not enough to cover his operating expenses.

Mourad became involved with his current entrepreneurial venture by accident. One year, his brother Rachid rode home from Spain with a Moroccan who was bringing used clothes into the country. The friend needed money and asked if Rachid would be interested in buying some of the shipment to resell. Rachid paid for part of the shipment and asked Mourad to help him transport it from Tangier to Fes. Mourad had a knack for sales, and he familiarized himself with the entire business, which entailed purchasing regular shipments from Moroccans who traveled between northern Morocco and Spain and would sell him, sight unseen, the contents of cars filled with clothes. Using money borrowed from his mother as start-up capital, Mourad rented a tiny shop that was well placed for pedestrian traffic in an outlying neighborhood of Fes. At first he also took his wares to Suq al-Ahad, the Sunday market on the outskirts of town, but now his shop in Hay Zahra does so well that he does not need to travel with his merchandise. He eventually developed connections with northern Moroccans who regularly deliver clothes to Fes and are reliable suppliers who can be counted on to bring merchandise of acceptable quality. In the past, to increase his stock, he took out small loans that were part of microcredit programs designed to help small businesses. But Mourad avoided these whenever possible, because he had seen other small businessmen sucked into a cycle of perpetual borrowing and repayment.

"I've only taken those loans when I couldn't borrow from family," he explained. "And only if I was sure I could pay them back. They want you to take out more and more, and then you're stuck." Indeed, many social scientists have described the cycle of indebtedness that microcredit loans engender. Women are often the preferred customers for microloans because they are more likely to repay them than men.[4]

With this income, Mourad supports his wife and two elementary school–aged children, who attend an inexpensive private school. They rent rather than own their apartment, but his income is sufficient for his wife to always wear fashionable clothes, work out at a gym, and have a housekeeper who comes once a week to clean the small apartment. For Mourad, these are signs that demonstrate he has been successful.

"I didn't want her to have to work," he said. "She can stay home and be there for the kids when they're done with school. And we can buy what we need for the children: a good education, they can each have their own room, and we take them to McDonald's sometimes. This to me means that I have achieved success." I found it interesting that he voiced the material aspects of a successful existence in terms that were highly recognizable to someone from the Global North: the commodification of an education, the desire for space and a move away from communal sleeping arrangements, and the ability to afford fast food.

Mourad talked about expanding into a larger shop but worried that the increased rent and possible loss of his current customers through relocation would make expansion a risky choice. It was true that a bigger shop would allow him to bring in more merchandise and potentially hire an assistant, but after having lost a job and failing at his cyber café, Mourad was content to be conservative and stay in his current location. He has good relationships with his fellow shopkeepers, street vendors, and customers, and he worried about having to reestablish those relationships elsewhere. He shrugged when I asked whether a larger shop would allow him to employ Khaled or Rachid, and said they were both busy with their lives and had no interest in working with him, even though it had been Rachid's shipment of clothes that had originally helped him to get started.

While Mourad is occupied with his own entrepreneurial venture, his brother Khaled has not worked for many years. His degree in English makes him a skilled conversationalist, but he has been unable to link his education to fields where it might be useful, such as in tourism.

"I don't want to guide people around the medina," he said. "That's not me—I am not interested in showing off history. I wanted to be part of the future, but how, I don't know. I couldn't see myself as a guide, and even the hotel jobs go to people with degrees in hotel management, not people with English degrees! Even in the hotels, unless you are with a union, they won't keep you. There are too many unemployed graduates. I applied for many jobs over the years and nothing ever happened." Unlike Rachid, Khaled was not willing to work at any job that was available, but he also seemed at times to be depressed, mentally paralyzed by years of being unable to find work. He lived in a small apartment with his mother and had a routine that revolved around his home, his neighborhood, and local cafés, where he held court and talked with his fellow *chommeurs* (unemployed) about the dire state of the world. A cousin, Hassan, had been in a similar situation: both graduated around the same time with English degrees, but Hassan delivered pizzas while tutoring children in English on the side at the local American Language Institute. Finally, Hassan found work as an English teacher at a language institute in Casablanca, where he has now been employed for several years. Family members held up Hassan as an example of what Khaled could have done if he set his mind to it.

Finding work in Morocco often requires creativity, a willingness to work for years at a salary well below one's educational level, or the ability to do something that might have only a tangential relationship to one's university degree. Mourad, for example, acknowledged that his accounting degree was useful for keeping track of his operating costs and merchandise, but the sales and networking aspects of his job were not skills that he learned at university. There was a disconnect between what students could study at the public universities and the availability of jobs. Examining the major sources of Morocco's GDP, it is often difficult to see the relationship between those industries and the current state of higher education in Morocco. Morocco's main sources of income are agriculture, phosphates, tourism, and manufacturing. Approximately 40 percent of the overall population, and 80 percent of those in rural areas, work in agriculture, which accounts for 20 percent of Morocco's GDP and 30 percent of the country's exports ("Morocco" n.d.). The European Union is the preferred trade partner, accounting for about 80 percent of Morocco's exports.[5] Most of the jobs in agriculture are unskilled and tend to be clustered in rural areas, such as the rich farmland outside Casablanca.

As noted earlier, phosphate mining is another important sector of the economy, and Morocco is thought to hold 85 percent of the world's phosphorus, the key ingredient in fertilizer. During the 1970s, phosphates were Morocco's primary export, but after the implementation of structural adjustment in the 1980s, tourism and manufacturing increased in importance. The government's private holding company, OCP, owns 94 percent of the country's phosphate interests.

Neither agriculture nor the phosphate industry, however, would be destinations for most recent university graduates, especially in urban areas. More likely is the prospect that university graduates will find themselves working in the private sector. In Morocco, as in other Global South countries, employment in the private sector is high, representing 88 percent of the country's GDP, but most of the available nongovernmental jobs are in the informal economy (Woodward and Safavi 2015, 64). The informal economy, representing jobs that are untaxed and unaccounted for by the government, carries with it little protection for its workers, and the labor is often likely to be both unskilled and dangerous.[6] Wages are low, and participants are likely to be poor. While Mourad was fortunate that he was able to rent an actual shop with a door that he could pull down and lock up at night, other vendors in Fes haggle for prime sidewalk space and truck their merchandise home every evening. These informal shops are constantly under threat from theft or raids by the authorities.

In Morocco, the informal economy has grown dramatically: from 1980 to 1984, 56.9 percent of the population was engaged in work in the informal sector, but between 2005 and 2010 that proportion had grown to a staggering 78.5 percent. Globalization has definitely contributed to the ballooning of the informal economy, yet it appeared in its nascent forms as a response to modernization. After World War II, the modernization model, in which states encouraged large-scale economic development, led to dual economies in Global South countries such as Morocco: "the formal economy of large enterprises subsidized by government and small-scale producers (craftspersons, artisans, small-scale agriculturalists, not yet an entrepreneurial class)" (Ilahiane and Sherry 2008, 247). In the 1970s, the anthropologist Clifford Geertz wrote about the *suq* or the traditional bazaar, where artisans bargained and sold their wares within a complex mosaic of relationships that included urban elites as well as Jewish tradesmen (Geertz 1979). When government industries shut down or privatized under structural adjustment, displaced workers entered the informal economy in droves, and informal suqs sprang up all over Moroccan cities. No longer just the province of artisans and tradesmen, the suqs became sites of commerce for all those pushed out of the formal economy, where people bought, sold, and traded a wide range of goods, particularly those made newly available by globalization, such as electronics, cell phones, and products purchased in the free trade zones of northern Morocco.[7]

Gender and Employment

While globalization has led many Moroccans to seek work outside the public sector, how has it specifically affected the type of work women do? More Moroccan women are present in the workforce than ever before, but their numbers are still quite low compared with other countries in the Global South. In part this is because the vast majority of women work in the informal sector, which is not reported in official statistics.[8] According to official statistics, only 22.7 percent of Moroccan women work outside the home, and wage inequalities for women are thought to be very high; it is estimated that they rank 130th of 142 countries studied (Majdi 2014). Only 12 percent of company managers are women, and 50 percent of the listed companies in Morocco contain no female members on their board of directors. Most of the increase in women's employment in Morocco is found in low-skilled occupations and in the informal economy.

Within the informal economy, women's positions are also of lower status than men's, and they are more likely to be found in smaller-scale enterprises such as selling food, whereas men are more likely to deal in nonperishable goods (Carr and Chen 2001, 3). Carr and Chen note the substantial gender gap in wages within the informal economy, because even within this economy, "women worldwide are under-represented in higher income employment statuses . . . (employer and self-employed) and over-represented in the lower income statuses (casual wage worker and industrial outworker" (3).

Moroccan women often receive no benefits or protection in work that can come with significant dangers, such as in factories that are not reported to the authorities but are nonetheless producing goods for export, often contracted with multinational companies. In Morocco, women's informal work typically involves agriculture, domestic labor, or food production (Charmes 2012, 116). During Ramadan, for example, in any of the old cities of Morocco, one might see women seated on stools in the alleys, tending a low table or blanket spread with stacks of pancakes for sale for breaking the fast. I asked Mourad about the women who sold food in the area close to his shop. There were two or three different regulars, he told me, women in their forties and fifties who were divorced or who needed to help supplement their family's income. One woman had worked in factories throughout the 1990s but now sold food, since factory jobs had become unreliable. They were all fairly poor, he said, and lived either in the medina or in the far outskirts of Fes in a neighborhood called Hay Agadir.

"They know this is a good location and they can probably sell more here than they would in their own neighborhoods," he said. "Also, they don't want their neighbors to see them."[9] The neighbors would know they were working, he said, and the women would have felt "ashamed" at being seen all day out on the streets selling food.

At a much higher status than the informal market are the coveted public sector jobs that are now extremely rare in Morocco. Hanane, the only public sector employee in the Benjelloun family, is also the only child to follow in her father's footsteps, as the late patriarch of the family was employed by the government. Ilham, who stays at home, is similar to the official majority of women who are recorded by Moroccan statistics as homemakers. Although Latifa, their mother, has never worked in a formal job, she was known around the neighborhood for her sewing and embroidery work, particularly her intricate traditional tablecloths and napkins. A family member with a fabric shop in the medina sold the tablecloths and napkins for her, which earned a small amount of extra income for the family.

Latifa did this work done on the side, when she took a break from her labor-intensive efforts to run a Moroccan household in the era before washing machines (still not present in every household) or prepared foods. Her embroidery was not something she did out of economic necessity, nor did she consider it part of any sort of "informal sector" employment. But the story of a family friend, Shadia, shows how many Moroccan women have transitioned sewing skills to the market. When Latifa's children were still living at home, Shadia and her mother, Oumaima, often came to help with washing clothes in the small courtyard of the family house. Oumaima collected the family laundry and scrubbed it vigorously on a washboard before hanging it out to dry on the clotheslines that snaked above the courtyard. Oumaima's husband had been injured in a construction accident and could no longer work. Her young daughter, Shadia, helped her on the weekends, although she went to school during the week until she was about fourteen. She then attended a community school for sewing, where she learned how to operate machinery, training for the jobs in privately owned factories that were becoming widely available throughout the 1980s and 1990s.[10]

Shadia was around the age of the youngest Benjelloun children, and throughout her twenties she operated a sewing machine in various textile factories in Fes. She found the work repetitive but preferred it to the unpredictability of her mother's work, which involved travel to different neighborhoods and cracked and brittle hands from being in contact with soapy water all day. Shadia was hard-working and responsible, so her employers generally left her alone, although she said they were harsh with their employees, not permitting them the breaks that the law required. Each day at five in the morning, a bus came to pick up Shadia and other women from her neighborhood, taking them to the industrial side of Fes, where the factories were located. She ate her lunch at the factory with the other employees, finished late in the day, and came home exhausted. The work paid only eight dirhams per hour (eighty cents), but it provided a consistent income for her family, which included an unemployed brother, father, and mother.[11]

After 2008 many of the factories that prepared clothes for export began to go out of business. In the last place Shadia worked, the factory shut its doors without explanation, leaving its workers unpaid for the last two weeks of their employment. Shadia went with the other employees to demand their severance pay, but when it became apparent that the factory owner had fled to Casablanca and could not be found, she gave up. (The factory later reopened in a different incarnation, making cassettes of Moroccan music for export to migrants in Europe.) Since 2011 she has had only had short-term, sporadic factory work. An injury to her wrist caused by repetitive labor made her disinclined to search for a job in Fes's remaining factories, and she was now helping her mother with her laundry business while taking in sewing projects at home. She never married; although she had been asked a few times, her parents were dependent on her income, and she feared that anyone she married might not allow her to work.

Shadia's experiences reflect the increase throughout the Global South in women's employment in low-skilled jobs such as those in textile manufacturing, food production, and other service industries (Assaad 2004, 13). As in most of the Global South (although not in the rest of the Middle East), Morocco has also experienced the feminization of its labor force, and the growth of female employment is found mainly in blue-collar professions. The Moroccan textile industry is a good example of one that shows the feminization of labor that often accompanies globalization. Coinciding with the beginning of implementation of structural adjustment, from 1983 to 1990, textile exports increased 358 percent (Arndt 2013, 4). In 1977 manufactured exports accounted for 7 percent of Morocco's foreign exchange revenue, a proportion that grew to 33 percent in 2002 (Assaad 2004, 17). Over the ten-year period from 1990 to 1999, women's presence in textile manufacturing grew from 38.7 percent to 62.7 percent (13).[12]

The textile industry meets many of the goals of structural adjustment, particularly increasing foreign investment and encouraging investors because of the availability of cheap unskilled labor. Women are less likely to unionize and demand higher wages, and are preferred in factory work in much of the Global South, including in Morocco. Moroccan factory workers are mostly young, unmarried women, predominantly from urban areas, and with varying levels of education: indeed, some have participated in training programs, and a few even have university degrees (Cretois 2013).

Moroccan textile factories, both formal and informal, serve as suppliers for retailers throughout Europe, including in Great Britain, Spain, and France. Some factories produce clothes that are not for export and may imitate foreign brands, occasionally using clothing models stolen from factories that produce name brand merchandise. Morocco has been an attractive destination for clothing manufacturers because of its proximity to the European market (Arndt 2013, 7). Manufacturers can respond instantly to rapid shifts in demand, a practice perfected by the Spanish clothing store Zara, which produces some of its clothes in Morocco, as well as in Portugal, Spain, and Bangladesh. Zara promotes "fast fashion," a practice that encourages consumers to visit the store frequently for constantly changing merchandise in response to runway trends (Berfield and Baigorri 2013). Both formal factories (registered by the government, often directly connected with a foreign brand) and informal (unregistered) factories exist in Morocco. The formal factories are often subsidiaries of foreign companies, and they tend to treat employees better, adhering to minimum wage requirements while also offering benefits (Arndt 2013, 25). Many of the informal factories, however, do not abide by Morocco's labor regulations, and workers are employed without contracts and in poor working conditions, often facing environmental and occupational hazards. In Fes, informal factories constitute 81 percent of the textile manufacturing sector (28). Unions in the Moroccan textile industry are rare, possibly due to the gendered nature of union organizing in Morocco (23).

In 2011 Shadia was one of at least 10,000 workers in Morocco's textile industry who lost their jobs within three years of the global recession in 2008 (Abdennebi 2011). By 2009 textile factories in Fes were estimated to be operating at approximately 30 percent of their capacity (Saad Allami 2009). An additional factor contributing to the crisis in the Moroccan manufacturing sector was the expiration in 2005 of the Agreement on Textiles and Clothing (ATC), a trade pact limiting the amounts that Asian countries could export (Arndt 2013, 12). This meant that cheaper labor was now available elsewhere, leading many manufacturers to outsource their production to places such as China. In Sale, a city near Rabat, a lingerie factory that had been a supplier for companies like Victoria's Secret and had been open for thirty years abruptly closed in 2011, leaving workers without their final pay (15). During this period, some factories tried to remain open by paying their employees less and working them longer hours, threatening that closure would happen if they could not become more competitive. Shadia had experienced this firsthand, stating that she had seen her wages go down steadily from the time of the crisis until she quit working entirely. She also had her hours increased at times of greater demand, without paid overtime.

"Our manager used to tell us that we would lose our jobs to China if we couldn't work fast enough," she said. "They made it sound like we were lazy and that the Chinese workers were so much better than we were, but we were doing our best. We were exhausted."

While the textile industry has begun to recover from the days of the recession, formal factories have increasingly been replaced by informal factories, which offer jobs that carry considerable risks for workers, are unstable, and offer no benefits. Nonetheless, survival necessitates that Moroccans find work wherever it is available, and in the textile industry, as in other industries whose prevalence has increased due to globalization, women are the preferred job candidates.

Conclusion

In the many years that I have been studying Morocco, I have witnessed almost no social mobility among the many families I have followed. Middle-class families seem to stay middle class, in part because of their reliance on social networks and family resources. But their status is precarious, particularly for those who more recently arrived in the city and lack extensive networks and resources to assist them during times of hardship. Education, while important, helps to maintain class position but does not always lead to employment. Social and familial networks, however, are most crucial at times of economic stress, for supporting new ventures or maintaining survival and dignity. Even middle-class families like the Benjellouns are not immune to economic difficulties. While their father came from a generation for whom education served as a certain guarantee of employment, the Benjelloun siblings grew up in an era when public sector jobs had largely disappeared, and the private sector jobs that replaced them did not require a skilled, educated workforce. Only one of the five children has a public sector job, while two do not work and two are in the informal economy.

Both middle- and underclass Fassis are largely dependent on the informal sector for employment. The underclass in Fes draws on networks for support wherever they can, yet their existence is precarious. The informal economy in Morocco has become dominant across social classes, and while someone like Mourad has the capital and resources to turn his informal venture into a modest entrepreneurial success story, the vast majority of Moroccans are more like Shadia, seeking work where possible, increasingly in the informal sector, where there are fewer protections and even lower wages. Examining the changes in women's employment in Morocco, it seems that most of the increase comes from underclass women who have to work out of necessity.

While the media and official rhetoric criticize the educational system for not preparing Moroccans adequately for jobs, the on-the-ground experience of the Benjellouns and other Fassis I have known indicates that the jobs simply do not exist. Over the past few years, there have been a few promising developments in the private sector, including the opening in 2012 of the largest Renault plant in North Africa, which employs 5,000 people; but aside from a small number of jobs in management, factory labor is not an option most university graduates would want to consider. Much of the investment in Morocco seems to be producing only more low-skilled jobs in service, construction, and manufacturing, fields in which government regulations to protect labor are not always enforced. Watching over the years as Benjelloun cousins graduated from university, I observed that some took service jobs well below their educational level while searching for something better; some moved to other cities to pursue unpaid internships; and yet others began what could amount to years of unemployment. After a few years of unemployment, many of the promising female cousins, although they had done well in school and although their parents had talked for years about the types of work they hoped their daughters would pursue, ended up getting married in their mid-twenties to men already established in their careers who were in their thirties or older. For these women, who at home were still considered girls, marriage offered security and a chance at adulthood. For men like Khaled, unemployment led to a seemingly endless stage of not-quite-full adulthood, where they existed in limbo for years, unable to envision an end to their perennial status as unemployed bachelors.

Highly skilled positions do exist but are in high demand, and educated graduates compete not only with talent but also with family connections for the few available spots in private firms. Migration, which crosses all social classes, provides a safety valve for family members who are able to find work outside the country's borders. But at times of worldwide economic stress, Morocco is also affected: by the inability of its migrants to send remittances home; by the decrease in tourism, resulting in a hit to that industry; and by the loss of jobs in firms making products for international markets. These blows strike all social classes but hurt those without resources the most.

Moroccans seem simultaneously to accept neoliberal discourses that blame people for their inability to find work and to decry how the government has abandoned them. Although Khaled had, for example, applied for numerous jobs in any possible field he might have been qualified for, the fact that he had given up looking for work, while his cousin Hassan had eventually succeeded, was cited by many as an example of his laziness. But when not speaking about specific cases, people tended to flip-flop from one point of view to the other. Those who were employed often put forth arguments that their own persistence and hard work had led them to employment, while the unemployed simply were not trying hard enough. Yet the same people might complain that it was a shame that the government had not done more for its citizens in terms of helping them to find jobs. Globalization has transformed the economic landscape of Morocco, leading to an uncertain future for its citizens across all social classes, except perhaps for those at the very top.

NOTES

1. A widely cited study of microcredit loans in rural Morocco shows no change in net income when comparing loan recipients with groups that did not receive loans. See Banerjee, Karlan, and Zinman 2014; Crépon et al. 2015.

2. There is even a government ministry dedicated to Moroccans living abroad, the Ministère délégué auprès des affaires étrangères et de la cooperation chargé des Marocains résidents à l'étranger. This ministry is charged not only with maintaining ties with migrants but also with facilitating bureaucratic paperwork and investment in the home country.

3. Although beyond the scope of this chapter, much could also be said about the ideas migrants have brought back from elsewhere and disseminated among family members and friends. These can range from, on the one hand, an increased sense of religiosity, learned in mosques in Europe that are often Saudi-funded and highly conservative, to, on the other, a more Westernized attitude toward topics such as consumption, politics, or moral issues.

4. See Poster and Salime 2002. Poster and Salime argue that the very same neoliberal system that offers microcredit loans as a solution to poverty is also one that has created the conditions causing that poverty in the first place.

5. As such, because the European Union has stringent requirements for minimal usage of pesticides, the Moroccan agricultural export market is highly attuned to European demands for organic produce (Codron et al. 2014).

6. The term "informal sector" first appeared in the early 1970s and refers to employment that is often self-directed, uses local resources, operates on a small scale, and draws on skills learned outside formal educational systems (International Labor Office 1972). Nuanced debates about the meanings of this term question whether "informal" versus "formal" creates an inaccurate dichotomy, whether people remain in the informal sector due to choice or coercion, or whether those working in the informal economy seek merely to evade taxation. For a summary of these debates, and a discussion of alternative terms, see Belhorma 2014.

7. For an ethnographic study of the new entrepreneurs of the Moroccan street markets, see Ilahiane and Sherry 2008.

8. A study of ninety women involved in the informal economy in Fes showed that 8 percent had a university degree, while 19 percent had at least reached high school (Belhorma 2014, 10). Of these women, 86 percent were employed in making traditional handicrafts (47 percent) or in the service industry (39 percent). Sixty-four percent worked at home, which the women surveyed said they preferred to do, as it allowed them to maintain family responsibilities such as taking care of children and the household. Sixty-seven percent of those surveyed were not the primary breadwinners in their family, but most still cited economic necessity as their primary reason for working. The majority of the women stated that they spent their income on food, medical costs, and clothes for the family, suggesting that for many

women, the informal economy is a necessary supplement to family income. Many also reported poor working conditions and a lack of access to markets.

9. For a rich ethnography about the lives of market women in the city of Beni Mellal, see Kapchan 1996.

10. For a firsthand ethnographic study of factory work in Fes, see Cairoli 2011.

11. As a seamstress, Shadia made more than the workers who ironed or cut fabric, whose wages were three to five dirhams per hour lower.

12. Over the same period, women's participation in restaurant and hotel work expanded from 7.4 percent to 23 percent (Assaad 2004, 20).

CONSUME

The End of the Mediterranean Diet

1995. Latifa roused her daughter Ilham from sleep just as the sun was brightening over the rooftop of the three-story apartment building in the center of Fes. Rubbing sleep from her eyes, Ilham followed her mother into the small kitchen, where she put a pot of water on the two-burner stove for tea and hot chocolate. Ilham threw a djellaba over her pajamas, stepping into plastic slippers that would take her a few doors down to the *hanoot*, the small dry-goods shop that she and her mother visited multiple times a day. There she handed the grocer a few dirhams and received a baguette and two round loaves of bread. Back in the kitchen, Latifa, Ilham, and her sister Hanane piled a breakfast tray with bread, small dishes of butter and apricot jam, and thermoses filled with tea and hot chocolate. As the sun poured into the room, they woke their other siblings, the boys who slept in the smaller of two salons, where they would all eat breakfast. Latifa's husband, Si Mohammed, exited their master bedroom and joined the children at the breakfast table. Noise from the television, tuned to one of the three Moroccan stations available to them, filled the room, and the Benjelloun children scrambled to eat their breakfast and get ready for school or work.

All except Ilham were out of the house and on their way an hour later. Ilham, who was eighteen and planned to marry the next year, stayed home with her mother. After they washed the breakfast dishes and put them away, Ilham and Latifa picked up woven straw bags and began their ten-minute walk to the Marché Central (Central Market), a honeycomb of market stalls located in the center of the Ville Nouvelle. Each stall was heaped with baskets of red onions, carrots, tomatoes, lettuce, and potatoes, but also fruits and vegetables particular to the season—cantaloupes and watermelons in the summer, oranges in winter, apples from the Middle Atlas Mountains in the fall. The women bantered with their favorite sellers, choosing from among the different stalls the produce that looked the best that day. Then they climbed the steps to the center of the market, where the offerings were more diverse, ranging from pet parakeets and goldfish to spices. Glistening fish trucked in from the coast, fresh on Tuesdays and Saturdays, lay on stone slabs in one central area. They examined the fish and decided they'd wait for a fresher supply before preparing *l'khout b'tamatem*, baked fish with a lemony cilantro sauce and tomatoes. Bypassing the meat stalls where hunks of beef and lamb hung from hooks behind the butchers, they headed for the chicken seller closest to the exit, from whom they bought a young capon.

Bags laden with food, the two women walked home to begin cooking the family lunch. Although Latifa's daughters always helped her around the house, it was not until marriage preparations for Ilham began in earnest that Latifa started the work of transferring her knowledge of Moroccan cuisine to her daughter. Hanane, who was twenty-three and had a job teaching in a primary school, knew how to make the basics but had just finished college and was not ready to marry yet. Now, Ilham was learning how to prepare labor-intensive dishes like *bstilla*, the chicken, almond, and cinnamon–filled pie, her mother's favorite *tagines*, and hand-rolled couscous. She would learn how to use every part of a newly killed sheep during Aid El Kbir, the Feast of the Sacrifice, and how to make dishes like *sharia m'dfouna* (buried noodles), in which noodles are successively steamed over broth and then served with chicken and a powdered cinnamon and sugar mixture. Her mother wrote nothing down, transmitting her knowledge orally and through gestures, Ilham following Latifa's commands and visually memorizing how much paprika or ginger to add to this or that dish, and at what point. After months of instruction, Ilham was able to prepare her mother's dishes as well as Latifa could and would enter her husband's household ready to cook for her new family, reflecting honor on her parents, who had raised her so well.

2013: Fes has spent millions of dirhams on a beautification campaign that is most obvious on the main routes into and out of the city. A toll highway now connects the city with Rabat, and thousands of high-rise apartment buildings have mushroomed, the city now sprawling out into areas that until recently had been farmland. In the city center, the grand Boulevard Hassan II has been completely transformed with fountains, a central garden, and blinking lights that extend the palm tree–lined avenue almost to the ancient medina. Yet Mohammed V Avenue, the other central artery off which one finds the Central Market, is in disrepair, its cobbled sidewalks missing stones here and there,

barely able to support the traffic that pours into it during rush hour. The
Central Market itself is falling apart. Many of the stalls are empty, with wire
netting over naked stall fronts, where only dust-covered wooden tables remain. Some of the same salesmen who were known to Latifa and her family
are still present, though many whisper that the city is attempting to freeze
them out for being unseemly amid all the cosmetic renovations. Fires have
damaged one wing of the market, and in its margins emaciated stray cats wind
their way among fish bones and rotting garbage that sometimes does not get
picked up by the city's new industrial garbage collection company.

Latifa is now widowed, her children grown. The family apartment in
the center of town will soon be torn down and replaced with a luxury high-
rise where single-family apartments will sell for 800,000 dirhams or more (the
equivalent of $80,000). The developers have compensated residents with ap-
proximately $20,000 per family, which Latifa uses to keep an apartment in a
neighborhood on the outskirts of town, close to the highway. Ilham, now the
mother of two children, lives in an affordable suburb about ten minutes' drive
from the city center. Latifa alternates among her children's residences but
spends much of her time with Ilham's family. When they shop, it is at one of
the many new supermarkets located on the outskirts of the city, easily reach-
able by car, though difficult by public transportation and impossible on foot.
The most prominent among these is the European-style Marjane, which has
three locations in Fes. Marjane has everything from televisions to canned tomatoes, multiple varieties of breakfast cereal, and an entire aisle dedicated to
packaged cookies. Of course, what Marjane carries is specific to the Moroccan
market and mirrors what can also be found in the small dry-goods shops still
on every street. There are different types of couscous, Knorr bouillon cubes for
flavoring tagines, housedresses, plastic flip-flops, and buckets for the *hammam* (public steam baths). There are even premade jarred tagine sauces. In the
produce section, customers select fruits and vegetables, fill plastic bags, and
then take them to be weighed by an attendant. There is a bakery and a deli
counter for cheese, lunchmeats, and even pork. There is a beer, wine, and li-
quor room, ostensibly for foreigners, though it is not uncommon to see well-
dressed professional Moroccans filling their carts with wine. The supermarket
is a clean, brightly lit warehouse, and it is a social event to shop there or even
just to walk around, buying nothing. Latifa and Ilham shop there together
on the weekends, Ilham driving the small family Fiat. Ilham's fifteen-year-old
son and ten-year-old daughter come too and are rewarded for their good behavior with packages of cookies. Rather than shopping every day, as they used
to, they have learned to stock up on groceries. The meat is cleaner there, they
say, refrigerated and already cut up rather than hacked apart on a butcher's

table in the Central Market, where temperatures in the summer can be 100 degrees Fahrenheit.

Food is still central to the family experience but with crucial differences from a generation earlier. Ilham and Latifa still prepare a Moroccan lunch together for the family, though daughter Sara eats her lunch at her school, and Ilham's husband, Brahim, a bank employee, works from 7:00 a.m. until 3:00 p.m. and does not come home until later, when he eats his tagine by himself in front of the television before going out to a café with his friends. Ilham worries about him; in his early fifties, he has developed the hereditary diabetes that has plagued other members of his family, yet he never seems to have time to take walks or exercise. Government offices and banks now follow a European schedule, abandoning the old custom where offices were shut down from noon until 2:00 p.m. for lunch. At a typical lunch, we usually find the two women and Ilham's son, Samir, who often refuses the tagine and wants a panini sandwich instead, with cheese and an unnaturally pink lunchmeat substance known as *cacher*, grilled on white bread, accompanied by a bag of potato chips. When Sara comes home after school, she often eats something similar or a package of cookies while she watches television. Ilham shrugs, saying it's just the way kids are these days.

"It's just modern life," she tells me.

FOOD AND ITS CHANGING MEANINGS

I share a glimpse of how a typical everyday routine has changed over a twenty-year period for part of the Benjelloun family to indicate some profound, globalization-related shifts in the way Moroccans shop, cook, and eat.[1] In numerous households, I have witnessed the rise of individualistic eating, where children's tastes are catered to and everyone has something different to eat. In urban settings, some schools and workplaces expect students and employees to remain for lunch, whereas others allow them to return home for the traditional two-hour lunch. Food in Morocco is intimately linked to both Moroccan identity and gender, yet under globalization, the Moroccan diet has become less healthy and is increasingly characterized by consumption of packaged foods.[2] The elaborate but time-consuming traditional cuisine, of slowly simmered meat and vegetable stews, cold salads, and fruit for dessert, now appears more often only on ceremonial occasions, and for many, a fast-food diet has become the order of the day.

The changing Moroccan diet is accompanied by evolving conceptualizations of time, family, and gender as well. As women's self-definition changes from an affiliation with the private to the public sphere, subtle links among food, citizenship, and identity are altered as well. Moroccan cuisine is an integral part of Moroccan culture, yet larger political and economic processes are affecting ways of shopping for, preparing, and eating food. As the public sphere becomes increasingly commodified, as gentrification alters residential patterns, and as regimes of time modeled on globalization-enhanced productivity come to replace traditional Moroccan schedules, where time was carved out for returning home for a family lunch, the ways that Moroccans shop, cook, and eat have changed as well. Cooking and childrearing are still part of women's identities, but there has been a radical generational shift. The citizen-consumer who asserts her identity through the products she buys has increasingly come to replace the woman for whom long hours in the kitchen (and the spectacular, time-consuming meals she produces) were a crucial part of female self-definition.[3]

Many Moroccans are aware that their eating patterns have changed, and they often cite time constraints as the reason. David Harvey's concept of time-space compression is useful in considering the rise of convenience foods and the shift away from a long, family-centered meal in the middle of the day. With time-space compression, as production is accelerated, so too are exchange and consumption (Harvey 1989, 285). The consumption of fast food and convenience food, as well as the production of disposable packaging and silverware, creates a constant supply and demand while also adding nonbiodegradable waste to the environment. This change in habits, according to Harvey, affects social relations as well, as it entails "being able to throw away values, lifestyles, stable relationships, and attachments to things, buildings, places, and received ways of doing and being" (286). For Moroccans, the decline in the face-to-face interactions that characterized the old ways of consuming food—interactions with known vendors in the central market, and with extended family in time-intensive preparations—affects social relations as well. Cuisine preparation becomes more about the status of what one can buy (in terms of the types of food and outsourced labor one can afford) and about taking care of the immediate family rather than spending time communally maintaining extended family relations.

Whether Moroccans looked favorably or unfavorably on the changes to the national diet, most described the reasons for these changes as time-centered: in the words of Mourad Benjelloun, who often does not come home for lunch because he keeps his clothing shop open for business, "There's no time for a long lunch like we had when we were growing up." Latifa also observed that although young mothers and housewives did not spend as much time each day preparing a big family meal as they used to when she was raising her family, "now that everyone comes home at different times, she [the wife] has to be there for them and make sure that everyone gets fed, and the new foods save her the time so that she can do this." For urban Moroccans, when time appears to be speeding up due to transformations in capitalist production, it seems only "natural" to many that the food industry should gracefully accommodate the needs of citizens to eat quickly and return to their daily tasks.

Although the snapshot of Ilham's family describes an urban, middle-class situation, commonalities remain across social classes: work schedules have changed for most of the population, and the traditional Moroccan family lunch is disappearing for a large majority of people, even among the poor, who are not only unable to afford food of acceptable quality but also frequently work in service-related occupations located far from their homes. Even in rural areas, convenience products have come to replace fresh produce, and in roadside hanoots (convenience stores) located over an hour from the nearest city, the available merchandise largely consists of packaged chips, crackers, cookies, and candy bars. Formerly, men and women purchased produce daily from local markets, via face-to-face interactions with small-scale entrepreneurs. Now, corporate-owned supermarkets have created a convenient yet anonymous shopping experience. While women still cook together, convenience has become an operative term in how Moroccans feed their families. Larger societal shifts are altering both the substance and the style by which Moroccan food is considered and consumed as part of daily life.

These changes have affected people throughout the country. A 2004 study of women from southern Moroccan households near the town of Er Rachidia revealed that although most were grateful for advances in medical care and acknowledged that technology had facilitated the traditional ways they had done housework, they felt that the change in diet had been detrimental to their health overall (MacPhee 2004, 376). Saharan housewives linked illness, fatigue, and indigestion to changes in diet and food preparation, as well as to changes in the organization of time. Traditionally, tasks were accomplished according to the rhythms of prayer and the cycles of light and darkness, but when men from the villages began to migrate to Europe for work, they would return not only with new cooking technologies but with new conceptualizations of time, and an insistence on following a Europeanized work schedule.

Concepts of individualism also came to affect residential patterns, as people ceased to live collectively and moved into nuclear households (MacPhee 2004, 381). Just as in Ilham's urban household everyone in the family had different tastes that she provided for, in the Moroccan Sahara, "contemporary housewives in town spend their time and energy preparing multiple versions of breakfast and lunch in catering to the individual schedules and tastes of the members of the household" (385). As people turned away from a traditional diet, members of the older generation complained that "now even the bread is plastic," also adding foods such as "yogurt, Coca-Cola, French fries, and spaghetti" to this category (388). Similarly, among the Benjellouns, everyone agreed that food was not the same anymore, although some were more worried about the change than others. When I was interviewing people about their everyday diets and their relationship to "traditional" Moroccan cuisine, Tariq, a cousin of the Benjellouns who was in his fifties, came over for lunch one day with Ilham and Latifa, and spent a good hour with me detailing all the foods that had disappeared. He spent some time describing a particular dish from the past that involved wheat berries and fermented milk that sat for several days before being consumed. To him, the time involved in the preparation, plus the natural ingredients used, led to better health outcomes.

"Today it's not like that, and this is why people are getting sick," he explained. "Cancer, high blood pressure . . . it's because we're not eating the same foods as we used to. And we used to work harder and walk more."

I want to be careful not to romanticize the past, since some aspects of dietary change were viewed positively (and were not generally connected with negative health outcomes). As with other globalization-related changes, supermarkets and convenience foods are viewed positively by many, and people have mixed feelings about the effects of new ways of consuming foods, not all of them negative. Citing supermarkets' cleanliness and orderly presentation of food, most Moroccans also say that just as those in the West have grown accustomed to shopping at one place for many items, Moroccans like to have the same opportunities as well. The old system of shopping in Fes involved a walk to the Central Market, the new system a trip in an often air-conditioned car. The old system necessitated bargaining via interactions with multiple merchants, whereas in the supermarkets interaction is minimized, and aside from the weighing of produce or the purchase of charcuterie, the mega-supermarket offers one-stop shopping. In the Central Market, one is besieged by beggars, and poverty is everywhere, whereas in the supermarket, security guards remove such unsightliness from view.

Yet the presence of mega-supermarkets such as Morocco's Marjane is accompanied by other, less welcome changes. The Moroccan diet has been transformed from a healthy Mediterranean-based diet of grains, lean protein, and vegetables to one increasingly dependent on processed foods, made readily available in the superstores. Studies are already documenting these changes via an increase in heart disease and diabetes, and rates of obesity are alarmingly high, particularly among women in urban areas (Mokhtar et al. 2001). But what has also been altered is the Moroccan experience of shopping, cooking, and eating, at every step connected with food from its natural state to its transformation into a cultural product, one in which regional and familial distinctions abound.

Though men were once the ones who went to market, market-based shopping has been the domain of women in cities for over thirty years, constituting a gendered experience of movement through men's space and back into the home, generally considered women's territory. Although all Moroccans must eat, food preparation has traditionally been a woman's task. What sensory pleasures are lost as the social repartee attached to purchasing food has disappeared, or as mothers, sisters, and daughters no longer spend hours together involved in food preparation? Is it a welcome trade-off, exchanged for economic independence or greater autonomy in women's personal lives? How has this migration away from lengthy preparations altered not only the sensory experience of cooking, but also specifically gendered forms of identity?

Food and Moroccan Identity

To those who know the country well, different types of Moroccan cuisine are mapped on separate territories and associated with regional forms of identity: for example, the imperial cuisine of the cities, each one a national capital at some point in history. All of the imperial cities—Fes, Rabat, Meknes, and Marrakech—pride themselves on individual variations and the distinctiveness of their locality's preparations. There is also the fare of the countryside: the blackened discs of Berber flatbread baked in communal ovens and served with hearty, meat-based stews.

Moroccan food has also been influenced by its history as a crossroads of cultures. When I ask residents of Fes how their cuisine originated, women and men alike tell me how Arabs expelled from Andalusia in the fifteenth century brought their Iberian tastes and refinement to the great civilization that was first established at the end of the eighth century. As Pierre Bourdieu has written, "Taste, a class culture turned into nature, that is, embodied, helps to shape the class body" (1984, 210). Moroccans are not a homogeneous group, and class differences are often additionally tied up in regional distinctions.

Fassis assert a regional identity in which they are essential to a vision of a nearly continuous nation-state, broken up briefly by French colonialism (1912–1956). Although the capital has been located in Rabat since 1912, and although the economic heart of Morocco is now in Casablanca, Fassis emphasize a vision of history, continuity, and identity that expresses what it means to be from Fes. Cuisine is a crucial part of this identity. Indeed, food is central to a wider Moroccan identity and citizenship. Islam, the country's long history as a stable monarchy, and its cosmopolitanism as a crossroads between Europe,

Africa, and the Middle East are offered as general attributes, but food and
family life are also frequently mentioned. Family, hospitality, and cuisine are
traits Moroccans will bring up when asked what makes Moroccan culture
distinctive. Cuisine in particular is singled out, and the international attention that Moroccan food receives is often cited as proof of the strength of the
country's history and traditions.

"Have you ever seen an Algerian restaurant in New York?" Rachid asks
me one day as we sit back on the banquettes after a delicious lunch prepared by
Latifa and Ilham. "What about a Tunisian restaurant in Miami? No, it's always
a Moroccan restaurant." Moroccans boast that their food not only tastes better
than the cuisine of neighboring countries but also, in the words of one woman
I asked, demonstrates that "Morocco has been a country for over a thousand
years." While Sami Zubaida and Richard Tapper note the tendency among
some food writers "to be drawn to explanations in terms of origin and to
assumptions of cultural continuity in the history of a people or a region" (1994, 7),
Moroccans themselves make these assertions about the continuity of cuisine
and culture I cite here.

Moroccans are proud of their heritage. Untouched by Ottoman occupation, they consider their culture to have a long, relatively uncolonized history,
although the forty-four years of French occupation left a legacy of bread- and
pastry-making that has enhanced the traditional repertoire. Moroccans show-
case "imperial" cuisine, a reference to the imperial capitals of the country
where Arabs expelled from Andalusia from the fourteenth through the six-
teenth century settled and developed distinctive regional cuisines. Their food
also has Berber, African, and Spanish influences. In Berber regions of Morocco, for example, such as in Marrakech, the city's Berber origins are highlighted as evidence of the deliciousness of the food. Fes, the imperial capital
until 1912, is another city renowned for its cuisine, though here Arab influences are emphasized.[4]

A Moroccan meal served to guests in an urban home, such as in the city
of Fes, can be very elaborate. Guests sit at tables covered with white cloths and
napkins embroidered with burgundy or deep-blue thread. A delicate, sweet
scent of roses fills the air as the host first pours rosewater over the guests'
hands from a ceremonial silver teakettle. Rosewater, distilled from flowers
that come from the Valley of Roses in southern Morocco, is also used to flavor
desserts and occasionally meat dishes, and roses are said to have been culti-
vated since the tenth century, when Moroccan travelers brought them back
from pilgrimages to Mecca. The first course consists of cold cooked salads of
carrots and eggplants or tomatoes and peppers, often followed by bstilla, the
chicken, cinnamon, and ground almond pie that is both sweet and savory and

was originally made with pigeon. The first entrée is often a chicken tagine, such as chicken with olives and lemons. Traditionally, Moroccans eat with their hands and use bread (rather than couscous, which is usually eaten only on Fridays) as a spoon to scoop up the food and absorb the rich sauces. A second course might be a meat dish, such as *lham b'il barquq*, lamb with prunes. Dessert is usually fresh fruit in season, with perhaps a glass of mint tea to round out the meal. By contrast, an everyday family meal would be much less elaborate. It might consist of one salad and one tagine, followed by fruit, but even the single salad and tagine can demand a morning's worth of preparation and slow simmering on the stove.

The type of meal described above would be beyond the means of a poor family, yet the ethics of hospitality in Morocco dictate that even in modest households guests should receive the best the host can afford. Even in isolated villages, I have experienced incredible meals: breakfasts of eggs freshly laid by hens that morning, blackened flatbread dipped in home-pressed olive oil, and glasses of strong, sweet tea. Nevertheless, the earlier description of the meal served in an urban home is reflective of a middle- or upper-class aesthetic. As Jack Goody (1982) has noted, cuisine represents a specific assertion of social class and identity. For Fes, such a meal is indicative of the city's position in Morocco's rich history. On the many occasions I have been present at these formal dinners, I have been told that "our ancestors have been preparing food this way for centuries," and with a foreigner present, the meals themselves seem to conjure up mythical narratives of Fes's centrality to Moroccan history, emphasizing the Arab, Muslim, and urban content and eliding Berber and rural influences. As Arjun Appadurai has commented on the tendency in many nations to emphasize refined, urban cuisine, such "high cuisines, with their emphasis on spectacle, disguise, and display, always seek to distance themselves from their local sources" (1988, 4).

The anonymous labor of women has historically been at the heart of these repasts, and women have historically transmitted culinary knowledge to the next generation. Much of this knowledge is not, however, being passed on within families today. In the past, ceremonial occasions such as a baby's naming-day ceremony or a boy's circumcision required the labor of multiple women to serve a large family and their guests. However, among the middle and upper classes in urban areas, this labor is increasingly becoming the domain of caterers. Additionally, there has been a generational shift in this traditional pattern,[5] with younger generations of women no longer acquiring the know-how to re-create many ceremonial dishes. Mourad's wife, Yasmine, who is ten years younger than him and does not work outside the home, told me once that she only knew how to cook basic tagines and couscous. I asked her if she wished she knew how to make more of the ceremonial dishes people tended to have on holidays and special occasions.

"No, I have no interest in learning how to make those," Yasmine replied. "I have my hands full with my children, who come home and need help with their schoolwork. You need a lot of people to make dishes like that. Who would help me out?" Her mother was not in good health, and she had two brothers but no sisters. "There's no time to make things like that anymore. Those times are gone."

Changing culinary habits are therefore not limited to ceremonial dishes. Many Moroccan women who do not work outside the home (and who in the past would have considered the preparation of tagines and couscous to be part of their regular domestic repertoire) state that they are preparing Moroccan meals less for their families, in part because their children prefer more "modern" or Western foods, but also because in urban areas the work schedule for many families no longer accommodates a long midday meal.

The apprenticeship of daughters to mothers in the kitchen constitutes a type of hereditary knowledge, an invisible labor through which culture is transmitted from one generation to another.[6] Girls and young women also learn rules surrounding the preparation and consumption of particular foods according to culturally held Galenic notions of "hot" or "cold" foods and their various effects on health (Greenwood 1981). In the past, middle- and upper-class women were defined by their contribution to the domestic sphere, their worth measured in motherhood and their finesse with food preparation. While marriage and childbearing are still important goals for most women, women's entry into the public sphere over the past sixty years has affected how the labor of the home is experienced in important ways.

Today, 30 percent of women over age fifteen participate in the labor force, but many also work in the informal economy, which is not measured by official statistics (Roudi-Fahimi and Moghadam 2011). At the university level, male and female students can be found in equal numbers. As mentioned in previous chapters, the average number of children Moroccan women will have in their lifetime has decreased from 6.6 births in 1980 to 2.5 in 2004 (Ayad and Roudi 2011). Overall, literacy remains a problem for women, who have a 60 percent illiteracy rate, yet much of the illiteracy is found in the countryside, where schools are often located far from remote rural areas. Among the middle- and upper-class Moroccans whose lives I am describing here, it is expected that girls will attend school, and possibly university, after which they will work prior to marriage.[7] In urban areas, women play an active role in the public sphere, and their presence in education, work, and commerce has been actively encouraged by the government since the 1940s (Mernissi 1987, 55).[8]

In addition to the entry of women into the public sphere, capitalism and globalization have also rapidly altered living arrangements, as well as the experience of shopping and food preparation. Sixty years ago, the nuclear household would have been unheard of, and on their marriage women could expect to live as part of an extended family in a large house. Today, living with extended family is much less common. The mother-daughter relationship remains a strong and important bond, with women and their mothers continuing to spend extensive periods of time together, particularly when the daughters do not work outside the home. Yet with the decline of extended family households, the labor pool for the preparation of traditional foods is considerably smaller than it once was. Thus, urban middle-class women are now unlikely to have prepared the food for ritual occasions. As other scholars have noted, caterers are increasingly preferred not only for ceremonial occasions but also for large family dinners (Salih 2002). A measure of prestige is associated with hosting catered events, prestige that is often attached to the husband's wealth and the outsourcing of this formerly domestic labor. At one such dinner, held to celebrate the arrival of an uncle from France who had not been home in a year, the hostess told me that they had hired a caterer "because we wanted to do something truly special for our guests."

Even women who are not employed in the public sphere will use caterers. There were multiple explanations for why this was the case. As one Moroccan told me on the occasion of yet another catered dinner that did not mark a traditional ritual, by hiring a caterer the husband was showing that he cared for his wife, "making things easier for her so she doesn't have to cook for all these people." At ceremonial occasions, the wife demonstrates her household management skills by directing the caterers in how and when to serve guests, while she is also able to enjoy socializing to a greater degree than would have been possible had she been in the kitchen the entire time. Women typically don their best djellabas and caftans for these events, and the hostess is no exception. The time not spent working in the kitchen, Hanane explained, can be used instead for the hostess to make herself beautiful, so she can attend her own event without being drenched in sweat or exhausted from the labor of cooking. While older women reminisced fondly about how many guests they had single-handedly served at events in the distant past, younger women were more likely to talk about the importance of socializing. Another woman said that with a caterer, wives could have extra time for "childrearing [tarbiya], rather than spending all their time on the food." But not all were positive about this trend. Another explanation highlighted the disappearance of the sociability previously associated with cooking together as an extended family. Yet among those I interviewed, nostalgia for the past was mainly expressed by older women who took pride in their cooking skills, and by men who romanticized the cooking of female family members.

"In the old days," Khaled Benjelloun told me, "if you had to feed a lot of people, all the women in the family would come together, you might hire a maid for a few days, and neighbors would come to help out, free of charge. But now everyone wants to be paid, or there's no family around to help, so that's why we have to hire caterers." This is unquestionably a recent shift, since as recently as the 1980s or 1990s women in an extended middle-class family would have prepared food at such events. Even in wealthy households of the past where it was common for servants to cook, women of the family still supervised the food production in the household's kitchen. With caterers, food is cooked elsewhere, delivered, and served primarily by men (and a few women) dressed as servers. Although the food can still be delicious, several people commented to me that it is lacking in something. The most common criticism of the caterers was that, while they excelled in presentation, some nebulous aspect of taste was lost in the process. Many Moroccans expressed nostalgia for food prepared by family members, in which a signature familial touch could be detected—for example, in Aunt Khadija's salad of roasted eggplants and tomatoes, or in Latifa's famous almond cookies.

Khaled told me that "with caterers, it's all about the presentation. If someone had an ice cream sculpture at a party, you have to outdo them with something more spectacular. It's about the way it looks on the plate, but the food isn't very good anymore. It doesn't taste the way it did when your aunts and grandmothers were making it." Aesthetics and prestige, as well as the ability to afford leisure time while others prepare the food, are increasingly central to decisions about how ritual labor is determined.

One ritual period during the year where women are more likely to come together for traditional food preparation is the fasting month of Ramadan, as other writers have noted (Buitelaar 1993, 28). Most women still possess the knowledge of how to prepare the traditional foods consumed during this month, such as *harira*, a hearty, tomato-based soup with meat and chickpeas, and the many varieties of honeyed pancakes, such as *bghrir* and *rghief* or *malawi*. As with most holidays around the world, Ramadan is a time for family, so mothers and daughters often cook together to prepare dishes that are eaten only at this time of year. Yet outside of Ramadan, the norms for everyday food preparation and eating have changed.

THE DISAPPEARING MEDITERRANEAN DIET

The Moroccan diet has changed dramatically, not only in terms of ceremonial foods but also in what people eat every day. Altered patterns of food consumption have led to health changes as well. Researchers have documented a "shift from traditional diets high in grains, fruits and vegetables and low in fat to diets high in sugar, refined grains and fat" (Batnitzky 2007, 446). The consumption of animal products and sugars has also increased. And whereas meat was once a luxury available only to the upper classes, there has been an increase in the amount of animal products consumed across all social classes. More than half (51.3 percent) of all women in Morocco are categorized as overweight or obese, a rate that has tripled in the past twenty years, and 65–67 percent of women's diets are composed of carbohydrates (Mokhtar et al. 2001).[9] Ironically, at the same time there has been a cultural shift from a preference for heavier women toward an appreciation of slenderness, particularly among the middle and upper classes. As in the United States, at a moment when people are statistically heavier than ever, the younger stars of Moroccan media, from cooking shows to musical competitions, are mostly slender.

This process of moving toward a Western diet, known as the "nutrition transition," affects Global South countries that have recently reduced their mortality and fertility rates, seen declines in the number of those suffering from infectious diseases and malnutrition, and increased their life expectancies. These transitions are accompanied by a shift to a diet high in fats, sugars, and processed grains, and a more sedentary way of life, causing a rise in chronic "lifestyle" diseases such as diabetes and heart disease. Morocco has experienced an increase in average daily calorie intake from 2,410 in 1968 to 3,031 in 1997, and a rise in per capita daily consumption of fats from 42 to 59 grams (Benjelloun 2002, 136).[10] In Morocco, obesity coexists with malnutrition, particularly in the countryside. Among the poorest of the population, people are more likely to be underweight, while obesity and being overweight correlate with economic wealth (139). Hypertension, diabetes, and high cholesterol are also on the rise, with higher rates in urban areas (139). Ilham's family is a reflection of this, as her husband, who is moderately overweight, has developed Type 2 diabetes, which he controls with medication rather than a change in lifestyle. Although boys and young men in Morocco avidly participate in sports at school, play street soccer, and lift weights at gyms, exercise is less common for girls and young women and almost unheard of among adults of both sexes. Similarly, Latifa and her son Mourad both have hypertension, and a heart attack killed Si Mohammed Benjelloun when he was in his sixties.

In addition to the nutrition transition that Morocco has experienced, the rising obesity statistics relate to other factors as well, including the availability of packaged convenience foods, increased rural to urban migration, and greater numbers of women in the workforce. Changing residential patterns, such as those detailed in the next chapter, have contributed to the recent success of supermarkets. Rising real estate costs in the center of the new city (Ville Nouvelle) of Fes, for example, have meant that many middle-class residents have been displaced to the city's suburbs. While this social class was previously the main clientele for the Central Market, the wealthy residents who have bought up real estate in the city center prefer to shop in the supermarkets.

The first decade of the new millennium witnessed a construction boom in Fes, with new, high-end developments springing up everywhere, and accompanying beautification programs that have altered the façade of the Ville Nouvelle. At the other extreme of the socioeconomic spectrum, local governments in many cities have also tackled the unsightliness of shantytowns by bulldozing them and forcing residents to take out loans to move into housing projects, the construction of which has been contracted out to developers willing to build them at the lowest cost (Bogaert 2011). In either case, these practices have not only displaced residents but also destroyed neighborhood social networks, increasing social fragmentation as well as the distance residents are now required to travel between work and home. National policies of adopting a work schedule more like Europe's have also meant that the traditional midday meal taken at home is now a relic of the past. New labor and urban dwelling practices have thus led to different diets, predisposing Moroccan citizens to choose foods made easily available in order to accommodate regimes of productivity.[11]

In 2013, along with students from my university, I interviewed a group of about fifteen students in Fes, all of whom attended a private business university. Fairly affluent, and between nineteen and twenty-two years of age, all but one of them said they did not know how to cook. The only one who could cook was a young woman who wore a headscarf and dressed in a modest Islamic style, while the others all wore casual Western clothes. She described her background as being "traditional," while the other students said they associated tradition with their grandmothers' generation. When asked what kind of food they liked, most cited fast food, and one said he ate lunch at McDonald's every day. Only one student, Fatiha, said she preferred her grandmother's cooking.

"My mother," Fatiha said, "doesn't know how to cook. We have a maid and she cooks for us. But my grandmother makes us the traditional Moroccan foods, and I love them. Maybe when I have more time, I will get her to teach me how to prepare them."

The theme of not having enough time appeared multiple times in our interviews. The university café served a limited menu of paninis, fries, tuna sandwiches, and ice cream, and many said they also went to cafés outside the school for lunch, eating pretty much the same thing there: panini sandwiches of processed meat and cheese, French fries, or pizza.

"We don't have a lot of time between classes," one male student said. "Most of us don't go home for lunch. So we have to get lunch quickly between classes."

The Moroccan students, additionally, were fairly unconcerned about their diets. In that way, they were not dissimilar to some of the American students in our group.

"I'm young, and I lose weight quickly," one young woman said.

"There'll be plenty of time to worry about what I'm eating once I get older," a male student told us.

This trend was noticeable among other age groups as well. A friend who sent her two children to a private primary school (which, it should be stressed, is much more common and less expensive in Morocco than in the United States) told me that there were children in her kids' school who had their family driver drop off meals from McDonald's to them. And although McDonald's was too expensive for less affluent Moroccans to eat there on a regular basis, it was reported to me among public school students that the wide availability of sandwich shops and street food meant that many other children who did not go home for lunch could also eat fast, deep-fried food.

THE RISE OF THE CITIZEN-CONSUMER

The ideal Moroccan citizen has become a "citizen-consumer." The citizen-consumer participates in a form of nation-state identity through which individuals affirm their membership in the nation by their ability to purchase products. Morocco has historically undertaken economic reforms without a foundation for political accountability and transparency, thereby "depoliticizing the public sphere," in the words of Abdeslam Maghraoui (2002, 24). Demands for accountability, democratic participation, and a "debate on the sources and distribution of power in the Moroccan political system" are marginalized by the monarchy in favor of "technical" economic reforms (24). One result of this depoliticization among Fassis is an apathy toward politics, replaced by an interest in belonging and national identity that can be asserted through the purchasing of particular products. A productive Moroccan citizen-consumer has an income, is able to drive to supermarkets, and purchases labor-saving packaged foods as well as desirable imported goods, such as packaged cookies or cereals.

The types of products advertised and purchased in Morocco are often culturally specific and are emphasized in media depictions showing an idealized Moroccan family consuming a meal that is a blend of both traditional and modern influences. Moroccans assert their identity through selections of particular products. As Kaela Jubas has noted, consumption has become "increasingly a stand-in for citizenship under contemporary neoliberal, consumerist ideologies" (2007, 231). Despite the supposed time-saving convenience of supermarkets, the ritual of shopping often takes longer because supermarkets are likely to be further away from home, and Moroccans tend to spend a long time looking at products. More energy, time, and enthusiasm now seem to be invested in the ritual of going to the supermarket than in subsequent food preparation.

Marshall's now-classic definition of citizenship limits the concept to those who are considered full members of a community and possess equal rights and status (Marshall 2009 [1950], 149). Much like the concept of a neutral public sphere that in reality often excludes persons on the basis of race, class, or gender, access to full citizenship also varies. Jubas has noted that citizenship has often been constituted according to production and consumption, with production belonging to the realm of the public (male) sphere and consumption to the private (female) realm (2007, 236). With globalization, both men and women are constituted as consumers, in part because production has been outsourced. As part of free trade agreements, as countries increase their imports, national economies no longer emphasize the production and consumption of domestic products alone, and encourage their citizens to purchase things produced elsewhere. Consumption is considered important in supporting a country's economy, even when products are not produced locally.

The consciousness of Moroccan citizens has shifted from a self-definition that previously emphasized other elements of sociality to one emphasizing the self as a citizen-consumer. Following Maghraoui, economic liberalization and consumer choice have become substitutes for true democratic participation that would constitute a classic vision of democratic citizenship. Citizen-consumers are subtly encouraged through media to buy particular products that are linked closely with Moroccan identity but which, in the end, become stand-ins for labor-intensive traditional cuisine. "Traditional" values that constitute Moroccanness have not simply disappeared, as hospitality and food are still central to Moroccan identity. However, these values are increasingly accompanied by media suggestions that certain products are essential to maintaining a strong family or creating a hospitable environment for one's guests. This is reinforced by advertisements that show Moroccan products consumed in traditional family settings, updated slightly to demonstrate a vision of the nation-state's ideal modern family, one in which the wife and mother wears "modern" Western clothes but is central in providing nutrition for her family.

The government-sponsored vision for Moroccan femininity was articulated on a national government website, The Moroccan Woman, that appeared from 1999 to 2003, in French, Arabic, and English versions. This website expressed the idea that the Moroccan woman should be "the guardian of Moroccan cultural values at home and the proponent of modernity outside her house" (Newcomb 2009, 25). Suggesting that the Moroccan woman could participate in society in a range of public positions, including "bus drivers, physicians, judges, notaries, engineers," the website also framed her as the "true keeper of traditions. . . . She keeps the upper hand over her home [as housekeeper] but she also performs other tasks outside home."

Many commercials for food products typically consumed by most Moroccans—processed cheese, yogurt, or tea, for example—show an idealized modern Moroccan family. The family's modernity is defined by the wearing of Western clothes, with perhaps one family member wearing something Moroccan, by the woman not wearing a headscarf, and by the presence of men at the table. This is the idealized blend of tradition and modernity to which women are expected to adhere. Many years ago, men and women would have eaten separately, and although for most families this had changed by the 1980s, today the eating pattern in middle-class urban households is rarely gendered. Eating separately today is less likely to be a factor of gender and more often reflects the constraints of work and school schedules.

Supermarkets are also an integral part of the rise of the citizen-consumer in Fes. Despite being a large urban area, the traditional city of Fes was initially slow to adopt chain supermarkets or corporations that might alter its traditional identity. The French/Moroccan chain Marjane first opened in the capital city, Rabat, in 1989; its first location in Fes did not open until more than fifteen years later. When I lived in Fes from 2000 to 2002, there was only one large supermarket, Makro, a membership-based warehouse that sold large appliances and food in bulk. It was not considered a pleasure to shop there, and the Moroccans I knew described it as dingy and badly organized. There was also Supermarket Squalli, a small, family-owned specialty market in the center of town where one could buy imported goods such as Dutch oats and peanut butter, which were not easy to find elsewhere. Before the rise of the large supermarkets, it was popular with upper-middle-class Moroccans and foreigners, but the middle-class Moroccans I knew rarely went there. During that time period, my middle-class Moroccan interlocutors did their shopping at the Central Market, at local butcher shops, or in smaller markets that were set up in parking lots or on the street in different parts of town. There were no foreign fast-food outlets.

By 2010 Supermarket Squalli had gone out of business, and there were three branches of Marjane as well as several other supermarket chains open in Fes, spread throughout different middle- and upper-class neighborhoods. There was a two-story McDonald's, always packed with customers, built to look like a traditional Fes medina house. Upper-class families ate there regularly, while for middle-class families it was an occasional treat, particularly to reward children for good behavior or a positive school performance. While I recall that in visits to Makro in 2000, the store was never very full, Marjane on a weekend was almost always packed, the density of customers frequently resembling what in the United States I would associate with a crowded supermarket the day before Thanksgiving.

Over the past several years, I have accompanied Moroccans I know into the Marjane supermarket to ask them what they're buying and why, and, with the help of research assistants, also conducted an informal observational study of what Moroccans were shopping for. On weekdays, the Marjane could be very empty, but, as mentioned above, on the weekends, shopping at Marjane became a social experience, with many families simply wandering around admiring goods and comparing prices but not buying anything. The Benjelloun family, however, had learned to stock up: on packets of cookies for their kids, sweetened yogurt drinks, jelly, tea, olives, tomatoes, couscous— all items that were also available in the local corner store. They bought meat shrink-wrapped in packets, and vegetables, though Latifa said she still preferred to go to an informal street market "where the vegetables are fresher," even though it was a twenty-minute walk from her house. Ilham, however, did not shop at street markets. She bought soft drinks and bags of chips, pasta, muffins, and croissants, and, for her son, panini sandwiches and frozen French fries, although sometimes she would still make homemade fries for him as a treat. She still purchased fruit for dessert, although usually Ilham and Latifa were the only ones who ate it. In other carts, I would see more of the same, with packaged goods far outnumbering fresh fruits and produce.

"I just like to buy everything all at once," Ilham's sister, Hanane, told me. "It's so much easier to come here than get a little here, a little somewhere else. They have all the products that I like, and some things I've discovered that I never would have known about." She then showed me a breakfast cereal, imported from France, that she told me was "good for digestion and helps you lose weight." It had little protein, some fiber, and a lot of sugar, much like American breakfast cereals. I asked both Hanane and Ilham if the types of foods they bought at Marjane differed significantly from what they would have purchased in the old neighborhood.

"At Marjane, you can buy food that doesn't spoil," Hanane explained. "You can get things to have on hand in case anyone is hungry. We could always go to the hanoot near our house before, if we needed something last minute, so we bought some of the same things, like butter or flour, but now we can buy a lot and keep it on hand so we don't need to go to the hanoot except for things we've forgotten." The hanoots, which sell single items of products, such as single-serving yogurts, small containers of milk, and baguettes, and which are also well stocked with packaged goods, are still a feature of all Moroccan neighborhoods, and seem not to have disappeared yet, despite the presence of the supermarket.

"We don't buy as many vegetables as we used to," Ilham said. "When I was growing up and we all came home for lunch, you needed more vegetables: more onions, and whatever you were putting in the tagine that day. Now that my kids don't often eat tagine, I don't make it as often, so I don't need to have the vegetables around because they would just rot." I asked her if she missed the sociality of the old days, with the entire family coming home from school and work to eat together at lunch. She shrugged and sighed.

"Of course I do, but I also miss my father who used to support us, God rest his soul, and he is gone and the world is a different place. There's no time anymore. And we have to focus on our children now. Their success in school is everything. If they don't do well, they won't be able to get a job, so we have to focus on them." Again, Ilham made an important comment on time and on the increased labor she needed to invest in her children. The convenience of the supermarkets, she implied, allowed her to spend time focusing on these other tasks that were now crucial to securing a future for the next generation.

Globalization has irrevocably altered the retail landscape in emerging economies such as Morocco's. Free trade agreements with the United States and Europe have resulted in a wave of international retailers entering the Moroccan market over the past fifteen years. During the same period, satellite media have also become ubiquitous, influencing Moroccans through advertising and brand consciousness to adopt more consumer-centered habits. Supermarkets, first introduced in Morocco in the 1980s, did not initially take off (Amine and Lazzaoui 2010, 564). A 2010 study by two Moroccan scholars found that while upper-class Moroccans shopped exclusively in supermarkets, and middle-class Moroccans did most of their shopping there, lower-class Moroccans visited the supermarket out of curiosity, bought little, and expressed their primary purpose there as social (2010, 569). Upper-class Moroccans, by contrast, not only bought most of their food there but also purchased products of social distinction that were not Moroccan in origin (fine cheeses or salmon), and considered choosing to shop at the supermarket as asserting something about their social class. Interestingly, interviews with upper-class Moroccans revealed that they did not like the presence of lower-class Moroccans who, they said, were turning the supermarket into a suq (the traditional weekly, chaotic country market) (Amine and Lazzaoui 2010, 570).

Yet despite the transformation of many Moroccans into citizen-consumers, globalization has not resulted in a total Western-style homogenization of the Moroccan market. There are large Moroccan-owned supermarket chains that adapt themselves to local values, such as not selling alcohol, or encouraging customers to feel comfortable shopping in casual neighborhood dress (Amine and Lazzaoui 2010, 572). For many Moroccans, the supermarket is also a social space, where many come just to browse and to see and be seen by others. By failing to purchase anything, they turn a space of commerce into a public space, one whose primary purpose of commercial interaction is not fulfilled. Some customers try to import tactics generally used in neighborhood hanoots, breaking up packages and attempting to buy them as single items (572). For the lower classes, even the event of going to a supermarket like Marjane, regardless of the amount of goods actually purchased, is significant. As Amine and Lazzaoui write, "The fact of having crossed the psychological and socio-logical barriers to access such places of consumption and make some small purchases is an act highly charged with meaning" (571). While the upper class distinguish themselves by their ability to fill their carts with luxury goods, the lower class are often simply glad to be present. Shopping "is a way to fill a sense of exclusion long perceived and experienced by this segment of the popula-tion, for long unable to access the consumption. This behavior comes also from a desire to achieve an ideal image of oneself, reflected by going to the same places as the upper social classes" (571).

While markets such as the Marché Central are in decline, some lower- and middle-class Moroccans still favor the traditional shopping experience for a number of reasons. Supermarkets are frequently accessible only by car, and many Moroccans prefer to patronize the local grocer because of the personalized interactions they have with him. Local grocers frequently offer credit and have a more intimate knowledge of their stock and when they will receive shipments of goods that clients expect and are looking for. A visit to a central market or suq in any Moroccan town or city involves a completely dif-ferent sort of sensory engagement from a supermarket. In the suq, different odors range from the pleasant to the not so nice, from the honeyed scent of the flower market to the acrid stench of freshly slaughtered chickens. In Fes, the market closes in the afternoon but is usually open in the morning to accommodate the traditional midday meal. Commerce quiets down around the time of the midday call to prayer, then picks up again briefly as shoppers grab a last-minute ingredient on their way home from the mosque. Shopkeepers meet the eye of every passerby, calling them by name or by honorifics, such as *Hajja*, a term of respect for older women, technically those who have been on a pilgrimage to Mecca. Banter, conviviality, and the exchange of smiles and inquiries after one's family members can win a savvy shopkeeper more customers. The produce, crated in directly from the countryside, is sometimes still coated with dirt, and the shopper examines carrots of varying sizes, some knobby and ugly, others straight and uniform. The shopper tosses handfuls of fat orange carrots into the shopkeeper's scales, ordering a kilo of onions, a bunch of parsley, a few lemons, a head of lettuce for a salad, and two kilos of tomatoes. For the fresh fruit that always rounds out a traditional meal, she might buy a kilo of apples, oranges, and bananas.

What is most notable in these shopping trips is the absence of prepared foods. On a visit to the market in May 2011, I counted only one shop among the thirty or forty stalls in the market that sold anything that could be defined as prepared. This one-of-a-kind shop, which used to cater to Europeans and elite Moroccans before the big supermarkets arrived, sells products such as ketchup, imported cheeses, cereals, and jams. The eclectic offerings of the Central Market further include a shop that sells pet fish, one that features houseplants and cacti, and another two that sell baskets. There is also a spice seller, a very old man in a dimly lit corner whose storefront displays jars filled with twigs and other mysterious substances. His offerings are limited, but his knowledge of medicinal herbs is voluminous. Of the remaining stalls, there are a few butchers and spice sellers, but the majority sell fresh vegetables and fruit, essential ingredients in Moroccan cuisine.

Conclusion

Women were always central to the maintenance of a Moroccan identity through cuisine, though in a notable shift, the former equation of "you are what you eat" is shifting to become "you are what you buy." Yet these shopping trips are less a part of everyday life than they were even a decade ago, and families like the Benjellouns are depending on the ritual of daily shopping and cooking much less than they used to. Moroccan culinary citizenship has become less about the ritual of local market banter, communal food preparation, and food sharing, and more about the consumption of prepared foods and the feeling of being pressed for time. The close association of brands with food is now ubiquitous in Moroccan culture, and in the generation of children growing up now, a diet of packaged foods (cookies, soft drinks, processed meat sandwiches, breakfast cereal, and drinkable yogurts) has become an assertion of household modernity. One woman who worked as a housekeeper in the apartment of a friend told me that she preferred to feed her young children sandwiches every day for their main meal instead of Moroccan tagines because they were cheap, affordable, and took little time to prepare.

Restaurant culture has also become a part of life in Fes, even though its reputation as a conservative city means that there are far fewer restaurants or types of restaurants than one might find in Casablanca or Marrakech. On the weekends, people often go to McDonald's, or to "family" restaurants where kebabs, salads, and pizzas are common menu items. Buying sandwiches from street vendors or cafés to consume later at home is also common. In a study of residents of Oujda, Said Mentak found that the advent of restaurant culture was mourned as "a loss of the traditional family gathering around a 'healthy' meal. It is 'healthy' because people believe that restaurants are not controlled and clean enough" (2013, 145). People also equated restaurant culture with homemakers neglecting their houses or respect for the family. Restaurants like McDonald's were viewed positively by some, who thought they changed people's mentalities and "made them more open to new food cultures" (144). The negative health outcomes associated with the McDonald's diet, however, were not mentioned.

Traditional cuisine is increasingly associated with ceremonial occasions or holidays, and is also likely to be prepared by caterers or nonfamily members. As such, an essential way of knowing and experiencing the world is changing. The close linkage of cuisine with Moroccan identity has correspondingly been altered to one in which Moroccan identity is increasingly expressed through the choice of where to shop, the ability to buy, and the types of food products purchased. Both women and men are constituted as citizen-consumers by the nation-state, but the national media represents Moroccan female modernity through particular products and the types of food a mother buys for her children. Moroccan media images give the impression that children eat only processed cheese, yogurt, and jam on toast, and aside from the yogurt, the reality is not much better.

For women, it is not only the shopping experience that has been transformed but the time spent in food preparation as well. Although the shopping experience at the supermarket can take hours, much longer than a quick trip to the Central Market, the result is that the shopper now comes home with premade goods rather than produce and meat that require transformation. Whereas in the past, Moroccan identity was linked to cuisine, with women playing an integral role in the preparation and serving of this cuisine, much of this labor is now outsourced. Moroccan women are still expected to perform much of the labor in the house, even if they work in the public sphere; yet the means and type of cuisine prepared are changing to accommodate a different work regime in which not all members of the family return home for lunch and not all eat the same things. As such, women are increasingly encouraged to be citizen-consumers, purchasing convenience foods that reflect the new, fast-paced lifestyle of the modern family, one in which convenience, productivity, individuality, and new regimes of timekeeping have displaced cuisine as central to citizenship. The changing meanings attached to shopping and food preparation are further signs that globalization and global capitalism have penetrated the corners of Moroccan social life, not always for the better.

Notes

1. For more on the topic of food and globalization, see Inglis and Gimlin 2009; Nützenadel and Trentmann 2008; Kiple 2007; and Phillips 2006.

2. For a comprehensive survey of the anthropological literature on food and the senses, see Sutton 2010. On food and memory in anthropology, see Holtzman 2006. Regarding food and national culture, see Belasco and Scranton 2002 as well as Howell 2003.

3. Parts of this chapter previously appeared in Newcomb 2013 and are reprinted here with permission of the publisher.

4. Further sources that consider the culture of food in the Middle East and North Africa more broadly include Zubaida and Tapper 1994 and Heine 2004.

5. "Traditional" is not the most appropriate word, since it implies that culture once existed in a timeless, static state. One hundred years ago there would no doubt have been significant changes: it would have been men encountering one another in the market to buy food, which they then would have taken home to the women for preparation. Casting our observations back several centuries, certain key ingredients in Moroccan cuisine, such as tomatoes and potatoes, came from the New World and would not have been known in Morocco in the past (or in Italy, for that matter, where tomatoes are now considered essential to "traditional" cuisine).

6. Holtzman (2006, 10) notes the danger in overly romanticizing women's special connection with food, which often falls back on Western stereotypes emphasizing women's special connection with the domestic realm.

7. As a result of these changes, women's presence in the public sphere is now accepted, although an implicit divide between domestic and public is still present such that the public space of the street and the private space of home are still considered in some sense men's and women's worlds, respectively. Women tend to move quickly through public space, whereas men can linger, yet boundaries are much more fluid than they were previously. For more on this dynamic, see Newcomb 2009.

8. For more on changing gender dynamics in the Moroccan public space, see Newcomb 2009; Kapchan 1996; Mernissi 1987; Rassam 1980; and Maher 1978.

9. Moroccan women have higher rates of obesity than men for a number of reasons: they are less likely to work outside the home, and after multiple pregnancies frequently do not exercise or work to lose the weight. In the middle and upper classes, they often employ someone to do housework for them, thus having almost no sources for physical activity (Benjelloun 2002, 138).

10. There are variations in data between urban and rural areas. Rural areas still exhibit malnutrition, higher infant mortality, and a lower life expectancy than urban areas. And while meat consumption has increased steadily in urban areas, it has been uneven in rural areas. Across both urban and rural areas, consumption of sugar and grains has remained high, generally in the form of sweetened tea and bread (Benjelloun 2002, 137). Daily caloric intake tends to be higher in rural areas due to a more strenuous agricultural lifestyle, but consumption of fats and animal products is lower (138).

11. Although this study is concerned with urban areas, rural areas are experiencing the same phenomenon. In a village about an hour outside the southern coastal town of Sidi Ifni, the anthropologist Jamila Bargach took me to a few local groceries that serve several hundred villagers, showing me that the shops sold primarily packaged foods.

5

DWELL

Urban Nostalgia as Neoliberal Critique

*We may not be able to trace the track of modernity before it is
laid down, but once it is we shall have explanations enough . . .
for the course it has taken.*
— Clifford Geertz, quoted in Miller 2009

NOT IN MY BACK YARD

Khaled circulated among the tables in the Floria café, petition in hand, talking
to longtime residents about the most recent threat to the Lux neighborhood's
rapidly fading character. A Moroccan businessman who was not local to Fes
wanted to construct a bakery on a site whose rightful owner had disappeared.
The original owner was a Jewish resident of the neighborhood who had
emigrated forty years before to Israel and could not be located to give his permission for such a major change to the space. The city was ready to go ahead
with the permits and had publicly posted a notification, which residents had
only one week to challenge. Khaled and his neighbors were protesting the proposed construction, arguing that the bakery would bring unnecessary early
morning smoke and noise to the once quiet residential neighborhood.

With his petition, Khaled was trying, single-handedly, to challenge the
latest blow of gentrification. The spacious Floria café is located on a busy corner of Hassan II Boulevard, the main street of the Ville Nouvelle of Fes, and it
serves as both a habitual dwelling point for Lux residents and a place of tran-
sience, where tourists stop by for a quick coffee before heading to the ancient
medina. Along the boulevard, the grand art deco facades have been recently
refurbished, and families sit on marble benches while their children play in
artfully designed fountains or buy sunflower seeds and balloons from street

vendors. The Floria café looks out over this boulevard, with the Lux neighborhood, now an uneven mix of grandeur and decay, tucked just behind it.

Yet all this Mediterranean beauty, nothing about it specifically or uniquely Moroccan, has its costs. Many neighborhoods in the immediate vicinity of Hassan II Boulevard have become prime real estate. Numerous smaller, French-built three-story buildings have been torn down to make way for gleaming high-rises, displacing small businesses and tenants alike, while even the original buildings' owners, despite the supposed gold mine on which they sit, can almost never afford to live in the new construction.

Khaled's petition represented one small political statement against the disrupted patterns of social life in his neighborhood. It generated various nostalgic responses from residents about the neighborhood's disappearing architecture, and the meaning of the old structures to the residents' sense of identity. In responding to both encroaching gentrification and city beautification projects, many residents expressed a form of urban nostalgia: nostalgic reflections on an ideal urban past that simultaneously critique the city that exists in the present.[1] Urban nostalgia offers a complex commentary on new urban forms representing neoliberal economic projects that are increasingly exclusionary. With the financial encouragement of governments, cities become beautiful spaces of commerce, and the messy and unsightly patterns of everyday life are shoved to the margins, to suburbs that sprawl further and further away from the spaces where people work. Communal memories have the potential to become politicized, serving as critiques of systems of power, although whether or not they can result in an effective political response is another issue. To whom does the city now belong?

The forces of gentrification that have altered the landscape of the Ville Nouvelle, or New City, represent a symbiotic relationship between government and business characteristic of neoliberal economies. This arrangement disrupts traditional class identities, since many of the residents displaced from the city center were once part of the city's elite. However, the city center previously boasted more economic diversity than it does now. The hodgepodge of small local businesses and mobile street entrepreneurs that were once a thriving part of the Lux neighborhood are missing from the Ville Nouvelle. And in terms of living spaces, gentrification practices are even more exclusionary than past residential practices, since for the past fifty years it was common to find buildings whose residents hailed from different social classes. By contrast, apartments in the new buildings are available only to the wealthiest. Many of those able to afford these residences are from elsewhere, thus disrupting the local character and sense of place through which many Fassis trace their identities.

Khaled's outrage about the bakery resulted in his becoming a temporary activist. This was the summer of 2011, when the uprisings popularly known as the Arab Spring were also taking place throughout the Middle East and North Africa.[2] These revolutions in other countries have resulted in regime change, instability, ongoing wars, and border conflicts, but Morocco had its own protest movement, the February 20th Movement, which fizzled out after several months. At the time Khaled was protesting locally, however, the February 20th Movement was also organizing ongoing demonstrations. Across the region, activists were giving voice to some of the same problems that concerned people like Khaled: unemployment, the rising costs of goods and services, inequality, corruption, and social exclusion.[3] Yet Khaled and his friends and family members seemed completely disinterested in the February 20th Movement. Instead, they wanted their neighborhood to be as it had been many years before. How, I wondered at the time, could revolutions be taking place, about issues I had heard people like Khaled complaining about for years, while he was distressed about the opening of a bakery?

Urban nostalgia—a longing for an ideal city of the past—serves as a critique of neoliberal gentrification in a globalized world. This nostalgia contains the possibility for political action, yet because of social fragmentation, political action tends to be localized and directed at symptoms (such as the bakery) rather than causes. Residents are not longing for a perfect world but wish to return to an urban setting in which fostering cooperation, conviviality, and community were all preeminent concerns. Urban nostalgia is provoked by changes to the urban landscape, by ruins, new construction, and gentrification.

Nostalgia is often framed as a passive and unreliable emotion, rooted in individual psychology or attached to a conservative vision of the past, reflecting a sentiment of longing for a time that is impossible to re-create. Yet this belies its potential to serve as a source of political critique or even action. While it remains to be seen whether, in the Moroccan context, discontent over new forms of urbanism can be transformed into positive social change, at the very least it is still important to think about what this dissatisfaction might mean. Urban nostalgia not only reveals a snapshot of past ways of moving and dwelling in cities but also represents a pointed critique of how social relations of the past, albeit hierarchical, become even more stratified and exclusionary under neoliberal economic practices.

Theorists of the city have described the creation of "global cities" central to transnational flows of capital and political influence (Sassen 2001). These theories posit that as the production of commodities becomes spread throughout the world, cities like London and New York have developed as financial and informational centers in order to manage this spread of capital. A focus on cosmopolitan global cities, however, tends to affirm an implicit distinction between "First World" and "Third World" cities, leaving out smaller cities in Global South contexts. Other scholars have called for a greater understanding of how cities in the "periphery" are also important sites for understanding urban processes as well as globalization (Robinson 2002; Bell and Jayne 2009). Arturo Escobar suggests that the focus on global cities leads to a deterritorialization of culture, or what amounts to a loss of focus on cultures rooted in particular places. He describes an "erasure of place" that privileges the global over the local, making global processes seem both neutral and apolitical (2001, 141). Examining local conflicts over space, Escobar highlights the very political nature of both globalization and efforts to lay claim to territory. Following Escobar, but also Kimberly Smith (2000), who argues for the political potential of nostalgia, I read Fassi nostalgia for modern urban forms that have disappeared or are in disrepair as a critique of globalization-related processes that have not benefited residents on a local level. Conflicts over space may seem rooted in nostalgia for a utopian past, but they are, in their own way, another form of protest against globalization.

This chapter moves beyond conceptualizing space solely in its pre- and postcolonial forms. Khaled's and his family's attachment to their neighborhood in the Ville Nouvelle did not stem from an appreciation of colonization, although they frequently mourned the destruction of French colonial architecture. In Morocco, the colonial project was completed more than fifty years ago, long enough that in the Ville Nouvelle, memories of French occupation belong only to the oldest residents.[4] Interestingly enough, however, Khaled and others of his generation did speak fondly of the former Jewish presence in the neighborhood. Lux neighborhood memories focus on disappearing architectural elements of the past that have recently been demolished by developers. Through talk about place, the neighborhood is re-created in its former glory, and a map of the past is created that challenges the contemporary identity of Fes itself. Memory, as Jöelle Bahloul has written, "becomes the construction of a social and cultural identity whose symbolic terminology tends to challenge the experience of the current reality" (1996, 2). Alongside these memories, residents actively discuss the visible changes to their city today, changes that have pushed many Fassis out of the city center and to its margins. A space for critique and political action can be found in this discourse on the city's new architectural formations. In critiquing gentrification as well as city beautification projects, Moroccans are not rejecting an abstract idea of modernity but rather a vision of the city that excludes almost everyone except the very rich.

The backdrop to Khaled's petition was the active protest movement in the spring of 2011.[5] Named the February 20th Movement after the date when the first demonstrations began, the protests did not demand the overthrow of the king but asked that his advisers be removed from their official roles (Belghazi and Moudden 2015, 38). Movement leaders called for judicial independence as well as for a constitutional monarchy. As was the case elsewhere in the region, unemployment and a lack of economic growth were among the key causes motivating protesters, many of whom came from families who had experienced persecution at the hands of the previous king, Hassan II (Lawrence 2016). At the first protest, movement organizers boasted crowds of 200,000, while the government estimated that there were only 35,000 demonstrators (Molina 2011). The king responded almost immediately by announcing a commission to begin revising the constitution, ultimately giving the prime minister more power. As Cohen and Jaidi note, King Mohammed VI has consistently tried to give the impression that he is leading a peaceful transition to democracy, even if in actuality the country may not be headed in that direction (2006, 1).

Mohammed VI's proactive responses caused a split within the movement, as some accepted his assertions on good faith, while others believed that the government would make only cosmetic changes. Another factor in the movement's lack of cohesion was the multiple social actors who participated, "namely, the non-partisan youth, the traditional opposition, the radical left, the moderate Islamists, and the radical fundamentalists"; these groups frequently disagreed about tactics and goals (Belghazi and Moudden 2015, 38). The new constitution was accepted on July 2011, after which only smaller protests took place among those who supported the king versus others unhappy with the extent of the reforms. Often violence broke out between the few remaining factions, and the monarchy's role was no longer that of active participant in the conflict but rather of arbiter and peacemaker (Abdel-Samad 2014, 801).

I had been eager to visit Morocco that summer to find out how my friends felt about the February 20th Movement and the instability that was sweeping the region. Although the weekend demonstrations had been more intense in the spring months before I arrived, they were still going on while I was there. Yet only one person in Khaled's large extended family was involved with the protests. Khaled's cousin Zahra, a well-educated woman in her twenties who lived in another city, was, like many of the protesters, educated and unemployed, angry at seeing her better-connected peers finding work while she bounced from one low-paying internship to another. She had a master's degree in chemistry from a Moroccan university, which everyone felt should have been a guarantee of a good job. After all, people said, chemistry was a practical degree, unlike English literature. Her parents, who still lived in Fes, were worried about their daughter's involvement in the protest movement and urged her to come home and stop protesting, which she eventually did. But other family members simply rolled their eyes when I mentioned her. In their opinion, she had fallen in with the wrong crowd, or she was spoiled and looking for a government handout. In general, the middle-class Fassis I knew were impatient with the protesters and did not feel they had a legitimate claim to change.

Even those who did not have a job or an income did not sympathize with the movement. One man called them "atheists who believe human rights means eating in public during Ramadan." University colleagues and others whom I knew from previous work with nonprofits were more supportive but said they felt that the king had addressed the protesters' grievances already.[6] In general, criticism of the government might include city officials, the king's advisers, or the prime minister, but for the most part, people in the Lux neighborhood that summer were not talking about the protest movement. Instead, their ire was directed at businessmen from outside Fes and the mayor who was allowing them to come into Fes and destroy its character.

SAVING THE VILLE NOUVELLE

Most tourists who come to Fes are interested primarily in the city's medina, which was founded in 789 CE by Moulay Idris I, one of the first Arab rulers of Morocco (O'Meara 2007, 6). The medina contains most of the ancient historical sites of import, its winding alleys and suqs offering a glimpse of a "traditional" Arab city, in which neighborhoods were once organized by trades. In scholarly literature as well, attention has focused on the medina, primarily for its deep historic character or for how well it represents the typology of the "Islamic City."[7] Fes served as the capital of Morocco from 1666 until the beginning of the Protectorate (1912–1956), when the French decided to relocate the capital to Rabat. The Ville Nouvelle, built a short distance from the medina, attracts little attention in guidebooks and is primarily a site for hotels from which day trips to the medina can be organized. Yet Morocco's villes nouvelles also have their own unique history, since they were part of France's idea of the Protectorate, which was not a full-fledged colony. Rather than razing the city or building alongside traditional architecture, throughout Morocco, the French constructed their "new cities" as experiments in urban planning, often at a distance from the medinas.[8] This led to what Janet Abu-Lughod (1981) once termed "urban apartheid," in which a sort of de facto segregation was instilled, one in which the sites of both French residence and power were located in the Ville Nouvelle, while Muslim Moroccan natives lived in the medina. The *mellah*, the historic Jewish quarter of the medina, was already in

shops offer higher-end goods that average Fassis would not use on a regular basis. They are additionally owned by non-Lux residents, many of whom have connections to the new buildings' owners.

"Our neighborhood is being sold away to outsiders [*berrani*]," Khaled argued. "We need to tell them we don't want the smoke from the oven. The noise and the pollution from the oven should not be so close to where we live."

Other residents told me they objected to the way in which the proposed transaction was being, in the words of one man, "sneaked through the municipality behind our backs." It was only by chance that the residents had even learned about the proposed bakery. The entrepreneur who wanted to build it had only to post a notification at one of the city's administrative offices, without seeking the approval of neighborhood residents. Another neighbor had been applying for a copy of his birth certificate and saw the notification. When Khaled found out about it, he had decided to take action.

"It's not that we don't have businesses here already," Miriam, another Lux resident, told me. "We do. But the owners are known to us. Some have been here forever. Some come and go. But the newer ones have no connection to the neighborhood."

Residents told stories that expressed nostalgia for past patterns of commerce and residence currently on the wane. In the Lux neighborhood, for example, just in front of the cinema, a Jewish man and his wife had owned a clothing shop. Although they lived in another part of the city, they had rented and operated the shop for over thirty years, selling men's dress shirts and ties. Lux residents spoke highly of the merchandise, and said the shop's owner was "part of the neighborhood," even if he did not live there.

"I had one shirt from them, and it lasted almost twenty years," said Khaled's brother Mourad. "It was from Italy. They really sold quality stuff. There is nothing you can buy right now like that. Everything is imported from China, and it's poor quality." This was high praise coming from a man whose livelihood is derived from importing cheap clothes.

When the owner planned to sell the building that contained the clothing shop, the shopkeeper refused to leave or to take the compensation the owner tried to offer him. Although the law does not allow renters to be displaced without adequate compensation, if the city condemns architecture as being unfit to live in, residents can be forced to leave. This building was slowly demolished, until it remained a crumbling façade with only the shop remaining at the bottom. The city promptly condemned it, forcing the shopkeeper to leave. He received a small amount of money, though by now he was close to retirement age and could not establish a new shop. Lux residents who had supported the shopkeeper said there was nothing they could do. The shopkeeper was a renter in a building that had been sold.

"You see how quick the city was to tear the building down," Khaled said. "It was a dirty trick. They will do anything to help out the big businessmen. Even if it means destroying the city."

"Where could he [the shopkeeper] go?" another neighborhood resident, Mustapha, commented. "He's too old to start over. If he opens another shop out in a popular [sha'abi] neighborhood where he can afford the rent, he won't have the same type of clientele passing by. People won't appreciate what he sold like we did here."

Other Lux residents celebrated the shopkeeper's actions in remaining in his shop and were critical of the forces they imagined were behind his expulsion.

"This is why we don't have the heart to kick out our own renters," one man, whose family owned another building, commented. "Where would they go? It's shameful [h'shooma] they're doing this to such an old man. But the new owner doesn't care at all about the people who live here. It's all about profit, and the city government helps them out. In the past, a long time ago, we took care of one another."

On Nostalgia

Fassi urban nostalgia frequently followed this pattern: an altered space on the urban landscape provoked reflections about the absent places or people who had previously occupied it, often with the painful circumstances of how they had been displaced. Where the old Cinema Lux (now a high-rise) once stood, people recalled childish mischief in the theater or clandestine meetings between young lovers. In another location, people told me of how the man who hoped to be a new building's doorman faithfully guarded, day and night, both the rubble from the demolished building that had been there first and then, over several months, the construction of the building itself. When the new high-rise was completed, the owner, rather than giving the man the coveted position as doorman, unceremoniously banned him from the premises. People also recalled the Squalli supermarket, which had been in the neighborhood for years and sold a few luxury items not available elsewhere, such as oatmeal or special cookies from Spain. It went out of business when multinational supermarket chains began opening up throughout Fes. Then there was the dilapidated Central Market, still functioning but infested with flies, with tumble-down bricks and overflowing garbage at its margins. Once it had been a well-kept place where families bought meat and vegetables for the daily tagine and looked forward to their daily banter and bargaining with particular salesmen, a face-to-face experience completely absent from the sanitized shopping experience at well-stocked air-conditioned chains like Marjane.

Cities undergoing rapid social alterations are particularly prone to nostalgia. As Elizabeth Wilson has written, "The massive changes that take place in cities induce this emotion to an intense degree" (1997, 137). Urban nostalgia could be said to take the form of what some scholars have called "reflective nostalgia," a type of performative nostalgia that "lingers on ruins, on the patina of time and history, on uncanny silences and absences and on dreams" (Della Dora 2006, 210). Reflective nostalgia considers the past through still visible fragments as well as ghostly absences, which are also notable in the Lux residents' memories. Vidler (1992) writes of the "architectural uncanny," elements of urban landscape that arise from the unconscious despite attempts to suppress them, and this term has resonance in Fes. In narrative, Lux residents tend to dwell on what is absent, and many of their stories figure around former Jewish residents of the neighborhood. Those who are older than thirty-five still have significant memories of the neighborhood's original residents, and recall seeing their unleavened breads at the public ovens at Passover, or the neighbors who grew up "like our brothers," until the entire family immigrated to Canada.

Residents found a parallel to the departure of the neighborhood's Jewish residents in their own situation. It is not inconsequential that one of the issues at the heart of Khaled's petition was the missing owner of the space in which the bakery was to open. Although efforts had been made to locate the man, no one could find him, nor did the few remaining members of the Jewish community know how to reach him. He was said to have immigrated to Israel and perhaps died there, yet the central defense against the bakery was that this long-departed owner might return to claim his rightful property. The Lux area, in fact, was at one time a majority Jewish neighborhood. Khaled's grandfather had bought his own family's apartment building from a Jewish family, and at one point six out of the eight families residing in the apartments had been Jewish. One by one, Jewish families left, and tenants and family moved in. Around 125 Jews remain in Fes today, though their population once numbered in the thousands. Fes is now central to Jewish heritage tours that often bring back the Sephardic descendants of people who lived in Morocco for centuries. They primarily visit the mellah, old synagogues, shrines, and cemeteries, yet occasionally someone drifts off the tour and into the Lux neighborhood, carrying a scrap of paper bearing an address of a building or the names of a few former residents. Lux residents speak excitedly of these visits, perhaps not recognizing the visiting nephew of the uncle who once occupied an apartment just above the motorcycle repair shop, but sensing in his visit a connection to a past in which a certain order of things remained unquestioned.

A longing to return to an illusory past is common to the human condition, but the concept that we think of today as nostalgia has arisen in more recent history. The roots of the word "nostalgia" come from two Greek words meaning "to return home" and "pain in the body" (Della Dora 2006, 209). The term originated with a Swiss physician, Johann Hofer, who described the psychological distress among Swiss soldiers fighting abroad as "a sad mood originating from the desire to return to one's native land" (Zwingman 1959, 12). Nostalgia was characterized by physical symptoms as well, including anorexia, anxiety, and depression. During the eighteenth century, soldiers of other nationalities also became afflicted, and many physicians believed the condition could lead to insanity or death (K. Smith 2000, 510).

By the mid-nineteenth century, conceptualizations of nostalgia as a severe medical disorder were becoming less common. The first glimmerings of something resembling our current understanding of nostalgia date to an 1873 study by Haspel (K. Smith 2000, 512). Haspel argued that nostalgia was a childlike attachment to place that was also an attachment to the past. The hardships faced in the present created an illusory sense of an idyllic past. By the 1920s, psychoanalytic understandings were eventually layered onto the interpretations of nostalgia. By 1950 the original sense of homesickness was lost, and a famous study by Nandor Fodor gave rise to something fairly close to our current understanding of nostalgia as an unrealistic longing for a utopian past that never existed (K. Smith 2000, 513). Fodor writes that nostalgia is the desire "for a far-away fairy land where all strife ceases and life rolls smoothly in a state of perfection and bliss" (1950, 26).

Kimberly Smith argues that nostalgia, rather than being a neutral analytic device, is acutely political, arising in the context of nineteenth-century resistance to modernization and industrialization (2000, 505). Nostalgia was generally expressed for a lost way of life, typically rural and agrarian, and represented a critique of modernity. While also containing the seeds of a potential political stance, Fassi urban nostalgia differs from this in important ways. Fassi urban nostalgia, reflective though it may be, represents a desire to return not to some ancient, imagined past but to a more recent past and to an urban sociability that is increasingly on the wane. The destruction of local architecture has brought with it the displacement of neighbors and kin who were present since the early 1960s. Svetlana Boym has written that nostalgia "is a rebellion against the modern idea of time, the time of history and progress" (2001, xv).

For Fassis, nostalgia is not merely a rebellion against time; it is a rebellion against the transformation of a landscape that aims to turn Fes into an exhibit—a pretty façade, but one in which most people can no longer afford to live. The ideal past is imagined as one of urban harmony, lived out in a French-built setting. The longed-for past is the postcolonial years, in which the architecture may have acquired a shabby veneer, yet social life was both fair and fully realized. Displacement was not a hallmark of the utopia of the past. Writing of Zanzibar, William Bissell notes a similar phenomenon: nostalgia for the colonial period, but a nostalgia that is rooted in very real socioeconomic grievances. "Throughout much of Africa," Bissell writes, "one also finds a widespread and profound sense of foreboding, a perceived crisis in the fundamental conditions of social production and reproduction brought on by neoliberal policies and market orthodoxies. From Angola to Zanzibar, people are confronting the restructurings of global capital in terms of an economics of impossibility that renders daily life ever more precarious" (2005, 222).

A Flower for Every Resident

A number of scholars have focused in recent years on the increasingly exclusionary characteristics of global cities, commenting in particular on the mentality of fear that leads to segregated and fortified urban landscapes.[11] These writers have decried the decline of public spaces and services for all that has accompanied the rise of fortified enclaves available only to the wealthiest. Fes is representative of these fears yet also differs from them in significant ways. In one sense, there has been an increase in some forms of public space, creating new sites of sociability: in particular, parks and the promenade in the center of Hassan II Boulevard. Yet despite the availability of public space for leisure and visual consumption, private space has become increasingly unaffordable, both in the city center and in the many gated communities and exclusive residential enclaves that have been constructed in other parts of the city since 2000.

When he took office in 2003, the mayor of Fes, Abdelhamid Chabat (who was not originally from Fes but was born in the nearby town of Taza), proclaimed that one of his primary goals was to beautify the Ville Nouvelle, which had grown shabby from neglect. One of his campaign promises was to plant a million flowers, one for each resident. Under his care, the Ville Nouvelle experienced a cosmetic renaissance. Hassan II Boulevard, the tree-lined street stretching from the exit of the new autoroute to the end of the medina, has been transformed, with new pavers, palm trees towering over flower gardens, and modern fountains that light up at night. Women crack sunflower seeds on the marble benches as their children play in the fountains, and vendors walk by selling balloons and other cheap toys. Smaller fountains send up intermittent spray to the delight of the children who run in and out of them, and in the summer months, people come to the boulevard to escape the heat. Ice cream shops and cafés line the street, where families sit and eat enormous parfaits with multiple scoops of ice cream, granola, and fruit toppings. In the late afternoons, Andalusian music blasts from speakers attached to a government building. It is the traditional music of Fes, said to date back to when the Arabs were expelled from Spain, a reminder of Fes's Arab origins as well as its glorious place in national history. Hassan II Boulevard has become a better-used public space, free, available to everyone, and kept almost scrupulously clean by the new trash companies that have everywhere sprung up to deal with Morocco's rubbish.

Chabat also transformed smaller spaces throughout the city. A dirty and forbidding park behind Chefchaouni Street, close to the public market and once a gathering spot for prostitutes and alcoholics, is now replete with a flower garden, a café, and fake cliffs and waterfalls set into a manufactured hillside. Rosemary bushes send up their minty fragrance to passersby. These are also spaces where families congregate, and where women feel at ease visiting with their sisters or their mothers. One could argue that this creation of pleasant public spaces in which families feel comfortable is a positive development. I mentioned this to Nadia, a middle-class housewife who liked to take her two small children to play in the park and in the fountains. She lived in a newer apartment building in another neighborhood and was not a Lux resident.

"I like it very much," she agreed. "Now when it's hot, we can take a break from the heat, and our children have a place to play." Indeed, many Moroccans were proud of Chabat's transformations of the public space. Others, however, were more circumspect in their response.

"Parks do not create jobs," one man from the Lux neighborhood commented. "You know who Chabat put to work? He brought poor guys from his own neighborhood to serve as parking attendants throughout the city. Now, even if you park on the street, there's some redneck ['arobi] thug standing there demanding you pay him. Otherwise, what jobs did any of this bring? We need jobs, not flowers." Indeed, his political opponents commented that Chabat "has succeeded in hiding the city's miseries" (Bennani 2012).

Others noted that even though Hassan II Boulevard has been renovated, many other significant roads remain unchanged. One has only to veer off the boulevard onto one of the other large streets, Mohammed V Avenue, to see a different story. There, traffic-clogged side streets feature open manholes, pockmarked pavements, and a large number of beggars. One of the city's landmarks, the Central Market, is slowly decaying, as described in the previous chapter. Now, a Fassi told me, "the government is letting it fall apart" because they want the market to die, and for people to shop in the supermarkets on the outskirts of town that reflect the vision of modernity and capitalist success.

"We won't need the market anymore because life will be like it is in America," Nadia tells me proudly when I ask her about the rapidly decaying Central Market. "We can use our cars to shop for groceries instead."

"What about the people who don't have cars?" I ask. She shrugs.

"I don't know. They can take the bus."

Critics of modern Moroccan urban landscapes have drawn attention to the haphazard quality of construction, the pollution, a lack of design for lived spaces, and the absence of aesthetic beauty or unity. Describing the impact of factories on the Moroccan landscape in the 1960s, Edmond Amran El Maleh once wrote, "The artificiality of a false modernity is in the process of uniformalizing, of slowly laminating society as a whole, destroying the original configurations of our culture and its landscapes" (1997, 14).

The anthropologist Clifford Geertz also documented the flaws of Moroccan urbanization during the 1980s in Sefrou, a city located not far from Fes, which Geertz called a "miniaturized version" of Fes.[12] In 1986, Hassan II, the father of the current king, gave a speech decrying the pace and direction of Moroccan urban planning, specifically singling out Sefrou for criticism. Geertz himself criticized the ugly direction of urban development in Sefrou, saying, "What was once a chiseled jewel set in a paradisian garden was now a sprawling, disorganized, anything but jewellike bourg" (1989, 296).

The creation of unseemly new architecture in Sefrou was necessitated by massive rural-urban migration but was funded in part by remittances from Moroccans living abroad, in an otherwise stagnant Sefroui economy. But to Geertz, disputes over the city's architecture during this period were largely about a battle between migrants and long-standing residents, at the heart of which was the desire to be "included within the body of the city and inscribed in its landscape" (1989, 297). While this tension between outsiders and natives is evident nearly three decades later in Fes, exclusion from the city's central landscape altogether is an even greater factor. In the face of this, ethnic divisions (such as that between Arab "insiders" and Berber "outsiders") that were once significant to locals take a backstage role, and capital becomes more important. In fact, although "original" Fassis may still distinguish themselves from those with non-Arab, non-Andalusian ancestry, in the recent acts of urban displacement I have witnessed greater solidarity among Lux residents of different ethnic backgrounds.

Lux residents, despite their class and ethnic differences, have experienced rising costs of living, the decline or elimination of local business, and stagnant employment prospects. The exclusion of locals from neighborhoods that have "belonged" to them for the past forty years is part of a larger process of neoliberal capitalism, in which government and industry closely work together to bring investment and tourism to Fes. While the populist mayor of Fes may have been the public face of this gentrification, the Moroccan Ministry of the Interior maintains control over urban development throughout the country (Bogaert 2011, 9).

Beginning with the sociologist Ruth Glass, who coined the term "gentrification" in 1964, scholars for many years have studied the process of middle-class residents in Western cities gradually buying up and changing the character of lower-income neighborhoods. Other scholars have examined this process globally for non-Western locales.[13] By the 1990s, Neil Smith has argued, gentrification had become "a crucial urban strategy for city governments in consort with private capital in cities around the world" (2002, 440). Yet the connection between gentrification and neoliberalism has remained understudied in scholarly literature. Despite gentrification having become a widespread phenomenon, also lacking are ethnographic studies of the particular ways the "gentrification blueprint" (Davidson and Lees 2005, 1167) plays itself out in local contexts. In focusing on neoliberalism, an ideology that also supports privatization, free trade, and open markets, I am here interested in the specific ways in which nation-states encourage and coerce economic investment and enterprise while simultaneously absenting themselves from the regulatory process. Local studies of how individuals are responding to these processes are now needed more than ever.

The displacement experienced by Lux residents and business owners, while painful, is nowhere near as extreme as other examples from the literature. Many displaced Lux residents, even renters, received compensation for their property, although developers will sell the redeveloped property at a much higher rate. The situation is more complex for those who have no claim to property rights to begin with. The urban poor in Mumbai, for example, who occupied an area zoned for economic development, were unceremoniously relocated to slums on the outskirts of town (Harris 2008, 2419). Closer to home, Bogaert has documented how urban slum dwellers in Casablanca have been relocated from sites marked for development, then compelled to take out housing loans to buy apartments in projects funded by private investors who had offered winning bids accepted by the government (2011, 16).

The difference in the case of Casablanca slum dwellers and the middle- and lower-middle-class residents of Lux is that slum dwellers bear the added stigma of being a population considered a possible terror threat if not managed by the government. Thus, slum dwellers are encouraged to enter the formal economy by getting "on the books"—responsible for paying back housing loans, monthly electricity and water bills, and other expenses that, as slum dwellers, they previously did not have to contend with.[14] Under neoliberalism, authoritarian governments clear the path for private capital while simultaneously, if the situation merits it, "managing" the displaced population. Expelled from their unsightly housing, slum dwellers are simultaneously included, albeit marginally, in the structures of the neoliberal economy, although this "inclusion" inevitably leads to further indebtedness and poverty (Bogaert 2011, 3). Most Lux residents, by contrast, are still scraping by, clinging to their economic and class positions, but only barely. Although many criticized the mayor or the local administration, they did not extend their criticism to the nation-state and its policies. Instead, they blamed investors, both Moroccans from "outside" Fes and transnational companies such as the Barcelo hotel chain, which had razed another block of land on Hassan II Boulevard, several blocks away from Lux. There appears to be a genuine confusion about who is behind this process, making local efforts to fight incidents such as the proposed bakery even more difficult to organize.

Longtime Fes resident and architect Jean-Paul Ichter has been highly critical of urban development since the beginning of the millennium. In the Moroccan newspaper *Maroc Hebdo*, Ichter (2010) notes the astoundingly swift pace of development, particularly the construction of entire neighborhoods, some priced well out of reach of the majority of Moroccans. He observes the tendency of developers to cram high-rise buildings so close together that residents can almost reach out and touch adjoining buildings. Construction takes place without any plan for collective social life. Recreational areas are also erased from the landscape, as they are not profitable as real estate, with the exception of a new, exclusive golf course recently constructed in Fes, but he notes that a golf course is hardly green space for all the people. "We are heading for an 'urban (totalitarian) segregation," Ichter writes. He terms this process a return to "Haussmann urbanism."[15]

The comparison of construction projects in modern-day Fes to Haussmann's public works projects in Paris is apt in more ways than one: the relocation many residents of the Ville Nouvelle face was also part and parcel of Haussmann's plan for Paris. As the scholar David S. Barnes has written, "'Haussman[n]ization' turned Paris into an immense construction site, displacing tenants from the crowded central districts and causing rents in the city to rise dramatically" (2006, 49). Haussmann also proposed wide, open boulevards as a way of maintaining hygiene, staving off disease, quelling possible riots, and fighting crime. Surveillance is also a hallmark of neoliberal gentrification, and the idea that a city should allow for maximum surveillance of its inhabitants is also evident in the Fes mayor's plans. In 2011 Chabat announced that 265 security cameras would be installed in various locations throughout the city in the coming year. Additionally, the Haussmannian architecture of the Ville Nouvelle makes it easy to deploy military personnel. During the February 20th Movement protests, organizers frequently found their protest routes blocked and access to the center of the city effectively obstructed.

Conclusion

Khaled's nostalgia and outrage about the bakery spurred him to a form of activism, in gathering signatures to take to the city government. Yet he made no connections among neighborhood gentrification, displacement, and the February 20th Movement. And while the city worked hand in hand with investors to create a beautified yet unaffordable Ville Nouvelle, the ancient medina nearby fell further into disrepair. Although parts of it have been declared World Heritage sites, many buildings are structurally unsound and overoccupied by poor rural-urban migrants, another example of the lack of jobs and poverty that still plague Fes despite surface appearances to the contrary.

Conflict over the bakery and the shopkeeper's efforts to remain in his place of business both stimulated reflections on what residents were losing in a changing city. Pollution, a diminished quality of life, and poor-quality merchandise characterized the future, whereas harmonious social relationships and businesses that fit snugly within the fabric of social life were all cited by Lux residents as evidence of a more organic past. People criticized the mayor's extensive efforts to rehabilitate the city as cosmetic, and as a project that was not really intended to benefit the people to whom Fes belonged.

"What good are the parks and gardens when we have no place to buy vegetables?" one woman, Amina, asked. "Or when they don't bring jobs? I will take a job for my son any day over a park or a garden."

"Pretty soon, we will have to take a bus just to see this garden," I overheard a man comment once in the café. "Who can afford to live here anymore?"

In remembering a different sort of Fes, nostalgia serves as a critique of the erasure of memory in neoliberal landscapes, as a certain way of life is destroyed to make way for investment capital. The Ville Nouvelle, a remnant of colonialism, is not a World Heritage site. Upon its foundations, to destroy and rebuild is a way of asserting a modern claim to what was originally a French city. The story of the bakery shows one instance in which this vision of the past was briefly maintained, although these are few and far between. The presence of a new kind of ruin—failed urban development projects—occasions another critique: that development itself is always partial and half-executed, and that the past has been torn down to make way for a present that is both false and inadequately realized.

Khaled's large extended family was one of a few holdouts, residents of the Lux neighborhood who still clung to their valuable Ville Nouvelle real estate, refusing to sell to developers. The dispute over the potential opening of a bakery, which the neighborhood's residents successfully blocked, represented a minor victory of David over Goliath. The presumed scourge the bakery represented, seemingly out of proportion to the offense it actually would create, offered an opportunity for the neighborhood's denizens to reflect on new processes of urbanization that are directly affecting postcolonial patterns of social life. The conflict also occasioned nostalgic reflections among the neighborhood's inhabitants. This nostalgia represented an attempt to create a narrative map of the past, one in which changing architectural forms offered comments on social reality, and on the neoliberal economic practices that are rearranging the Fes landscape.

In defense of the neighborhood, Khaled and his friends told stories about an idealized past, irrevocably sundered by recent urbanization. They spoke of the rhythms of everyday life in the microcosm of the Lux neighborhood, of familiar landmarks they passed on the way home from school, of homes in the neighborhood where they'd spent time, and of residents who had long ago moved away or died. Yet their critique was framed not merely in nostalgia for a way of life whose alteration was inevitable, but also in the particular ways they might fight what was happening and maintain something of the neighborhood's original character. In this case, the potential bakery's owner could serve as a scapegoat, a suitable figure to blame for a larger issue: the Moroccan government's desire to integrate itself into the global economy, often at great cost to its citizens.

Nostalgic responses to new forms of urbanization should not be read as a critique of a specifically Moroccan modernity but rather as a political response to neoliberal urbanization's local effects. Fassis employ nostalgia in discussing recent changes to the city in part because they feel that urban planning is no longer in their hands, that it is part of a present spiraling out of control in which urbanization does not improve social life but simply offers a cosmetic solution to urban blight that benefits others. Who these "others" are remains in dispute, and in these local instances I witnessed, blame frequently went to local government, foreign interests, or wealthy Moroccan investors who were not from Fes. This lack of agreement about who is behind this exclusionary future is also reflected in the fragmentation of the nationwide February 20th protest movement, which was unable to unite Moroccans behind a cohesive message, even as there are definite social ills that lower- and middle-class Moroccans have in common.

While smaller than protests in other countries, the February 20th Movement drew in part on frustration with the economic prosperity that seems to benefit only the tiniest segment of Moroccan society. Although protest movements in other North African countries resulted in the ousting of long-term dictators, in Morocco they remained largely fragmented. In Fes, a few people I talked to said they supported the demonstrators but stated that they themselves were too busy trying to make ends meet to take part.[16] Others referred to the demonstrators as "outsiders" and "atheists" who sought to destabilize the monarchy.[17] They did not connect the February 20th Movement's demands with their own local grievances, or perhaps the movement never managed to demonstrate its resonance with some of the pressing issues that troubled Lux residents.

The fragmentation of Moroccan political culture has been cited as one reason for the movement's failure to effect substantial change. As Belghazi and Moudden note: "The notion of the people as united by common goals, shared values, communal sentiments, or as victims of collective exploitation, and mass repression was thwarted in the aftermath of the euphoric period. The measures taken by the state to satisfy sections of society likely to amplify the protests drove home the idea that the people, far from being a united whole [with the] ability to effect change should be construed in terms of division, separation, and hierarchy" (2015, 45).

One might have thought, for example, that high levels of unemployment among university graduates would have made them natural allies of the movement. As noted earlier, unemployed university graduates have been protesting outside the Moroccan Parliament since the 1990s, yet the majority of them did not take part in the February 20th Movement, in part because some believed it would jeopardize their chances for employment. Many of these protesters are not actually unemployed, but are seeking public sector jobs or else are doing work not commensurate with their educational level (Badimon 2013, 197). The Moroccan government has historically handled the unemployed university graduates by giving some of them jobs, thus encouraging future generations of protesters to be hopeful that they, too, will be as fortunate. In fact, when Moroccan activists began organizing the first protest on February 20, the prime minister and the Ministry of the Interior, through its negotiators, even promised 1,000 of the unemployed graduates employment if they would not stand along with the others (Badimon 2013, 208). This strategy of divide and conquer, or divide and persuade, also seems to have been effective in peeling off other segments of the movement until only a small number of protesters were left.

Similarly, the Lux neighborhood's gentrification continued to provoke a kind of atomistic outrage disconnected from any larger political process. Five years later, even more residents had left the neighborhood, and Khaled's family, one of the last holdouts, had finally sold their building. The bakery was never built, yet the space was eventually appropriated from the city and turned into a fish restaurant, opened by an outside investor. The smell, I thought, must have been considerably worse than that of a bakery would have been.

The original owner, a spectral presence in 2011, had become more substantial in the memories of some. In 2011 nobody remembered his name. Five years later, someone thought it was Shlomo. His children were said to be living in Canada, or perhaps Israel. Someone had an address; someone in the dwindling community of Fes's remaining Jews was trying to get in touch with the family so that they could reclaim their property. They would be very upset, Khaled said, to know that they had been displaced.

Notes

1. There are some excellent studies on the Middle East and North African region exploring architecture as a means of recalling the past and commenting on the present, including Pandey 2003; Slyomovics 1998; and Bahloul 1996.

2. I place "Arab Spring" in quotes because the term is considered condescending, implying that the entire region was somehow sleeping through a winter from which it "woke up." Other terms are preferential, including "revolutions" or "revolutions for dignity" (*karama*).

3. Two useful works, by Spiegel (2015) and Willis (2012), focus on the politico-religious and historical contexts of the uprisings in Morocco, respectively.

4. Instead, the urban nostalgia expressed by Lux residents is generally premillennial, focusing on the period from the 1970s until the early twenty-first century. Over this time period, the national population doubled from 15 million to 30 million, and structural adjustment programs of the 1980s resulted in massive waves of migration to the city, thus flooding Fes's population with residents from rural areas, many of whom could only afford to live in substandard housing.

5. More detailed discussions of the February 20th Movement can be found in Molina 2011; Madani, Maghraoui, and Zerhouni 2012; Hivert 2013; and El Hachimi 2015. On the chronology of events and political outcomes of the protest movements, see Abdel-Samad 2014.

6. Through other channels, including social media, I attempted to find local people to talk to who considered themselves part of the February 20th Movement. However, some of them seemed afraid to reveal themselves in person to a researcher they did not know and insisted on talking only through direct messages on Twitter.

7. The classic study of the Fes medina is Roger Le Tourneau's *Fès avant le protectorate: Étude économique et sociale d'une ville de l'occident musulman* (1949). A more recent work that aims at an emic view of medina space and how architectural representations infuse and are

infused by residents' representations of the world is Simon O'Meara's *Space and Muslim Urban Life: At the Limits of the Labyrinth of Fez* (2007).

8. See Paul Rabinow's *French Modern: Norms and Forms of the Social Environment*, which discusses in greater detail the French social experiment and intentions behind the creation of the Moroccan villes nouvelles (1991).

9. For more on this idea of "original" Fassis who stake identity claims to the city in their ancestry, see Newcomb 2009. Although many of these families have illustrious family names and distant relatives who are now central to the ruling political and economic apparatus in Rabat and Casablanca, they themselves are now located firmly in the middle class.

10. In 1961 Fes had a Jewish population of 12,194, but by 1969 the population had declined to under 1,000. By 2000, there were less than 125 Jews in Fes altogether ("Fez" 2012). The Jewish residents of Lux figure significantly in neighborhood memories. See Bahloul 1996 for an excellent monograph on the subject of residents' memories of Jewish-Muslim household relations in colonial Algeria.

11. See, for example, Ghannam 2002; Davis 1992; Ellin 1997; Caldeira 1996, 2001.

12. In fact, many of the issues Geertz describes pertaining to Sefraoui identity are also present in Fes, including a long-established, gentrified bourgeoisie who blame the influence of rural-urban migrants on the city's decay.

13. See, for example, Thomas 1991; Escher, Petermann, and Clos 2001; Potuoglu-Cook 2006; and Sandler 2007.

14. For Morocco, Bogaert divides neoliberalism into two phases: roll-back and roll-out. Roll-back neoliberalism refers to the austerity measures and withdrawal of the state from public services under structural adjustment programs. Under roll-out neoliberalism, by contrast, there is increasing state intervention and an attempt to include subaltern populations within the capitalist system. In part, this shift was due to the violent response that roll-back neoliberalism received in the form of riots and other violent public movements.

15. Georges-Eugène Haussmann was appointed by Napoleon III in the 1850s to create a new urban design for Paris, characterized by the destruction of small neighborhoods and the creation of wide boulevards and monumental, uniform apartment blocks. The new plan was designed in part to prevent the spread of diseases in close quarters and to ease access to commerce for shoppers, but also to assist in military deployment and the erection of barricades in the event of civilian rebellions (Barnes 2006, 50). The plan also fostered close links between government and private industry, enabling them to work together to build a city allowing for maximum surveillance and order.

16. In fact, on one day that I was in Fes, a demonstration crossed quite close to the Lux neighborhood itself, and I was surprised to hear a few residents comment that the demonstrators themselves were outsiders, and that they were also a nuisance because they were bringing out riot police and thus creating an unstable environment.

17. Spadola (2013). has also noted a similar phenomenon among lower-middle-class residents of the Fes medina, who in other circumstances were critical of the monarchy yet nonetheless came to its defense when asked their opinions of the protesters.

CONCLUSION

IN 1994, IF YOU LIVED in Morocco and wanted to call someone in a foreign country, you had to go to the main post office in the center of the city, the Post, Telephone and Telegraph office, called the PTT. There, you gave your number to the government employee on duty, then waited, sometimes for two hours if there was a long line of people. Finally, when your call was connected, you were directed to one of several small booths where you talked for as much time as you could afford. For Moroccans separated from family members working abroad, these calls were expensive, and many could afford to make them only once a month. Quickly you would share your important news with your loved one: the birth of a new baby, perhaps, or a request for money, or possibly an announcement that someone from the neighborhood had found them a potential spouse. But it could be lonely in those days, when communicating with family abroad was such a challenge.

In Moroccan homes of 1994, when the streets emptied at midday and families gathered around the lunch table, the television was always on, like an additional family member who related cheerful stories about the government's latest accomplishments. The king was always busy, traversing the country, inaugurating development, endlessly cutting ribbons on new rural health clinics or schools. During Ramadan, the entire country tuned into the same special Ramadan series. Exposure to programming from overseas meant Latin American *telenovelas* or American prime-time shows that had been popular a few years earlier, like *Dallas* or *Knight Rider*. News broadcasts filtered what people learned about the world, always painting Morocco in a positive light, but newspapers did represent both government and opposition party views. Although negative news about Morocco was limited, international newspapers were available and avidly read by Moroccans, often in cafés. Many were knowledgeable about world politics, perhaps more so than the average American.

Cell phones, the internet, and satellite dishes were just a few years away. When they appeared, they changed everything, not just for Moroccans but for the rest of the world as well. In that old way of life, choices were limited. In some ways, this was simpler, people recall when talking about the past. There was more of a sense of shared culture when there was only a limited amount of culture to share. Soon there were hundreds of television programs to choose from, and cell phones and Skype could connect you to your family overseas almost instantly. These new resources, an important part of globalization, were also potentially threatening to authoritarian regimes, since they offer access to negative information about those regimes as well. These technologies were powerful tools used during the Arab revolutions of 2011 and in Morocco too, when demonstrators who were a few steps ahead of the government were able to organize protests through social media.

But in January 2016, the government decided to exercise its extensive powers, limiting access to Skype and other VoIP (Voice over Internet Protocol) technologies that allow voice communication with people anywhere in the world. Morocco's Telecommunications Regulatory National Agency (ANRT) claimed that Skype and other VoIP technologies were unlicensed to deliver phone calls, and determined that only three phone companies, owned by a mix of international and domestic investors, which included holding companies owned by the Moroccan government, had the licenses to offer voice calls.

Since Moroccans depend on these services for business as well as for social and familial connections, entrepreneurs and small businesses were particularly hard hit. Social media campaigns suggested that Moroccans remove their "likes" from the three phone companies' Facebook pages. Second-generation expatriate children sent messages to the king, letting him know how they felt about no longer being able to chat with their family in Morocco. Moroccans were also savvy enough to understand that talking over the internet was not the same as a phone call. People already paid for Wi-Fi connections in their houses; why charge an additional fee for something that most Wi-Fi users in the world took for granted? Moroccans joked that now the post office would also be limiting e-mails. The only way around the ban was to build a virtual private network (VPN), which requires considerably more advanced knowledge of the internet than the average consumer possesses. As of October 2016, the ban remained in effect but was intermittently enforced. Sometimes the ability to chat is available and sometimes it is not. In terms of commerce, this partial ability to communicate could make a Moroccan entrepreneur trying to do business with someone outside the country seem unreliable.

To me, the VoIP ban demonstrates the uneven nature of globalization's promises in countries like Morocco. While Morocco may have the same internet technologies available in the United States, the decision to limit one crucial aspect of internet usage to its citizens restricts technological access to the wealthiest, since Moroccan phone companies do not offer affordable international calling plans. There is a further digital divide with respect to internet usage, since although 60 percent of Moroccans have access to the internet, only 67 percent of the population is literate (UNESCO 2016).

People's ability to access certain aspects of globalization becomes more and more restricted as one moves down the ladder of social class. Globalization aims to replace public goods with private ones, and at its best, creates competition so that consumers get lower prices. This may be good for shoppers in the Moroccan suqs, flooded with plastic buckets and T-shirts made in China, but it does not benefit the women who used to work in Moroccan factories but no longer have jobs.

Privatization is supposed to help consumers by guaranteeing that many companies will compete to offer similar services at low prices. Outside investment is supposed to make local economies more competitive. But what about a European company that takes over a city's water supply and raises the rates so high that people cannot afford it? This has happened in Tangier, where the populace protested against the high costs of utilities in 2011 and 2015. Should water be a public utility or a private good? In many Global South countries, it is becoming increasingly defined as the latter.

Amendis, an affiliate of the French company Veolia, has controlled waste, water, and electricity in Tangier since 2002. Its other subsidiaries now operate in Rabat and the surrounding areas as well (El Yaakoubi 2015). Protests in Tangier during the Arab revolutions of 2011 and more recently in 2015 targeted the high costs Tanjawis (people from Tangier) pay relative to other cities where the government still operates utilities. Amendis has claimed to be offering a "social good" to very poor populations in Tangier by connecting their homes to water sources. A 2007 study the corporation conducted with the help of development researchers showed that when people in poor neighborhoods were offered interest-free loans to connect their households directly to the company's water pipes, they were happy to do so, since they often spent hours accessing public taps that were further away from their homes (Devoto et al. 2012). Researchers found that the water quality was not improved from the free water people already had access to, but that Moroccans now used more water and had more time for leisure. "Getting connected generated important time gains," the study summarized, "but did not lead to increases in labor market participation, income, or schooling attainment. The spare time was used for leisure and social activities. Because water was often a source of tension between households, home connections appeared to improve social integration" (ibid.). One wonders if convincing people to connect their households to a private water source where previously it was free created any social strains among those who now struggled to pay for the water on limited incomes.

Stories like these continue to be heard over and over. They cause Moroccans to compare globalization with colonization, since, coincidentally, most of Morocco's business and investment is with France. The stories told in this book are mostly those of middle-class Moroccans, the roughly 50 percent of the population whose incomes range from around $350 to $550 per month. This may be enough money to afford subsidized food, but what about other costs—affordable housing, health care, technology, water and electricity, and consumer goods? As incomes decrease, nearly every cent of many families' budgets will be spent on food and shelter.

The Moroccan government has an ambitious plan for the next five years, which includes creating 500,000 new jobs in manufacturing for multinational companies by 2020. "The plan," reported by a US State Department website focused on foreign investing, "aims to support the development of small and medium-sized enterprises (SMEs), improve youth employability, support integrated industrial platforms, and promote exports, using increased foreign investment to boost knowledge sharing and technology transfer" ("2015 Investment Climate—Morocco"). By focusing on developing industries such as aeronautics, electronics, and automotive manufacturing, the government hopes to make the country into a crucial economic hub mediating among Europe, the Middle East, and Africa. Indeed, the unemployment rate has declined in recent years, and this plan aims to build on this trend. But the language used to describe these types of projects also reflects a continuation of the neoliberal development Morocco has pursued in recent years: "trade liberalization" and "structural reforms" are the processes Morocco has actively pursued in order to achieve this economic progress. How is a ban on technologies like Skype going to help those small and medium-size enterprises the plan claims to want to support?

The United Nations' Human Development Index (HDI) provides another way of measuring globalization's progress in Morocco. The HDI examines "progress in three basic dimensions of human development: a long and healthy life, access to knowledge and a decent standard of living" (United Nations Development Program 2015, 1). This is reflected in life expectancy, education level, and gross national income. For 2014, the HDI focuses on work, encompassing not just work to earn a living but "contributing to the public good, reducing inequality, securing livelihoods and empowering individuals" (1). The UN HDI website notes that "a positive link between work and human development is not automatic. The link can be broken in cases of exploitative and hazardous conditions, where labour rights are not guaranteed or protected, where social protection measures are not in place, and when unequal opportunities and work related discrimination increase and perpetuate socioeconomic inequality" (1). The UN report further adds that many countries may fail to report the prevalence of child labor and lack of labor protections, for example, which are also indicative of the level of human development. Will Morocco's new industries fulfill all of these conditions? Under neoliberalism, have they fulfilled them in the past?

Morocco ranks 126th out of 188 countries in the Human Development Index, with an assigned HDI value of 0.628. (Norway is ranked first, at 0.944.) Morocco has managed to improve its HDI dramatically since 1980, when it was at 0.396. Since 1980, life expectancy has increased by sixteen years to an average of seventy-four years. Mean years of schooling have also risen by 3.7 years. And income level, as measured by the Gender Inequality Index (GNI), has risen almost 112 percent.

This certainly sounds like good news for Morocco. But because the HDI relies on averages, it "masks inequality in the distribution of human development across the population" (United Nations Development Program 2015, 4). To account for this, the UN tries to measure how much of that human development is lost due to income inequality. When inequality is figured into the statistics, Morocco's HDI falls to 0.441, a loss of nearly 30 percent. When "multidimensional poverty" is also included, which looks not just at income but also at household data for health, education, and living standards, the most recent data available (for 2011) shows that "15.6% of the population are multidimensionally poor, while an additional 12.6% live near multidimensional poverty. . . . Income poverty," the UN concludes, "only tells part of the story" (6).

Inequalities of gender are also measured under the GNI, which looks at economic activity, empowerment, and reproductive health. Morocco measures at 0.525, ranking it 117th out of 155 countries. (In a regional comparison, Libya is ranked forty-eighth and Tunisia twenty-seventh.) For every 100,000 live births, 120 women still die. (Compare this with seven maternal deaths per 100,000 live births for Germany, for example, and the disturbingly high twenty-one deaths per 100,000 for the United States.) In Morocco, 26.5 percent of women participate in the labor market, compared to 75.8 percent of men. As a Global South country, Morocco has been working hard to improve its performance on these kinds of indicators, and although the government pushes agendas that are supposed to enhance women's rights and integrate women into the labor market, Katja Žvan Elliott writes that "feminists and the development communities have failed to address the shrinking or, in fact, the non-existence of the welfare state, which could protect women from being exploited as cheap labor or from being denied the protection of their families for acting as autonomous individuals" (2015, 185).

What does all this mean for middle-class families like the Benjellouns? As part of the middle class, they earn incomes that are presumably high enough by Moroccan standards to live comfortably. Yet out of the five Benjelloun siblings, only one, Hanane, actually has a job in the formal economy. Mourad, although in the informal economy, can support a family on what he makes, but he does not have health insurance. Rachid has only sporadic income, and Khaled none at all. Ilham remains in the acceptable category of homemaker, and her husband provides for her. As unmarried men, Rachid and Khaled are unable to fulfill societal expectations of manhood such as heading a household or supporting a family. And if one of them were to come down with a major illness, the entire family would need to pool its resources to get him the medical care he needed.

Have the Benjellouns benefited from globalization? Yes, if cars full of clothes from China that cross the Straits of Gibraltar and end up in Mourad's shop are a benefit of globalization. Yes, if we consider that the higher standards of living have increased Benjelloun life expectancies (although only time will tell whether the increase in illnesses such as diabetes and heart disease will decrease these numbers). Yes, if we measure benefits in terms of access to cell phones and the internet, and the ability to buy frozen French fries at the Marjane supermarket. When Rachid is in Spain, Latifa will not have to wait two hours at the post office to call her son.

But if the question is whether the Benjellouns have full access to health care, work opportunities, housing, and meaningful careers promised by a dynamic neoliberal economy, the answer is no. Prior to Independence, by the standards of the day, their family had a higher social status than they do now. While others have climbed, the Benjellouns, like so many others in their social class, have tumbled a few rungs on the social ladder.

Other globalization stories could have been told in this book, of rural families, or lower-class families, or families with closer connections to politics, perhaps, or to religion. While the stories of the Benjellouns do not represent the lives of all Moroccans, they are reflective of the lives of many Fassis whom I have come to know since the beginning of the millennium. The Benjellouns' experiences mirror those of other middle-class people in Global South countries who are struggling to benefit from globalization's promises while supporting each other and staying connected to their families when some must migrate in search of work. Across Morocco, people assert a sense of local identity in the face of processes that threaten to erode what is distinctive and admirable about their unique way of approaching the world, an approach that we can still call Moroccan culture.

APPENDIX: GLOSSARY OF TERMS

Aid El Kbir—the feast of the sacrifice, a major holiday on the Muslim calendar that commemorates when Prophet Ibrahim (Abraham) believed he would have to sacrifice his son for God.

Amazigh—literally, "free people," the preferred term for Berbers.

Andalusia—a region of Spain, occupied by the Muslims (Moors) from the eighth through the eleventh century. From the eleventh through the fourteenth century, as Christians gradually reinvaded the region, al-Andalus or Andalusia was the part of Spain still occupied by Muslims. It was considered a golden age for Muslims.

ARTs—assisted reproductive technologies.

atfal anabib—"test-tube" babies, or babies from in vitro fertilization (IVF).

baraka—a blessing.

Berbers—indigenous people of North Africa.

berrani—outsiders

bghir—yeasted pancakes with hundreds of little holes on top that are dipped in butter and honey and traditionally eaten to break the fast during Ramadan.

bint an-nas—a girl of excellent character.

CEDAW—United Nations Convention on the Elimination of Discrimination against Women.

cherif or *cherifa*—a descendant of the Prophet.

chiqaq divorce—divorce for reasons of irreconcilable differences.

chommeurs—unemployed persons.

darija—vernacular Moroccan Arabic.

dirham—Moroccan currency.

djellaba—long, traditional garments worn by both men and women.

Fassi—resident of Fes.

February 20th Movement—Moroccan protests during the 2011 Arab revolutions that called for judicial independence, a constitutional monarchy, and economic growth.

Fes—ancient Moroccan city and the setting of this book. It was the capital of Morocco from 1666 until the French Protectorate, when the capital was moved to Rabat.

fqih—a Qur'anic healer.

French Protectorate—Although not called a colony, Morocco was under the control of France from 1912 to 1956.

Galenic medicine—originating in ancient Greece, the idea that the four humors of the body are out of balance. Moroccan beliefs in the power of heat and cold to cause illness are derived from this system.

Global South—developing countries, primarily in Africa, South America, and parts of Asia.

globalization—trade, world capital and investment movements, migration, and environmental degradation that influence world economies, cultures, and politics.

Hajja, Hajj—honorific terms for women or men who have completed the pilgrimage to Mecca.

hammam—public steam baths.

hanoot—a small dry-goods shop located in a Moroccan neighborhood.

harira—a hearty, tomato-based soup with meat and chickpeas.

Hassan II—father of King Mohammed VI of Morocco.

HDI—Human Development Index, a statistical measurement of life expectancy, level of education, and quality of life.

hijab—headscarf.

IMF—International Monetary Fund.

in sha allah—God willing.

Independence—Morocco achieved its independence from France in 1956.

intracytoplasmic sperm injection or ICSI—male-directed therapy that identifies viable sperm and injects them into the oocyte.

IVF—in vitro fertilization, an assisted reproductive technology in which the oocyte is fertilized by sperm outside the woman's body.

kafala—foster parentage of orphans.

khafeef—flaky; unsubstantial.

l'achoub—herbs.

l'brd—the cold; a traditional belief that cold enters the body and can cause illness and infertility.

Lux neighborhood—a neighborhood in Fes originally named for the Cinema Lux in the Ville Nouvelle.

Maliki jurisprudence—Muslim countries follow different legal schools for shari'a law. Morocco follows the Maliki school, which was developed in the eighth century and follows the Qur'an and the hadiths, in addition to the consensus of the people of the city of Medina during the time of the Prophet, as primary sources for determining laws. Shari'a law in Morocco is generally applied only in matters of marriage and family, and the laws for business and crime are based on European codes.

medina—the ancient city center.

mektub—fate.

mellah—historic Jewish quarter of the medina.

microcredit loans—very small business loans to patrons with no credit history or collateral who live in poor countries.

Mohammed VI—king of Morocco who has ruled since 1999.

mudawana reforms—the legal reforms to the family code, governing a woman's rights in marriage and divorce, ratified by the king in 2004. These reforms raised the minimum age of marriage from fifteen to eighteen, allowed women to petition for judicial divorces, and permitted marriage without a guardian or *wali*.

muhajer/muhajereen—Moroccan migrant(s) living in other countries.

MSA—Modern Standard Arabic.

m'sada—a traditional masseuse specializing in infertility.

nafaqa—support that a husband is required to pay for the amount of time he was married to his wife, as set by a judge during divorce proceedings.

neoliberal—favoring privatization and a free market.

NGOs—nongovernmental organizations.

nia—intention; goals focused toward the divine.

Prophetic medicine—medicine practiced according to the example of the Prophet Muhammed, including the idea that individuals may be attacked by negative spiritual influences that can be combated by recitation of the Qur'an.

Qur'an—sacred book of Islam with the teachings of the Prophet.

Ramadan—the ninth month of the Islamic calendar, commemorating the first revelations of the Qur'an to Muhammed. A month of fasting and prayer.

remittances—money sent home to one's country of origin by family members working in other countries.

rizq—daily bread; informal reference to income or livelihood.

ruqyah shariah—Qur'anic healing verses.

sadaq—bride price.

sfinj—doughnuts sold in the street.

shabakia—deep-fried, twisted pastries dipped in honey and sesame seeds

shari'a—religious law developed by Muslim scholars in the 300 years following Muhammed's death.

shaykh—a ruler of a tribe; an Islamic cleric.

shiqaq—discord; a new category of divorce available to women since the revisions of the mudawana.

STEM—science, technology, engineering, and math.

structural adjustment programs or SAPs—When the IMF granted loans to Morocco in the 1980s, it required program changes that would stimulate privatization and deregulation.

suq—traditional bazaar where people buy, sell, and trade a range of goods.

sura al-fatiha—The opening chapter of the Qur'an, this *sura* is a prayer for the guidance and mercy of God.

tagine—a traditional stew of meat and vegetables.

Tamazight—Berber language.

thqaf—to tie someone up through sorcery, potentially blocking them from acts like conception.

Ville Nouvelle—the "new city"; the modern section of most Moroccan cities built by the French during their occupation of Morocco.

wali—male guardian.

BIBLIOGRAPHY

"2015 Investment Climate Statement—Morocco." n.d. US State Department. Accessed October 2, 2016. http://www.state.gov/e/eb/rls/othr/ics/2015/241672.htm.

"2500 fécondations in vitro réalisées chaque année au Maroc." n.d. *La Vie Éco*. Accessed April 6, 2015. http://www.lavieeco.com/news/societe/2-500-fecondations-in-vitro -realisees-chaque-annee-au-Maroc-13250.html.

Abdel-Samad, Mounah. 2014. "Why Reform Not Revolution: A Political Opportunity Analysis of Morocco 2011 Protests Movement." *Journal of North African Studies* 19:5: 792–809.

Abdennebi, Zakia. 2011. "Moroccan Textile Sector Battles Tough Times." Reuters. March 17. Accessed May 31, 2013.

Abu-Lughod, Janet. 1981. *Rabat: Urban Apartheid*. Princeton, NJ: Princeton University Press.

Adam, André. 1968. *Casablanca: Essai sur la transformation de la société marocaine au contact de l'occident*. Paris: CNRS.

Adjamagbo, Agnès, Agnès Guillaume, and Fatima Bakass. 2014. "Decisions about Unplanned Pregnancies and Abortion among Women and Men in Morocco and Senegal: Influence of Norms, Practices, and Institutional Contexts." Working paper, IUSSP Scientific Panel on Abortion Research, June.

Akesbi, Najib. 2003. "Ajustement structurel et segmentation du marché du travail." *Annales marocaines d'economie* 7: 3–12.

Alam, Anwar. 2011. "Islam, Bread Riots, and Democratic Reforms in North Africa." *Islam and Muslim Societies* 4(1).

Allali, Réda, and Hassan Hamdani. 2006. "Société: Blad schizo." *TelQuel* 243: 42–49.

Althaus, F. 1994. "Moroccan Fertility Falls." *International Family Planning Perspectives* 2(2): 77–79.

———. 1997. "Rising Contraceptive Use and Age of Marriage Lower Fertility Rates in Morocco." *International Family Planning Perspectives* 23(1): 46–49.

Amine, Abdelmajid, and Najoua Lazzaoui. 2010. "Shoppers' Reactions to Modern Food Retailing Systems in an Emerging Country." *International Journal of Retail and Distribution Management* 39(8): 562–581.

Amster, Ellen. 2013. *Medicine and the Saints: Science, Islam, and the Colonial Encounter in Morocco: 1877–1956*. Austin: University of Texas Press.

Appadurai, Arjun. 1988. "How to Make a National Cuisine: Cookbooks in Contemporary India." *Comparative Studies in Society and History* 30(1): 3–24.

———. 1996. *Modernity at Large: Cultural Dimensions of Globalization*. Minneapolis: University of Minnesota Press.

Arditti, Rita, Renate Klein, and Shelley Minden, eds. 1984. *Test-Tube Women: What Future for Motherhood?* London: Pandora.

Arndt, Jordan. 2013. "Contending with Change: Moroccan Women's Participation in the Textile and Clothing Manufacturing Industry." Fulbright U.S. Student Program. Accessed December 3, 2015. http://www.solidaritycenter.org/wp-content/uploads/2015/01/Morocco. Contending-with-Change-report-on-women-in-textile-industry.9.13.pdf.

Assaad, Ragui. 2004. "Why Did Economic Liberalization Lead to Feminization of the Labor Force in Morocco and De-feminization in Egypt?" Working paper, Center of Arab Women Training and Research, Mediterranean Development Forum.

Assaad, Ragui, and Caroline Krafft. 2014. "The Economics of Marriage in North Africa." World Institute for Development Economics Research, Helsinki, Finland.

Ayad, Mohamed, and Farzaneh Roudi. 2006. "Fertility Decline and Reproductive Health in Morocco: New DHS Figures." Population Reference Bureau. Accessed April 6, 2015. http://www.prb.org/Publications/Articles/2006/FertilityDeclineand ReproductiveHealthinMoroccoNewDHSFigures.aspx.

Badimon, Montserrat Emperador. 2013. "Does Unemployment Spark Collective Contentious Action? Evidence from a Moroccan Social Movement." *Journal of Contemporary African Studies* 31(2): 194–212.

Bahloul, Joëlle. 1996. *The Architecture of Memory*. Cambridge: Cambridge University Press.

Bakass, Fatima, and Michèle Ferrand. 2013. "L'entrée en sexualité à Rabat: Les nouveaux 'arrangements' entre les sexes." *Population* 68: 41–65.

Banerjee, Abhijit, Dean Karlan, and Jonathan Zinman. 2015. "Six Randomized Evaluations of Microcredit: Introduction and Further Steps." *American Economic Journal: Applied Economics* 7(1): 1–21.

Bargach, Jamila. 2001. "Personalizing It." In *The Ethics of Kinship: Ethnographic Inquiries*, ed. James Faubion. Lanham, MD: Rowman and Littlefield.

———. 2002. *Orphans of Islam: Family, Abandonment, and Secret Adoption in Morocco*. Lanham, MD: Rowman and Littlefield.

Barnes, David S. 2006. *The Great Stink of Paris and the Nineteenth-Century Struggle against Filth and Germs*. Baltimore: Johns Hopkins University Press.

Batnitzky, Adina. 2007. "Obesity and Household Roles: Gender and Social Class in Morocco." *Sociology of Health and Illness* 30(3): 445–462.

Belasco, Warren, and Philip Scranton, eds. 2002. *Food Nations: Selling Taste in Consumer Societies*. London: Routledge.

Belghazi, Taieb, and Abdelhay Moudden. 2015. "*Ihbat*: Disillusionment and the Arab Spring in Morocco." *Journal of North African Studies* 21(1): 37–49.

Belhorma, Souad. 2014. "Self-Employed Women and Poverty Reduction in Morocco: What Relations for What Ends?" Working paper, Center for Women's

Policy Studies. Accessed July 10, 2016. http://www.centerwomenpolicy.org/programs
/poverty/documents/Self-Employed-Women-and-Poverty-Reduction-in-Morocco
-What-Relations-for-What-Ends-by-Souad-B.pdf.

Bell, David, and Mark Jayne. 2009. "Small Cities? Towards a Research Agenda."
International Journal of Urban and Regional Research 33(3): 683–699.

Benjelloun, Sabah. 2002. "Nutrition Transition in Morocco." *Public Health Nutrition* 5(1)
A: 135–140.

Bennani, Driss. 2012. "Portrait: Le fabuleux destin de Hamid Chabat." *TelQuel*,
October 11. Accessed July 10, 2016. http://telquel.ma/2012/10/11/Portrait-Le
-fabuleux-destin-de-Hamid-Chabat_539_4538.

Berfield, Susan, and Manuel Baigorri. 2013. "Zara's Fast-Fashion Edge." *Bloomberg
Business*, November 14. Accessed September 5, 2016. http://www.bloomberg.com
/bw/articles/2013-11-14/2014-outlook-zaras-fashion-supply-chain-edge.

Bissell, William C. 2005. "Engaging Colonial Nostalgia." *Cultural Anthropology* 20(2):
215–248.

Bogaert, Konraad. 2011. "The Problem of Slums: Shifting Methods of Neoliberal Urban
Government in Morocco." *Development and Change* 42(3): 2–24.

———. 2013. "Contextualizing the Arab Revolts: The Politics behind Three Decades of
Neoliberalism in the Arab World." *Middle East Critique* 22(3): 213–234.

Bogaert, Konraad, and Montserrat Emperador. 2011. "Imagining the State through
Social Protest: State Reformation and the Mobilizations of Unemployed Graduates
in Morocco." *Mediterranean Politics* 16(2): 241–259.

Boudarbat, Brahim, and Aziz Ajbilou. 2007. "Youth Exclusion in Morocco: Context,
Consequences, and Policies." Middle East Youth Initiative Working Paper.
Washington, DC: Brookings Institution, Wolfensohn Center for Development.

Boufous, Sawsann, and Mohammed Khariss. 2015. "The Moroccan Middle Class from
Yesterday to Today: Definition and Evolving." *Business and Economics Journal*
6(3).

Bouhga-Hagbe, Jacques. 2004. "A Theory of Workers' Remittances with an Application
to Morocco." IMF Working Paper 04/194.

Bouoiyour, Jamal, and Amal Miftah. 2014. "The Effect of Migrant Workers' Remittances
on the Living Standards of Families in Morocco." Working paper, Centre
d'analyse théorique et de traitement des données économiques. https://basepub
.dauphine.fr/bitstream/handle/123456789/12802/130064_2013_2014_10Migrant
_Workers_Remittances_on_Living_Standards_Morocco_JBouoiyour_AMiftah
.pdf;sequence=1.

Bourdieu, Pierre. 1984. *Distinction: A Social Critique of the Judgement of Taste*. Cambridge, MA: Harvard University Press.

Boutieri, Charis. 2014. "Arduous Journeys on Roads Not [Yet] Taken: Language,
Neoliberal Work Skills, and the Exhausted Educational Dream." *Farziyat*,
February 25. Accessed January 8, 2016. http://www.farzyat.org/arduous-journeys
-on-roads-not-yet-taken-language-neoliberal-work-skills-and-the-exhausted
-educational-dream.

Boym, Svetlana. 2001. *The Future of Nostalgia*. New York: Basic Books.

Buitelaar, Marjo. 1993. *Fasting and Feasting in Morocco: Women's Participation in
Ramadan*. Oxford: Berg.

Cairoli, M. Laetitia. 2011. *Girls of the Factory: A Year with the Garment Workers of Morocco*. Gainesville: University of Florida Press.

Caldeira, Teresa. 1996. "Fortified Enclaves: The New Urban Segregation." *Public Culture* 8(2): 303–328.

———. 2001. *City of Walls: Crime, Segregation, and Citizenship in São Paulo*. Berkeley: University of California Press.

Carlisle, Jessica. 2013. "Moroccan Divorce Law, Family Court Judges and Spouses' Claims: Who Pays the Cost When a Marriage Is Over?" In *Feminist Activism, Women's Rights, and Legal Reform*, ed. Mulki Al-Sharmani, 56–71. London: Zed Books.

Carol, Sarah, Evelyn Ersanilli, and Mareike Wagner. 2014. "Spousal Choice among the Children of Turkish and Moroccan Immigrants in Six European Countries: Transnational Spouse or Co-ethnic Migrant?" *International Migration Review* 48(2): 387–414.

Carr, Marilyn, and Martha A. Chen. 2001. "Globalization and the Informal Economy: How Global Trade and Investment Impact on the Working Poor." Background paper commissioned by the ILO Task Force on the Informal Economy. Geneva: International Labour Office.

Charmes, Jacques. 2012. "The Informal Economy Worldwide: Trends and Characteristics." *Margin, the Journal of Applied Economic Research* 6(2): 103–136.

Charrad, Mounira. 2001. *States and Women's Rights: The Making of Postcolonial Tunisia, Algeria, and Morocco*. Berkeley: University of California Press.

CIA World Factbook. 2017 Morocco. Accessed April 14, 2017. https://www.cia.gov/library /publications/the-world-factbook/geos/mo.html.

Claassen, Emil Maria, and Pascal Salin. 1991. *The Impact of Stabilization and Structural Adjustment Policies on the Rural Sector: Case Studies of Côte d'Ivoire, Senegal, Liberia, Zambia and Morocco*. Rome: Food and Agriculture Orgnization of the United Nations.

Cloke, Paul, Philip Crang, and Mark Goodwin. 2013. *Introducing Human Geographies*. 3rd ed. New York: Routledge.

Codron, Jean-Marie, Hakan Adanacioglu, Magali Aubert, Zouhair Bouhsina, Abdelkader Ait El Mekki, Sylvain Rousset, Selma Tozanli, Murat Yercan. 2014. "The Role of Market Forces and Food Safety Institutions in the Adoption of Sustainable Farming Practices: The Case of the Fresh Tomato Export Sector in Morocco and Turkey." *Food Policy* 49: 268–280.

Cohen, Shana. 2003. "Alienation and Globalization in Morocco: Addressing the Social and Political Impact of Market Integration." *Comparative Studies in Society and History* 45(1): 168–189.

———. 2004. *Searching for a Different Future: The Rise of a Global Middle Class in Morocco*. Durham, NC: Duke University Press.

Cohen, Shana, and Larabi Jaidi. 2006. *Morocco: Globalization and Its Consequences*. New York: Routledge.

Conway-Long, Don. 2006. "Gender, Power, and Social Change in Morocco." In *Islamic Masculinities*, ed. Lahoucine Ouzgane, 145–160. London: Zed Books.

Coontz, Stephanie. 1988. *The Social Origins of Private Life: A History of American Families*. New York: Verso.

Corea, Gena. 1985. *The Mother Machine: Reproductive Technologies from Artificial Insemination to Artificial Wombs*. New York: Harper and Row.

Cornell, Vincent. 1998. *Realm of the Saint: Power and Authority in Moroccan Sufism*. Austin: University of Texas Press.

Crapanzano, Vincent. 1973. *The Hamadsha: A Study in Moroccan Ethnopsychiatry*. Berkeley: University of California Press.

Crawford, David. 2007. "On the Sluggishness of Cities." *Anthropology News*, April.

———. 2008. *Moroccan Households in the World Economy: Labor and Inequality in a Berber Village*. Baton Rouge: Louisiana State University Press.

Crépon, Bruno, Florencio Devoto, Esther Duflo, and William Parienté. 2015. "Estimating the Impact of Microcredit on Those Who Take It Up: Evidence from a Randomized Experiment in Morocco." *American Economic Journal: Applied Economics* 7(1): 123–150.

Crétois, Jules. 2013. "Moroccan Women Face Hardships in Textile Factories." *Al Monitor*, April 15. Accessed June 2013. http://www.al-monitor.com/pulse/culture/2013/04/morocco-women-workers-hardships.html.

D'Addato, Agata V. 2003. "Progression to Third Birth in Morocco in the Context of Fertility Transition." *Demographic Research* 15(19): 517–536.

Davidson, Mark, and Loretta Lees. 2005. "New-Build 'Gentrification' and London's Riverside Renaissance." *Environment and Planning A* 37: 1165–1190.

Davis, M. 1992. *City of Quartz: Excavating the Future in Los Angeles*. New York: Vintage Books.

de Certeau, Michel. 1984. *The Practice of Everyday Life*. Berkeley: University of California Press.

De Haas, Heine. 2014. "Morocco: Setting the Stage for Becoming a Migration Transition Country?" *Online Journal of the Migration Policy Institute*, March 19. Accessed December 5, 2014. http://www.migrationpolicy.org/article/morocco-setting-stage-becoming-migration-transition-country.

Deiana, Manuela. 2009. "Improving Women's Rights in Morocco: Lights and Shadows of the New Family Code (Moudawana)." *International Journal of Interdisciplinary Social Sciences* 3(11): 69–80.

Della Dora, Veronica. 2006. "The Rhetoric of Nostalgia: Postcolonial Alexandria between Uncanny Memories and Global Geographies." *Cultural Geographies* 13: 207–238.

Dellal, Mohamed, and Amar Sellam, eds. 2013. *Moroccan Culture in the 21st Century: Globalization, Challenges and Prospects*. New York: Nova Science.

Devoto, Florencia, Esther Duflo, Pascaline Dupas, William Parienté, and Vincent Pons. 2012. "Happiness on Tap: Piped Water Adoption in Urban Morocco." *American Economic Journal: Economic Policy* 4(4): 68–99.

"Divorce Applications in Morocco Plummeted 72%." 2005. *Arabic News*. Accessed November 13, 2010. http://www.arabicnews.com/ansub/Daily/Day/050215/2005021526.html.

El Aoufi, Noureddine, and Mohammed Bensaïd. 2008. "Les jeunes: Mode d'emploi. Chômage et employabilité au Maroc." Rabat: Economie critique.

El Hachimi, Mohamed. 2015. "Democratisation as a Learning Process: The Case of Morocco." *Journal of North African Studies* 20(5): 754–769.

El Maleh, Edmond Amran. 1997. "Itinéraire: Critique de la critique." *Horizons maghrébins* 33/34: 10–15.

El Yaakoubi, Aziz. 2015. "Thousands Protest Utility Prices in Morocco's Tangier." Reuters, November 1.

Ellin, Nan, ed. 1997. *Architecture of Fear.* New York: Princeton Architectural Press.

Elliott, Katja Žvan. 2009. "Reforming the Moroccan Personal Status Code: A Revolution for Whom?" *Mediterranean Politics* 14(2): 213–227.

———. 2015. *Modernizing Patriarchy: The Politics of Women's Rights in Morocco.* Austin: University of Texas Press.

Ennaji, Moha. 2014. *Muslim Moroccan Migrants in Europe: Transnational Migration in Its Multiplicity.* London: Palgrave Macmillan.

Ennaji, Moha, and Fatima Sadiqi. 2004. "The Impact of Male Migration from Morocco to Europe on Women: A Gender Approach." *Finisterra* 39(77): 59–76.

Escher, Anton, Sandra Petermann, and Birgit Clos. 2001. "Gentrification in der medina von Marrakech." *Geographische Rundschau* 53: 24–31.

Escobar, Arturo. 2001. "Culture Sits in Places: Reflections on Globalism and Subaltern Strategies of Localization." *Political Geography* 20: 139–174.

Evans-Pritchard, E. E. 1976. *Witchcraft, Magic, and Oracles among the Azande.* Oxford: Oxford University Press.

Evrard, Amy Young. 2014. *The Moroccan Women's Rights Movement.* Syracuse, NY: Syracuse University Press.

"Female Headed Households." 2017. World Bank Demographic and Health Surveys. Accessed March 2017. http://data.worldbank.org/indicator/SP.HOU.FEMA.ZS ?locations=MA.

"Fez." 2012. *Jewish Virtual Library.* Accessed June 3, 2014. http://www.jewishvirtual library.org/jsource/judaica/ejud_0002_0007_0_06432.html.

Foblets, Marie-Claire. 2007. "Moroccan Women in Europe: Bargaining for Autonomy." *Washington and Lee Law Review* 64(4): 1385–1417.

———. 2008. "Marriage and Divorce in the New Moroccan Family Code: Implications for Moroccans Residing in Europe." In *Law and Religion in Multicultural Societies,* ed. Rubya Mehdi, Hanne Petersen, Erik Reenberg Sand, and Gordon R. Woodman, 145–175. Copenhagen: DJOF.

Fodor, Nandor. 1950. "Varieties of Nostalgia." *Psychoanalytic Review* 37: 25–38.

Friedman, Jonathan, and Kajsa Ekholm Friedman. 2013. "Globalization as a Discourse of Hegemonic Crisis: A Global Systemic Analysis." *American Ethnologist* 40(2): 244–257.

Gardiner, Michael. 2000. *Critiques of Everyday Life.* London: Routledge.

Geertz, Clifford. 1979. "Suq: The Bazaar Economy in Sefrou." In *Meaning and Order in Contemporary Morocco: Three Essays in Cultural Anthropology,* ed. Clifford Geertz, Hildred Geertz, and Lawrence Rosen. Cambridge: Cambridge University Press, 123–225.

———. 1989. "Toutes Directions: Reading the Signs in an Urban Sprawl." *International Journal of Middle East Studies* 21(3): 291–306.

Ghannam, Farha. 2002. *Remaking the Modern: Space, Relocation, and the Politics of Identity in a Global Cairo.* Berkeley: University of California Press.

Giddens, Anthony. 1990. *The Consequences of Modernity*. Stanford, CA: Stanford University Press.

Ginsburg, Faye, and Rayna Rapp. 1995. Introduction to *Conceiving the New World Order: The Global Politics of Reproduction*. Berkeley: University of California Press.

Glass, Ruth. 1964. *London: Aspects of Change*. London: MacGibbon and Kee.

Gomez-Rivas, Camilo. 2008. "Morocco's Imperfect Remedy for Gender Inequality." *Middle East Report* 247(38).

Goody, Jack. 1982. *Cooking, Cuisine, and Class: A Study of Comparative Sociology*. Cambridge: Cambridge University Press.

Greenwood, Bernard. 1981. "Cold or Spirits? Choice and Ambiguity in Morocco's Pluralistic Medical System." *Social Science and Medicine* 15(3): 219–235.

Harrell, Richard S. 1962. *A Short Reference Grammar of Moroccan Arabic*. Washington, DC: Georgetown University Press.

Harris, Andrew. 2008. "From London to Mumbai and Back Again: Gentrification and Public Policy in Comparative Perspective." *Urban Studies* 45(12): 2407–28.

Harvey, David. 1989. *The Condition of Postmodernity*. Oxford: Blackwell.

Haut Commissariat au Plan du Maroc. 2012. *Le Maroc en chiffres*. Rabat: Direction de la statistique.

Heath, Jeffrey. 1987. *Ablaut and Ambiguity: Phonology of a Moroccan Arabic Dialect*. Albany: State University of New York Press.

Heine, Peter. 2004. *Food Culture in the Near East, Middle East, and North Africa*. Westport, CT: Greenwood.

Highmore, Ben. 2001. *Everyday Life and Cultural Theory: An Introduction*. London: Routledge.

———. 2011. *The Everyday Life Reader*. London: Routledge.

Hivert, Joseph. 2013. "Se désengager du mouvement du '20 février.'" *European Journal of Turkish Studies* 17: 2–24.

Holtzman, Jon. 2006. "Food and Memory." *Annual Review of Anthropology* 35(1): 361–378.

Howell, Sally. 2003. "Modernizing Mansaf: The Consuming Contexts of Jordan's National Dish." *Food and Foodways* 11(4): 215–243.

Howes, David. 1991. *The Varieties of Sensory Experience*. Toronto: University of Toronto Press.

Hughes, Courtney Rinker. 2013. "Responsible Mothers, Anxious Women: Contraception and Neoliberalism in Morocco." *Arab Studies Journal* 21(1).

Ichter, Jean-Paul. 2010. "Chronique de Jean Paul Ichter Eviter un urbanism ségrégatif." *Maroc Hebdo*, April 9. Accessed June 16, 2011. http://www.maghress.com/fr/marochebdo/88112.

Ilahiane, Hsain. 2006. *Historical Dictionary of the Berbers (Imazighen)*. Lanham, MD: Rowman and Littlefield.

Ilahiane, Hsain, and John Sherry. 2008. "Joutia: Street Vendor Entrepreneurship and the Informal Economy of Information and Communication Technologies in Morocco." *Journal of North African Studies* 3(2): 243–255.

Inda, Jonathan Xavier, and Renato Rosaldo. 2008. *The Anthropology of Globalization: A Reader*. 2nd ed. Malden, MA: Blackwell.

Inglis, David, and Debra Gimlin, eds. 2009. *The Globalization of Food*. London: Bloomsbury.

Inhorn, Marcia. 2005. "Women, Gender, and Infertility as a Social Phenomenon: Arab States." In *Encyclopedia of Women and Islamic Cultures*, ed. Suad Joseph. Leiden: Brill.

———. 2006. "Making Muslim Babies: IVF and Gamete Donation in Sunni vs. Shi'i Islam." *Culture, Medicine, and Psychiatry* 30(4): 427–450.

———. 2007. "Reproductive Disruptions and Assisted Reproductive Technologies in the Muslim World." In *Reproductive Disruptions: Gender, Technology, and Biopolitics in the New Millennium*, ed. Marcia Inhorn. New York: Berghahn Books.

International Labor Office. 1972. *Employment, Incomes, and Equality: A Strategy for Increasing Productive Employment in Kenya*. Geneva: International Labor Office.

"International Migration at All-Time High." 2015. Press release, World Bank, December 15. Accessed January 2016. http://www.worldbank.org/en/news/press-release/2015/12/18/international-migrants-and-remittances-continue-to-grow-as-people-search-for-better-opportunities-new-report-finds.

Jay, Martin. 2012. "New Prime Minister Surprises Moroccans with Support for Abortion." *New York Times*, January 11.

Jubas, Kaela. 2007. "Conceptual Con/fusion in Democratic Societies: Understandings and Limitations of Consumer-Citizenship." *Journal of Consumer Culture* 7(2): 231–254.

Kagermeier, Andreas. 1989. "Décentralisation et réorganisation des espaces administratives au Maroc." In *Le Maroc: Espace et société*, ed. A. Bencherifa and H. Popp, 115–124. Passau: Passavia Universitätsverlag.

Kapchan, Deborah. 1996. *Gender on the Market: Moroccan Women and the Revoicing of Tradition*. Philadelphia: University of Pennsylvania Press.

———. 2007. *Traveling Spirit Masters: Moroccan Gnawa Trance and Music in the Global Marketplace*. Middletown, CT: Wesleyan University Press.

Kearney, Michael. 1995. "The Local and the Global: The Anthropology of Globalization and Transnationalism." *Annual Review of Anthropology* 24: 547–565.

Kiple, Kenneth F. 2007. *A Movable Feast: Ten Millennia of Food Globalization*. Cambridge: Cambridge University Press.

Korfker, Dineke G., Floor van Rooij, Simone E. Buitendijk, Symone B. Detmar, and Ria Reis. 2014. "Infertility Care in the Netherlands for Turkish and Moroccan Migrants: The Role of Religion in Focus." *Obstetrics and Gynecology: An International Journal*.

Larémont, Ricardo René, ed. 2014. *Revolution, Revolt, and Reform in North Africa: The Arab Spring and Beyond*. New York: Routledge.

Lawrence, Adria. 2016. "The Mixed Record of Morocco's February 20th Protest Movement." *Washington Post*, February 20.

Le Tourneau, Roger. 1949. *Fès avant le protectorate: Étude économique et sociale d'une ville de l'occident musulman*. Casablanca: Société Marocaine de Librairie et d'Édition.

Lewellen, Ted C. 2002. *The Anthropology of Globalization: Cultural Anthropology Enters the 21st Century*. Westport, CT: Bergin and Garvey.

Lindsey, Ursula. 2015. "The Berber Language: Officially Recognized, Unofficially
    Marginalized?" Al-Fanar Media. Accessed September 23, 2016. http://www.al
    -fanarmedia.org/2015/07/the-berber-language-officially-recognized-unofficially
    -marginalized/.
MacPhee, Marybeth. 2004. "The Weight of the Past in the Experience of Health: Time,
    Embodiment, and Cultural Change in Morocco." *Ethos* 32(3): 374–396.
Madani, Mohamed, Driss Maghraoui, and Saloua Zerhouni. 2012. "The 2011 Moroccan
    Constitution: A Critical Analysis." International Institute for Democracy and
    Electoral Assistance. Stockholm: IDEA.
Maghraoui, Abdeslam. 2002. "Depoliticization in Morocco." *Journal of Democracy* 13(4):
    24–32.
Maher, Vanessa. 1978. "Women and Social Change in Morocco." In *Women in the
    Muslim World*, ed. Lois Beck and Nikki Keddie, 100–123. Cambridge, MA:
    Harvard University Press.
Majdi, Yassine. 2014. "Morocco's Workplace Gender Gap Widens." *Al-Monitor*,
    December 21.
Mannon, Susan, Peggy Petrzelka, and Christy Glass. 2012. "Keeping Them in Their
    Place: Migrant Women Workers in Spain's Strawberry Industry." *International
    Journal of Sociology of Agriculture and Food* 19(1): 83–102.
Marshall, Thomas Humphrey. 2009 [1950]. "Citizenship and Social Class." In *Inequality
    and Society*, eds. Jeff Manza and Michael Sauder, 148–54. London: Pluto.
Mathews, Gordon. 2011. *Ghetto at the Center of the World: Chungking Mansions, Hong
    Kong*. Chicago: University of Chicago Press.
McMurray, David. 2001. *In and out of Morocco: Smuggling and Migration in a Frontier
    Boomtown*. Minneapolis: University of Minnesota Press.
McTighe, Kristen. 2011. "Help for Unwed Mothers in Morocco." *New York Times*, June 9.
"Meet Houda: The Student Who Got the Highest Score on the Baccalaureate Exams."
    2014. *Morocco World News*, June 25. Accessed August 5, 2014. http://www.morocco
    worldnews.com/2014/06/133419/houda-the-student-who-got-the-highest-score
    -on-the-baccalaureate-exams/.
Mentak, Said. 2013. "Crossing Borders or Eroding Places: Moroccan Cultural Geography
    and Globalization." In *Moroccan Culture in the 21st Century: Globalization,
    Challenges and Prospects*, ed. Mohamed Dellal and Amar Sellam, 137–152. New
    York: Nova Science.
Mernissi, Fatima. 1977. "Women, Saints, and Sanctuaries." *Signs* 3(1): 101–112.
———. 1987. *Beyond the Veil: Male-Female Dynamics in Modern Muslim Society*.
    Cambridge, MA: Schenkman.
Miller, Susan Gilson. 2009. "Of Time and the City: Clifford Geertz on Urban History."
    Journal of North African Studies 14(3): 479–490.
Ministry of Justice, Morocco. 2007a. "Actes de mariage et actes de divorce." Accessed
    May 3, 2011. http://adala.justice.gov.ma/production/statistiques/famille/FR
    /Actes%20de%20marriage%20et%20actes%20de%20divorce.pdf.
Ministry of Justice, Morocco. 2007b. "Evolution de actes de divorces durant les dix
    dernières années." Accessed May 3, 2011. http://adala.justice.gov.ma/production
    /statistiques/famille/FR/Evolution%20de%20actes%20des%20mariags%20
    durant%20les%20dix%20dernieres%20annees.pdf.

Mir-Hosseini, Ziba. 1993/2002. *Marriage on Trial: A Study of Islamic Family Law in Iran and Morocco*. London: I. B. Tauris.

———. 2007. "How the Door of *Ijtihad* Was Opened and Closed: A Comparative Analysis of Recent Family Law Reforms in Iran and Morocco." *Washington and Lee Law Review* 64(4): 1499–1511.

Moghadam, Valentine. 2012. *Globalization and Social Movements: Islamism, Feminism, and the Global Justice Movement*. Lanham, MD: Rowman and Littlefield.

Mokhtar, Najat, Jalila Elat, Rachida Chabir, Adelatif Bour, Khalid Elkari, Nina P. Schlossman, Benjamin Caballero, and Hassan Aguenaou. 2001. "Diet, Culture and Obesity in Northern Africa." *Journal of Nutrition* 131(3): 887S–892S.

Molina, Irene Fernández. 2011. "The Monarchy vs. the 20 February Movement: Who Holds the Reins of Political Change in Morocco?" *Mediterranean Politics* 16(3): 435–441.

"Moroccan Women No Longer Abashed to File for Divorce." 2013. Morocco World News, June. Accessed July 12, 2015. http://www.moroccoworldnews. com/2013/06/93893/moroccan-women-are-no-longer-abashed-to-file-for-divorce/.

"Morocco." 2016. UNESCO. Accessed October 1, 2016. http://en.unesco.org/countries /morocco.

"Morocco." n.d. Chap. 9 in *Agriculture, Trade and Food Security Issues and Options in the WTO Negotiations*. Food and Agriculture Organization of the United Nations. Accessed March 3, 2016. http://www.fao.org/docrep/003/x8731e/x8731e10.htm.

"Morocco Withdraws Reservations to CEDAW." Women Living Under Muslim Laws. Accessed April 14, 2017. http://www.wluml.org/node/4941.

"Morocco's Teacher Protests Trigger Political Crisis after Government Violence." 2016. *New Arab*, January 11. Accessed January 24, 2016. http://www.alaraby.co.uk /english/society/2016/1/13/moroccos-teacher-protests-trigger-political-crisis-after -government-violence.

Najem, Tom P. 2001. "Privatization and the State in Morocco: Nominal Objectives and Problematic Realities." *Mediterranean Politics* 6(2): 51–67.

Newcomb, Rachel. 2009. *Women of Fes: Ambiguities of Urban Life in Morocco*. Philadel-phia: University of Pennsylvania Press.

———. 2013. "Modern Citizens, Modern Food: The Rise of the Citizen Consumer." In *Senses and Citizenships: Embodying Political Life*, ed. Christine Dureau and Susanna Trnka. New York: Routledge Press.

Nützenadel, Alexander, and Frank Trentmann, eds. 2008. *Food and Globalization: Consumption, Markets and Politics in the Modern World*. New York: Berg.

O'Meara, Simon. 2007. *Space and Muslim Urban Life: At the Limits of the Labyrinth of Fez*. New York: Routledge.

Ossman, Susan. 2007. "Cinderella, CVs, and Neighborhood Nemima: Announcing Morocco's Royal Wedding." *Comparative Studies of South Asia, Africa and the Middle East* 27(3): 525–535.

Ouadah-Bedidi, Zahia, Jacques Vallin, and Ibtihel Bouchoucha. 2012. "Unexpected Developments in Maghrebian Fertility." *Population and Societies*, no. 286: 486–490.

Pandey, Annarose. 2003. "Nostalgic Lives: Memories of Maria in Sidi Ifni, Morocco." *Journal of North African Studies* 8(2): 92–114.

Pfeifer, Karen. 1999. "How Tunisia, Morocco, and even Egypt became IMF Success Stories." *Middle East Report* 210: 23–26.

Phillips, Lynne. 2006. "Food and Globalization." *Annual Review of Anthropology* 35: 37–57.

Poster, Winifred, and Zakia Salime. 2002. "The Limits of Microcredit: Transnational Feminism and USAID Activities in the United States and Morocco." In *Women's Activism and Globalization: Linking Local Struggles and Transnational Politics*, ed. Naples and Desai, 189–219. New York: Routledge.

Potuoglu-Cook, Öykü. 2006. "Beyond the Glitter: Belly Dance and Neoliberal Gentrification in Istanbul." *Cultural Anthropology* 21: 663–669.

Povinelli, Elizabeth A., and George Chauncey. 2009. "Thinking Sexuality Transnationally: An Introduction." *GLQ: A Journal of Lesbian and Gay Studies* 5(4): 439–450.

Quraishi, Asifa, and Frank Vogel, eds. 2008. *The Islamic Marriage Contract: Case Studies in Islamic Family Law*. Cambridge, MA: Harvard University Press.

Rabinow, Paul. 1991. *French Modern: Norms and Forms of the Social Environment*. Cambridge, MA: MIT Press.

Rassam, Amul. 1980. "Women and Domestic Power in Morocco." *International Journal of Middle East Studies* 12(2): 171–179.

Rinker, Cortney Hughes. 2013. *Islam, Development, and Urban Women's Reproductive Practices*. New York: Routledge.

Robinson, Jennifer. 2002. "Global and World Cities: A View from off the Map." *International Journal of Urban and Regional Research* 26(3): 531–554.

Rosen, Lawrence. 2000. "Marriage Stories." *Recht van de Islam* 17: 1–14.

———. 2016. "Islam and the Rule of Justice." Unpublished Manuscript.

Roudi-Fahimi, Farzaneh, and Valentine Moghadam. 2011. "Empowering Women, Developing Society: Female Education in the Middle East and North Africa." Population Reference Bureau. Accessed April 6, 2015. http://www.prb.org/Publications/PolicyBriefs/EmpoweringWomenDevelopingSocietyFemaleEducationinthe MiddleEastandNorthAfrica.aspx.

"Rural Population % of Total Population." *World Bank* 2015. Accessed April 9, 2017. http://data.worldbank.org/indicator/SP.RUR.TOTL.ZS.

Saad Alami, Youness. 2009. "Fès-textile: Plus de 40% des usines menacées de fermeture." *L'économiste* (Casablanca), no. 2969. Accessed July 15, 2015. http://www.leconomiste.com/article/fes-textile-plus-de-40-des-usines-menacees-de-fermeture.

Salih, Ruba. 2001. "Moroccan Migrant Women: Transnationalism, Nation-States and Gender." *Journal of Ethnic and Migration Studies* 27(4): 655–671.

———. 2002. "Reformulating Tradition and Modernity: Moroccan Migrant Women and the Transnational Division of Ritual Space." *Global Networks* 2(3): 219–231.

Sandelowski, Margaret. 1991. "Compelled to Try: The Never-Enough Quality of Conceptive Technology." *Medical Anthropology Quarterly* 5(1): 29–47.

Sandler, Daniela. 2007. "Place and Process: Culture, Urban Planning, and Social Exclusion in São Paulo." *Social Identities* 13(4): 471–493.

Sassen, Saskia. 2001. *The Global City: New York, London, Tokyo*. Princeton, NJ: Princeton University Press.

Sater, James. 2010. *Morocco: Challenges to Tradition and Modernity*. New York: Routledge.

Sciarra, John. 1994. "Infertility: An International Health Problem." *International Journal of Gynecology and Obstetrics* 46: 155–163.

Seremetakis, C. Nadia, ed. 1994. *The Senses Still: Perception and Memory as Material Culture in Modernity.* Chicago: University of Chicago Press.

Sherringham, Michael. 2006. *Everyday Life: Theories and Practices from Surrealism to the Present.* Oxford: Oxford University Press.

Silverstein, Paul. 2012a. "In the Name of Culture: Berber Activism and the Material Politics of 'Popular Islam' in Southeastern Morocco." *Material Religion* 8(3): 330–353.

———. 2012b. "A New Morocco? Amazigh Activism, Political Pluralism, and Anti-Anti-Semitism in the Wake of Tahrir." *Brown Journal of World Affairs* 18(2): 129–140.

Skalli, Loubna. 2006. *Through a Local Prism: Gender, Globalization, and Identity in Moroccan Women's Magazines.* Boulder, CO: Lexington Books.

Slyomovics, Susan. 1998. *The Object of Memory: Arab and Jew Narrate the Palestinian Village.* Philadelphia: University of Pennsylvania Press.

Smith, Kimberly. 2000. "Mere Nostalgia: Notes on a Progressive Paratheory." *Rhetoric and Public Affairs* 3(4): 505–527.

Smith, Neil. 2002. "New Globalism, New Urbanism: Gentrification as a Global Urban Strategy." *Antipode* : 428–450.

Sonbol, Amira al-Azhary. 1995. "Adoption in Islamic Society: A Historical Survey." In *Children in the Muslim Middle East*, ed. Elizabeth Warnock Fernea, 45–67. Austin: University of Texas Press.

Spadola, Emilio. 2013. *The Calls of Islam: Sufis, Islamists, and Mass Mediation in Morocco.* Bloomington: Indiana University Press.

Spallone, Patricia, and Deborah L. Steinberg, eds. 1987. *Made to Order: The Myth of Reproductive and Genetic Progress.* Oxford: Pergamon Press.

Spiegel, Avi Max. 2015. *Young Islam: The New Politics of Religion in Morocco and the Arab World.* Princeton, NJ: Princeton University Press.

Stoller, Paul. 1989. *The Taste of Ethnographic Things.* Philadelphia: University of Pennsylvania Press.

Sutton, David. 2010. "Food and the Senses." *Annual Review of Anthropology* 39: 209–223.

Temmar, Fatima, Bilkis Vissandjée, Marie Hatem, Alisha Apale, and Devorah Kobluk. 2006. "Midwives in Morocco: Seeking Recognition as Skilled Partners in Women-Centered Maternity Care." *Reproductive Health Matters* 14(27): 83–90.

Thomas, Gerald A. 1991. "The Gentrification of Paradise: St. John's, Antigua." *Urban Geography* 12: 469–487.

Thorsen, D. E, and A. Lie. 2006. "What Is Neoliberalism?" Department of Political Science, University of Oslo. Accessed June 24, 2012. http://folk.uio.no/daget/What%20is%20Neo-Liberalism%20FINAL.pdf 2012-06-24.

Tylor, Edward. 1920 [1871]. *Primitive Culture.* New York: Putnam.

"UN CEDAW and CRC Recommendations on Minimum Age of Marriage Laws around the World." 2016. Equality Now.org. Accessed October 2, 2016. http://www.equalitynow.org/sites/default/files/UN_Committee_Recommendations_on_Minimum_Age_of_Marriage_Laws.pdf.

UNESCO. 2016. Morocco. Accessed October 1, 2016. http://en.unesco.org/countries
    /morocco.
United Nations Development Program. 2014. *Human Development Report 2015: Work
    for Human Development: Morocco.* Accessed February 4, 2016. http://hdr.undp.org
    /sites/all/themes/hdr_theme/country-notes/MAR.pdf.
"Urban/Rural Division of Countries for the Year 2015 and 2025." 2015. United Nations
    Statistics. Accessed January 15, 2016. http://www.geohive.com/earth/pop_urban
    .aspx.
Vidler, Anthony. 1992. *The Architectural Uncanny: Essays in the Modern Unhomely.*
    Cambridge: Massachusetts Institute of Technology Press.
Waterbury, John. 1972. *North for the Trade: The Life and Times of a Berber Merchant.*
    Berkeley: University of California Press.
Willis, Michael. 2012. *Politics and Power in the Maghreb: Algeria, Tunisia and Morocco
    from Independence to the Arab Spring.* New York: Columbia University Press.
Wilson, Elizabeth. 1997. "Looking Backward: Nostalgia and the City." In *Imagining
    Cities: Scripts, Signs, Memory,* ed. Sallie Westwood and John Williams, 127–139.
    London: Routledge.
Woodward, Richard, and Mehdi Safavi. 2015. "Private Sector Development." In
    *Economic and Social Development of the Southern and Eastern Mediterranean
    Countries,* ed. Rim Ayadi, Marek Dabrowski, and Luc De Wulf. New York:
    Springer.
"Workers' Remittances and Compensation of Employees—received (% of GDP) in
    Morocco." 2016. Tradingeconomics.com. Accessed October 1, 2016. http://www
    .tradingeconomics.com/morocco/workers-remittances-and-compensation-of
    -employees-received-percent-of-gdp-wb-data.html.
Zhiri, M., and W. Benyahia. 1987. "Epidemiology of Tubal Sterility in Morocco." *Journal
    de gynécologie, obstétrique et biologie de la reproduction* 16(8): 975–980.
Zubaida, Sami, and Richard Tapper, eds. 1994. *Culinary Cultures of the Middle East.*
    London: Tauris Parke.
Zwingmann, Charles. 1959. "'Heimweh' or 'Nostalgic Reaction': A Conceptual Analysis
    and Interpretation of a Medico-Psychological Phenomenon." Ann Arbor, MI:
    University Microfilms, 1959.

INDEX

abortion, 44
Abu-Lughod, Janet, 131
adoption and foster parentage, 63, 68–69
adultery, 25, 44–45, 70
Agreement on Textiles and Clothing (ATC), 96
Aid el Kbir, 102
Alaouite dynasty, 7
Amendis (French company in Tangier), 150–51
Amine, Abdelmajid, 121
Appadurai, Arjun, 68, 69–70, 110
"Arab Spring" (2011), 1, 8, 22, 24, 128, 146n2
Arabic language: colloquial Moroccan Arabic
    (*darija*), 8, 86; educational system's
    Arabization project, 3, 8, 85–86; Modern
    Standard Arabic (MSA), 8, 85–86
assisted reproductive technologies (ARTs), 23,
    56, 61–62, 63, 64, 69–71, 75; affordability/
    costs, 2, 23, 56, 57, 61, 69, 76n10; and
    Appadurai's vision of "technoscape," 69–70;
    doctors' roles in explaining biomedical
    reasons for infertility, 70–71, 72–74; and
    doctors' roles in the marital relationship,
    64–65, 71–74, 75; fertility drugs to stimulate
    ovulation, 55–56, 57, 60; and Islam, 70;
    male-directed therapies, 70; pursued in
    combination with traditional practices, 2–3,
    23, 55–62, 65–66, 69, 71, 75; in vitro
    fertilization (IVF), 2, 57, 61, 69–70. *See also*
    infertility

Bahloul, Jöelle, 129
baraka (a blessing), 59
Barnes, David S., 142
Belghazi, Taieb, 145

Berbers (Imazighen), 6, 8; Moroccan cuisine,
    108, 109; Tamazight language, 8, 86
Bilkhayat, Abdelhadi, 40
bint an-nas (girl of excellent character), 40, 46,
    47
biomedicine. *See* assisted reproductive
    technologies (ARTs); infertility
Bissell, William, 138
Bogaert, Konraad, 141, 147n14
Bourdieu, Pierre, 108
Boutieri, Charis, 85–86
Boym, Svetlana, 137
bride price (*sadaq*), 30, 31, 33–34, 53n1, 66, 67

Cairoli, M. Laetitia, 21
*The Calls of Islam: Sufis, Islamists, and Mass
    Mediation in Urban Morocco* (Spadola), 21
Carr, Marilyn, 93
Casablanca, Morocco: displacement of urban
    slum dwellers for development projects,
    141–42; economic center of Morocco, 108;
    Jewish Moroccans of, 6; rise of an alienated
    middle class in, 21
Central Market (Fes's Ville Nouvelle):
    dilapidation and neglect, 102–3, 132, 135–36,
    139–40; traditional food shopping at, 88,
    101–4, 107, 118–19, 121–22, 135–36, 139–40
Chabat, Abdelhamid, 138–39, 143
Chen, Martha A., 93
Chinese-made consumer products, 84
Cohen, Shana, 130; on globalization and the
    Moroccan middle class, 12, 21, 25, 28n18; on
    participation in global market capitalism,
    19–20

RACHEL NEWCOMB is Professor of Anthropology at Rollins College in Winter Park, Florida. She holds the Diane and Michael Maher Distinguished Chair of Teaching and Learning.